Aberfeldy

The History of a Highland Community

Ruary Mackenzie Dodds

Published in 2010 by
Watermill Books
The Watermill
Mill Street
Aberfeldy
Perthshire PH15 2BG
www.aberfeldywatermill.com

British Library Cataloguing-in-Publication Data

A catalogue record for this book is available from the British Library

ISBN 978-0-9554358-4-3

Designed by Nickolai Globe, Globe Design, Isle of Harris

Printed and bound under the supervision
of MRM Graphics, Wimslow, Buckinghamshire

For Kari

CONTENTS

Page

Introduction 1

1 How did it all Begin? 3

2 Pitnacree, Fortingall and Croftmoraig 7

3 Hill-forts, Duns and Crannogs 11

4 Picts and Saints 17

5 Into the Mist 23

6 The Coming of Abyrpheallaidh 27

7 Six Men from Dusty Charters 31

8 Grandees 33

9 Life for Ordinary People 37

10 Lairds, Castles and Clans 41

11 Religion Splits the Valley 45

12 Ruin, Occupation and Restoration 49

13 Pale John 53

14 The Work of a Winter Dawn 57

15 Rebellion and Change 61

16 The '45 65

17 Profit Comes to the Valley 69

18 The Town Takes Shape 75

19 The Early 1800s 83

20 Royalty and Disruption 91

21 Threat of Famine, Fear of France 97

22 Stationmaster Fyfe 101

23 A Real Town 113

24 Home Rule, Women's Rights and War 123

25 Between the Wars 131

26 Wartime 137

27 Never had it so Good 143

28 Towards 2000 155

29 Now and Ahead 161

Acknowledgements 170

Bibiliography 172

Index 176

Introduction

On a windy March day, as I walked over General Wade's bridge, a sudden thought about my great grandmother Elizabeth Stewart stopped me. I had been over that bridge hundreds of times, but what brought me to a standstill that chilly afternoon was the realization that she had crossed those very same arches early one morning in 1858. She was leaving the parish; she had walked from Tummel Bridge where her father Donald Stewart of Crossmount was the man who maintained General Wade's Military Road. She was to catch the 7am mail coach by the Breadalbane Arms, which would take her down the Tay valley turnpike to the rail terminus at Dunkeld, and then on by train – her first time on the still-new railway – to take up a post in service in Edinburgh.

From the spot where I now stood, she would have looked back and wondered when she would next be able to come home. In Edinburgh she would meet and marry one of a new type of policeman, a detective. Now, her great grandson has his own line of detective work: to unravel the story behind the area so familiar to her.

This book covers the area of the upper Tay and the lower Lyon. There is a range of opinions as to the actual identity of this space: some say it has its own character and its own values, separate from the tourist corridor north and south from Pitlochry. Others maintain that Highland Perthshire as a whole – from Pitlochry to Dunkeld, and from Kenmore to Kirkmichael – is an entity with complementary strengths. What is certain is that this valley has been a trade route since the beginning of history; and, for well over 250 years now, Aberfeldy town has been its hub.

The area might more properly be divided into 'strath' and 'carse', 'lochside' and 'glen'. However, in the absence of another more encompassing word, I use the word 'valley' throughout this book as shorthand to denote the entire

Aerial photograph of Aberfeldy in 2003

area from where the Tay joins the Tummel by Logierait in the east, to the lower reaches of Glenlyon, and the Kenmore end of Loch Tay in the west.

What is history? It's certainly a slippery thing, often based on ancient opinions and old propaganda. I shall try to provide answers to questions I have found myself asking about the area, and to present a picture of the place as the years went by. I have talked to local people and read all the books I can find about the valley; but I'll tell the story my way, based on my own research. I'll try not to duplicate the work of previous authors, and to use as many previously unpublished photographs as possible, ones that haven't appeared in the other excellent local histories; and I will bring in a taste of events outwith the valley, especially when they had an impact here. It would be easy to paint a rosy picture of the area's development over the centuries, but there is too much blood and anger right from the beginning of the story.

This is the story of the valley as a whole, because Aberfeldy town only began to coalesce out of four separate hamlets – Easter Aberfeldy, Upper Milton, Nether Milton and Moness – as a result of the construction in 1733 of General Wade's bridge, the very bridge I was standing on that March day. Prior to that, other settlements were bigger and more important.

People have been living in the valley for something like seven thousand years. So who were its first inhabitants?

How did it all begin?

CHAPTER ONE

Who were the very first men and women who walked – or paddled – into this valley? When did they arrive? And what did they find? There may have been visitors before the last Ice Age; if so, any traces of them were subsequently erased by the grinding weight of gigantic glaciers. Indeed there are no real clues as to when people began to arrive in this area after the most recent Ice Age, but it is safe to make a few guesses.

The north of Britain kept its glaciers until about 10,000 years ago, but recent arrowhead finds in southern Scotland show that hunters were operating there about 4000 years before that. So the first hunters probably came into this valley even as the glaciers were retreating from it. They may have migrated from Ireland, or more likely across the then-existing land bridge from Scandinavia. Initially, they probably based themselves close to the seashore. The sea provided them with at least twenty species of fish, thirty species of birds, plus oysters, crabs, scallops, limpets and whelks. They used flint to make tools, including axes and arrowheads. They gathered nuts, leaves, seeds and berries. They wielded stone-headed clubs and threw antler-tipped harpoons. They hunted elk, reindeer and maybe mammoth, and it was the search for meat that tempted them inland along the river valleys.

The Tay was – and still is – the mightiest river in Scotland. It was an obvious route for early logboat travel. Its waters teemed with salmon, and its banks sheltered herds of red deer and wild boar. Hunter groups arrived to settle and exploit these resources. They had to protect themselves and their encampments from wolves and bears. Almost everything these people fashioned and used was made of wood, which rots and vanishes, so we can only surmise how they lived.

Why would these first-footers have been attracted to this particular valley? Certainly because of the good hunting, but also, being serious wood-users, they could see this land was covered with birch, pine, alder, hazel, willow, oak and elm. And for woodworking, they could obtain top-quality stone axes from a quarry, a logboat-paddle away, up at Craig na Cailleach at the other end of Loch Tay. A few 5000 year-old axeheads from this quarry, grey-green and polished, still exist, dug up as far away as Derbyshire and Buckinghamshire, an astonishing sign of early long-distance contacts.

Hazel trees were particularly useful, not only as a source of nuts but also for constructing wattle panels and forming the framework for skin-covered boats. Willow had similar uses, and was excellent for large baskets. Plants had many uses: bracken, ferns, heather, rush, reed, sedge, honeysuckle and lily-leaves were good for thatching, bedding, small baskets, insulation and twine. Nettles made fine ropes and were good in soups. Silverweed root, wild carrot roots, raspberries, blaeberries, cherries, sloes, crab-apples and blackberries were eaten in season and were dried for storage. Edible water-lily seeds and roots were plentiful. Moss served as padding and for all the things we now use Kleenex and Andrex for.

These hunters smoked their meat and fumigated their temporary dwellings with juniper. They wove floormats with heather. They used plants we hardly bother with now, which we know have been used by similar so-called primitive societies: Meadowsweet (to flavour drinks); Rosebay Willowherb (pith for sweetener, dried as tea, and leaves as a green vegetable); Marsh Marigold (leaves and stems, both boiled); Bracken (rhizomes toasted, shoots boiled like asparagus); Tormentil (for tanning); Sphagnum Moss (for wound dressings); Lesser Celandine (tubers boiled for food, or made into a paste to treat piles).

However, the key reason for hunters to come here was the herds of red deer, threading their way through the trees and roaming the higher slopes. A single deer could provide sufficient calories to feed three adults and two children for two weeks. Its skin could be used for a pair of shoes, or a tunic, or for covering a coracle. Liquid containers could be made out of the deer's stomach, its large intestine and its bladder. Cordage could come from its gut and sinews, and glue from its hooves. The brain could be used for tanning hides. Its fat would do for lamps. Countless other articles could be fashioned from the bones: mattocks, needles, awls, punches, tool-handles, toggles, tooth-picks, and barbed points for spears and harpoons.

The hunters burned woodland to create suitable pasturage for deer, in effect creating extended deer-farms. Hunting carried status: there's evidence from 6000 years ago that our ancestors were shooting deer with longbows of imported yew. Bows like that would have been coveted in the same way as modern hunting rifles. The yew-tree in Fortingall churchyard, reputedly 5000 years old, shows that yews began to be planted locally rather than imported. They were carefully tended, treated with respect and became focal points for ceremonies.

As people began to unlock the secrets of how to cultivate the land and grow crops, this well-watered and sheltered valley with its gentle sunny slopes was an obvious spot to spend time. Not that hunting suddenly stopped. There was a slow change. People began to plant cereals in the ash of the woodland they had burned: emmer wheat, bere barley, flax, maybe oats. They began to rear cattle and sheep. There was sufficient food for folk not to bother with too much weeding and crop maintenance. Indeed, they probably had a fair amount of leisure time. After a year or two, they burned the next piece of wildwood and planted again in the ash-rich soil.

These people habitually dug pits, and traces of very early pits have been found at Grandtully, the first faint evidence of human life in the valley. It's possible that pit-digging was some sort of ritual; sometimes a fragment of a pot was put in, sometimes a flint, sometimes half a jar, as if the other half needed to be kept above ground in memory of something or someone. Maybe our ancestors were hypersensitive to the whole experience of simply surviving, and so they revered items we now take for granted, like a pot or a tool or a shelter.

People gradually started to stay in one place. Rather than attack yet another piece of virgin forest, it was easier to return to previously cultivated land where trees had only newly sprouted. Hunting continued, but farming began to

take hold across Scotland around 6000 years ago. The development occurred precisely because of the success of hunter-farming and deer-management. Well-fed people with time on their hands produced larger numbers of children. Rather than fight all the time for control over bigger areas – which ultimately benefited neither hunter nor farmer – people began to stay in smaller spaces and devote their lives to more intensive cultivation. It needed much harder work, not simply because of weeding: when they started using draught animals for ploughing around 2000 BC, it needed 50 per cent of the ploughed cereal area just to feed the oxen themselves.

When people began to stay in one place, it seems they chose sites quite close to those already used by their earlier more mobile ancestors. The first real signs of people settling in the valley soon appeared.

Replica logboat, built by a team from Perth and Kinross Heritage Trust, with help from the Scottish Crannog Centre, copying techniques similar to those used by builders of a 3000 year old vessel found in the River Tay at Carpow

Fortingall Long Cairn, estimated 5,500 years old

Pitnacree, Fortingall and Croftmoraig

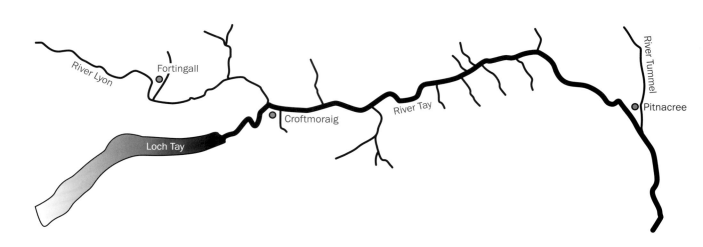

River Lyon · Fortingall · Croftmoraig · Loch Tay · River Tay · River Tummel · Pitnacree

Pitnacree Burial Mound, estimated 5,500 years old

Pitnacree, Fortingall and Croftmoraig

To get a feel for the very earliest settlers, go east to Pitnacree, or west to Fortingall and Croftmoraig: three of our earliest bits of hard evidence for people living here at least 5,500 years ago. Or rather dying here, as all three are burial sites.

The Pitnacree site is a pine-tree-covered mound. It stands just east of the Aberfeldy to Logierait roadbridge, opposite the junction with the old road from Pitnacree village. It was built as a burial-place by early local hunter-farmers. Originally it had two enormous split tree-trunks set about three metres apart, with a wattle-fenced corridor between them. Later, it was covered over with stones and turf.

The mound speaks: it says that the people here had the time and energy to build it. In this sunny spot with its gentle south-facing slopes, people were doing well. They used pottery, they cremated their dead; when customs changed, they left corpses out on ritual trestles to be eaten by birds and animals. It is possible that somewhere, ploughed under the fields nearby, are the remains of the hunter-farmers' huts. In any case, Pitnacree was a very important site. There would have been rituals connected with it. It would have been seen as the point that linked the living community with the souls of their dead; and it was used for a very long period.

Over at Fortingall, on the way to Fearnan, there is a whaleback-shaped east-west mound in a field, on the left, just before Lyon Bridge. It is a long earth-covered cairn, a communal burial barrow, dating from around 3,500 BC, the same period as the Pitnacree mound. Whoever built it possibly had links with the west as there are similar cairns in the Clyde valley. No doubt there were other such cairns and barrows throughout the valley, long since seen as obstacles and ploughed out.

Fortingall holds more messages from prehistory: a short distance from the long barrow, lie the remains of a round barrow with a large stone (2m x1m), lying flat in its circular ditch. This barrow has been dated to the Bronze Age, which followed the Stone Age and began about 4000 years ago. So people were still using the field 1,500 years after the building of the long barrow nearby.

There is evidence of other smaller stone-lined burials in the same field, but it is the large stone in the ring-barrow ditch that holds the real mystery. It has ten little conical indentations, called cup-marks. Nine are obvious, and there is one down the side. This valley has an exceptional number of these cup-marked stones, nearly 150, and more are being discovered. On some of the stones, the cup-marks have multiple rings cut round them, and in some cases additional odd and intriguing designs. They have an extraordinary magic, part of which is that no one knows what they signify.

The sheer number of the stones and the work needed to form each indentation sets the brain racing. There are hundreds of theories about them, from territory-markers to tide-indicators. They are usually sited in places with

'Cup-and-Ring' marks on a stone near Camserney, estimated 4000 years old

Standing Stone on the Haugh of Grandtully, estimated 4000 years old

good views. Whatever their function, they speak to us of people from thousands of years ago, standing exactly where we stand, chipping away, probably with similar joys and worries to our own.

There is another question about that large stone in the ditch: was it originally somewhere else? The cup-marks on the stone are older than the ring-barrow. Was it converted into a standing stone that then fell over? There is a standing stone, still upright, a short distance away. These standing stones were erected from about 4000 years ago; again we do not know what message these tall markers contain, but, as you walk round the valley, you begin to notice more and more of them. They are hard to spot from cars; there is one just visible from the road as it curves between Grandtully village and the modern bridge over the Tay, close to the old railway embankment.

Archaeologists armed with new techniques are bringing more of the valley's past to life, more for us to wonder at. Some time ago, at Balbridie in Deeside, a massive timber meeting hall (26m x 13m) was found, dating back 5,500 years, to the same period as Fortingall's long barrow and the Pitnacree mound. Possible signs of a similar meeting-hall (20m x 8m) have recently been discovered in a field between the Fortingall barrows and Fortingall's famous 5000 year old Churchyard Yew. Perhaps people were using this hall in conjunction with rituals at the three stone circles, whose stones still lie in another field just two minutes' walk away; or possibly the more permanent stone-built circles replaced the wooden hall.

Now to the Croftmoraig stone circle. Just south of the Aberfeldy-Kenmore road at the entrance to Tullichuil Farm, its huge uneven teeth are unmissable. The massive outer circle of stones is the first of four stages in the long life of this sacred place. Contemporary with Pitnacree and Fortingall, from the start it was a solar observatory. Early farmers needed to know the sun's movements in order to decide on the right times for planting and harvesting. There are two outlying stones to the south-east, perfectly aligned with the position of the equinoctial sunrise. A timber post circle was then erected inside the stones, also with a south-east alignment. These posts may have been the key supports for a building.

Later – possibly 3000 years later – some sort of ditched cairn or mound replaced the timber posts, with a new more refined axis facing south-west and marking sunrise, sunset and certain phases of the moon. Other possible astronomical alignments on the stones seem to show that this was not just a place for supplying data to farmers. The circle was a burial site, and there is a burial mound a few hundred yards away. Maybe there were specialists, priests of a sort, who spent their time ceaselessly watching the skies and supervising the communal rituals of life and death.

One thing is certain: Croftmoraig was a public building that required enormous amounts of communal labour to construct, repair and modify.

There is another circle above the Birks of Aberfeldy, and a third at Fortingall. They all have a scattering of white water-worn quartz pebbles. These could have been used for counting the days of lunar months, or as a gentle floor surface for bare reverential feet. In any case, with their sometimes-changing shapes, the length of time that these circles were in use was enormous, much longer than any cathedral. There are several more stone circles in the area, though none quite as impressive as Croftmoraig.

But there are also 'Four-poster' stones here, which are really rectangles of uprights rather than circles. Fourteen settings like this have been identified in the valley; and only fourteen more have so far been found in the whole of the rest of the British Isles. No one knows why there are so many here. The easiest one to see is as at Carse Farm on the road from Aberfeldy to Coshieville, in a field on the left. Also at Carse Farm, close to the junction of the Lyon and the Tay, there is another very unusual feature, a line of three tree-covered cairns, a linear cemetery, dating from about 1,500 BC. A similar, longer, better-known one exists at Kilmartin in Argyll.

Decent-sized stones are always useful, and smaller ones are all too easily shifted. So, much of what was erected by our prehistoric ancestors has since been carted away, re-used, broken up, or simply buried. As the *Red Book of Grantully* quaintly puts it: "On archaeological grounds, the destruction of such memorials of the past is too Gothic not to be regretted."

There are still significant archaeological messages lying undeciphered under local houses and farms. Archaeologists are finding traces of very early fields, farms and settlements both around Weem and on the hill slopes to the south of Aberfeldy town. Recent work at Dull and Fortingall has given a glimpse of how much more could be learned by digging a trench or two in various spots under the eyes of experts. But the remaining mounds, stone circles, standing stones and enigmatic cup-marks testify that the Aberfeldy valley has been home to hundreds of generations, a really long-lived farming-based community. Six thousand years' worth of morning glances at the sky.

Croftmoraig Stone Circle, begun roughly 4000 years ago

'Four-poster' setting of stones at Carse Farm, Dull

Hill Forts, Duns and Crannogs

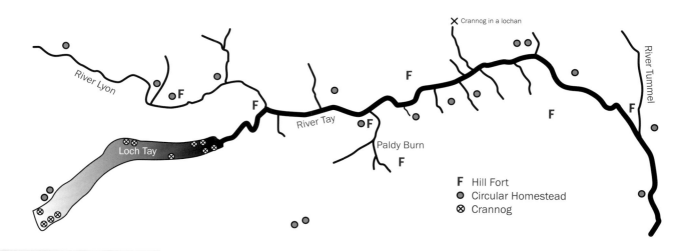

Crannog in a lochan ✕

F Hill Fort
● Circular Homestead
⊗ Crannog

River Lyon

River Tay

Loch Tay

Paldy Burn

River Tummel

Logierait hill-fort: first in use about 700BC: the tree line marks the substantial ditch that surrounds the fort. The cross is a memorial to the 6th Duke of Atholl (1814-1864).

Hill-forts, Duns and Crannogs

Flying over the upland hillsides of the valley, photographers have begun to reveal a very different picture beneath today's heather-clad slopes. 3,300 years ago, people were taking advantage of a fine and warm climate. It seems to have been a peaceful time. There were roles now for potentates, priests, smelters, smiths, traders and travelling tale-tellers, but most people remained involved in working the land. Extensive groups of huts and field systems have been identified high up in the hills. Similar hut groupings and surrounding fields probably also existed down in the drier parts of the valley, but signs of them will have long since been ploughed out.

However around 1000 BC, there was a change: the climate became colder and wetter. Archaeologists have pointed to the gigantic eruption of the Icelandic volcano Hekla in 1159 BC. The resulting massive dust-cloud may well have set off a decades-long permanent winter. As crops failed on the high grounds and people were forced to move into the valleys, there was much more pressure on land. Farming families needed protection and local chieftains, armed with bronze weapons, grew steadily more powerful.

Chieftains needed status symbols. Trade with other parts of Britain and the continent began to increase, especially in high-value imported goods like fine jewellery, bronze mirrors, jet necklaces and, significantly, heavy-bladed bronze slashing swords. Here in Perthshire, archaeologists have discovered Scotland's first wheels and dated them to this time. They were each made from three pieces of solid ash, so they probably came from a cart rather than a chariot. Nevertheless, the pace of life was speeding up.

The great days of monument-building were over, and when even more effective and dangerous iron weapons arrived three hundred years later – at the start of the Iron Age, about 700 BC – people started to construct defensive hill-forts to protect their livestock and themselves. They dug deep ditches, they erected massive stone walls, they cut down woodland to erect extensive timber palisades. All of these took huge amounts of work.

There are at least six such hill-forts overlooking our valley: Logierait and Castle Dow guard the eastern mouth; there is one on Cluny Rock; two look down on Aberfeldy from the south; another on the east end of Drummond Hill and yet another perched above Fortingall. There may be yet more to find: Weem Rock and the west end of Drummond Hill are prime suspects.

All these hill-forts are built on commanding heights with strategic views. All have virtually unscaleable crags or slopes in front, and serious defensive walls or ditches – or both – behind. All are a short distance from a higher point from which a beacon could alert at least one of the other forts. And all are within walking distance of field systems and settlements. Defensive palisades were thrown up around several of the previously undefended groups of huts.

Replica Crannog on Loch Tay, built with techniques in use in 600BC

Perhaps the Aberfeldy valley folk were preparing for attack from more warlike bands; or it may have been the start of clan-style life, with each little tribe jealously guarding its own territory. Maybe it was both.

Apart from the forts, settlements and field systems, two other rather grander sorts of building appeared a little later, from about 600 BC : 'duns' and 'crannogs'. These buildings were places that were lived in and used for enormous lengths of time, in some cases right into the Middle Ages, even into the seventeenth century. Both types are known as circular homesteads, with one group built on land and the other with its feet in loch water.

The land-based ones, the 'duns', were big buildings. Each had a diameter on average of twenty metres, a timber-raftered cone of thatch, and a circumference ringed by a thick, broch-shaped stone wall. They could comfortably accommodate an extended family of 30 people, plus their animals. A glance at the names of farms and houses dotted around Aberfeldy today gives a clue that the immediate area to the south of the town was well-populated in those days: Duntaylor, Dunskeig, Duntuim, Dunacree, Duntaggart, Dundai, Dundavie.

Some of these sites still have visible remains, but the best place to see a dun – not subsequently built over – is above Balnacraig, between Garth and Fortingall. Called Dun Geal, it sits on a south-facing shelf high above the valley. The outline of its walls remains perfectly clear. Its size and position immediately make one think of the massive amount of work involved in its construction, and the impression it would have made once completed. No doubt the most important locals lived there, and it may have served as a community gathering-place although it would have been a long hard climb for older members. Unlike the earlier hill-forts, these duns were not built specifically for defence. Indeed some of them are fairly easily attackable, but they were certainly status symbols.

Over at Kenmore there is a water-based version of a similar building, a crannog. A visit provides a clear picture of the enormous amount of labour required in its construction. Although there are two obvious original crannog islands in view from the water's edge, this one is new, only erected a few years ago. It is based on careful examination of one of the eighteen original crannogs in Loch Tay. Much of the knowledge about life in this period comes from painstaking local underwater archaeology. There is also a crannog site away in the hills above Strathtay, at Loch Derculich, and there may be others as yet unidentified.

These duns and crannogs were highly successful pieces of architecture. It is little wonder people used them right into mediaeval times. Some of them were converted into smelting shops and others into sheep-fanks. As homes and workplaces, they did the job; they were warm and waterproof, they kept out wolves and bears, and replacement building materials could be obtained quickly and locally.

As with their homes, when the local farmers went out to their fields they tended to stick to what they knew worked. Their labour scarcely changed for over a thousand years: they ploughed and sowed barley, wheat, oats and kale. They pastured sheep, cattle, pigs and goats. They used horse-drawn carts and ox-drawn single-stem ploughs. Dogs and cats did the jobs they still do. One or two new things appeared: chickens from further south, and new plants like coriander and dill.

Just east of Dun Geal, only a few hundred metres away, is one of the massive hill-forts. It is covered in a tangle of rhododendron branches, but the walls are still intact, and the crag on which it sits is as precipitous and breathtaking as it ever was. A better-preserved, more accessible fort is in sight,

*Dun Geal,
Fortingall:
(centre bottom):
first in use in
about 600BC*

Dun MacTuathall, Drummond Hill: dating from around 700BC. Aberfeldy in distance, upper right

perched on the east end of Drummond Hill: Dun MacTuathall.

There is a maddening anomaly here: Dun MacTuathall, a hill-fort – rather than a circular homestead – being called a 'dun'. There is another example of this immediately above Aberfeldy; the largest of the two hill-forts above the town is called just 'The Dun'. Quite when the linguistic mix-up occurred is unclear. The Pictish language was a form of Celtic. It was related to what later became Scots Gaelic, but in fact it was closer to Welsh. Presumably early Celtic speakers – or later Gaelic-speaking incomers – did not worry about the difference between hill-forts and circular homesteads; which accounts for Dunkeld, Dundee, Dunedin and so on. And, to add to the confusion, not all circular homesteads are called 'dun-something': Tomtewan, for example, up the hill from Grandtully Castle, still has a ten-metre fragment of its homestead wall.

The longevity of these big circular houses, the surrounding huts and fields, reflects how little life would have changed through the generations. Continuity would have been natural. The Aberfeldy valley was a settled farming community. Despite occasional adjustments in living patterns and beliefs, the seasons came and went.

Only in the first century AD do we begin to get the first faint feeling for the actual identity of our ancestors. Take the name of the village just mentioned: Dull is a Pictish name; it means 'meadow'. The 'Aber' in Aberfeldy is Pictish, too, meaning 'confluence'. It was the Romans who called people who lived in this valley 'Picts'. It means 'painted ones' in Latin, and they used the word generally to describe the peoples who lived in the North and North-East of what is now Scotland. It may either have referred to the way they decorated themselves, or it may have just been pejorative. There is a great deal about the Picts that is unclear, because they left no written history. However, they left a different sort of testimony, fascinating and enigmatic, and there is more on this in the next chapter.

According to the Romans, this valley's chieftains belonged to the Caledones super-tribe. The name lingers close by in Dunkeld, the 'dun' of the Caledonians, and Schiehallion, the magic mountain of the Caledonians. Over the hills south towards Perth, lay the lands and hill-forts of another super-tribe, the Venicones.

The Romans invaded southern Britain in 43 AD. Their battle-hardened troops with their superior weapons and tactics steadily advanced northwards and westwards. Despite several setbacks, they arrived just south of here in about 74 AD. It was a seismic event. No one knows how much resistance the Venicones raised, but like the tribes further south, their territories were occupied. The people of the Aberfeldy valley were suddenly very close to the Roman frontier, with its forts and its legions; and its patrols riding over the hills. The locals would have watched, bewildered, as the soldiers made notes on tablets made of wax, using a system called writing.

Under the experienced command of three leaders, Cerialis, Frontinus and Agricola, a line of forts and watchtowers was strung out along the Gask Ridge from the Forth near Stirling to the Tay at Perth. The legions erected outlying forts at the entrance to the different glens in front and to the west of the main line, and began to extend the frontier north-eastwards. The nearest forts to this valley were Fendoch in Glenalmond, and Dalginross near Comrie. Fendoch was within a day's march of the massive fortress of the Twentieth Valeria Victrix Legion (5,500 men, including 120 cavalry) at Inchtuthil, upstream from Perth.

Fendoch was also within a day's march of here. The Romans' chief aim in taking control of the most fertile parts of Scotland was obvious; they needed grain for wasteful, ever-hungry Rome. Units made their way over the passes to examine the food-production possibilities of this valley and to check whether or not the land was defensible. They will have marked the positions of the hillforts, duns and crannogs, and noted the importance of guarding the western approaches to the Aberfeldy valley from both Loch Tay and Glenlyon.

Other specialists appeared: officers from the Corps of Surveyors, stationed with the Twentieth Valeria Victrix came to check possible sites for future legionary advance encampments. Mineral Prospectors attached to the Second Adiutrix Legion, riding from Dalginross over the pass to the outcrops above Ardtalnaig by Loch Tay, were as interested in the veins of copper, lead, silver and gold as, much later, the 2nd Marquess of Breadalbane was.

There is increasing evidence that the Romans stayed in the area for about fifteen years. Like all empires, the Romans imposed their order on the tribes, by force if necessary. But like all imperial forces they also had huge requirements for their troops and their camps; they needed wheat, barley, vegetables, fruit, meat, milk and cheese. They needed endless supplies of timber for their buildings and leather for tents and shoes.

The demand for all of these provided something of a bonanza to the valley. The amount of goods taken over the hills by pack-horse and cart was huge. It is probable that the bases also became significant employers of local labour, both for services and construction. Locals will have come into contact with Roman auxiliaries from as far afield as what are now Hungary, Spain, Morocco and Syria.

Perhaps Aberfeldy had the best of the Romans being so close by: no occupation, but plenty of trade, and a certain amount of pleasant fraternization. Boece, an early chronicler, relates that a deputation was sent from the Emperor Augustus, first to Cymbeline, King of the Britons and, next, to Metellanus, King of the Scots. Metellanus supposedly had a castle at Fortingall. One of the

Roman ambassadors had a relationship with a local woman and their child later became Pontius Pilate, Governor of Judea. Even if this yarn is untrue, it may indicate how the locals felt about integration. Nevertheless, the possibility of being sold into slavery would have concentrated minds. Many Caledonians further north were subsequently sold as slaves, probably a few from this valley too.

As the Romans began to push northeast to take control of the fertile fields stretching coastwards towards Aberdeen, they met serious resistance at the point where the Grampians fall to the sea. The tribes united against them, and men from this valley will have joined the Caledonian fighters. The Battle of Mons Graupius took place in 83 AD; the most likely spot is near Benachie in Aberdeenshire. The Caledonians lost. This may have been the first of many times when fighters left the Aberfeldy valley to die on a distant field. In any case, the victory did the Romans little good. The Picts, with their beautiful, strange coded messages were still standing proudly on their hillsides centuries after the Roman Empire collapsed.

Picts and Saints

Just when the locals were settling down to steady trade and good employment, the Roman Empire departed. Almost immediately after Agricola's victory at Mons Graupius, the Roman legions with all their auxiliaries from different parts of the world began to pack up and leave. The advance post over the hill at Fendoch was deserted, the line of forts to the south was abandoned, and, even before some parts of it had been completed, the soldiers marched away from the massive legionary fortress further down the Tay at Inchtuthil.

At the very time when the power of the Empire was at its highest here, so its soldiers were suffering serious defeats elsewhere, in particular on the Dacian Danube frontier, in what is now Romania. During years of struggle, the Dacians had worked out successful hit-and-run tactics against the Roman army, and the Caledonians were soon to copy them.

Less than three years after Mons Graupius, the Romans had gone. The army retreated much further south and set up forts roughly along the line of the Tweed. But a child born in this valley in, say, the mid-70s AD would not have known life without the Romans until he was in his teens. If he lived to his mid-sixties, he would have seen them again, for in 140 AD they returned to rebuild and reoccupy the forts at Comrie and Perth, and to construct the Antonine Wall from the Forth to the Clyde. Once again, they stayed for about twenty years before they left, and once again it was due to a change of plan: Marcus Aurelius had become emperor. A philosopher and a highly experienced soldier, he insisted on keeping the empire within properly controllable limits.

More or less as soon as the Romans abandoned the fat lands between the Forth and the Tyne, the northern super-tribes – including the Caledonians – went on the rampage using Dacian hit-and-run methods. By 180 AD they were over the Antonine Wall and by 200 AD they were raiding the stone curtain of Hadrian's Wall. Just as men from the valley had probably gone north to join Calgacus's 30,000 strong Caledonian army in 83 AD, so young men would have joined Caledonian units heading south throughout this period, perhaps returning – if they were lucky – with plunder to show for it. Fourteen of Emperor Marcus Aurelius' silver coins have been found here.

These raids were too much for Emperor Septimius Severus. In 208 AD, he came to Britain in person and assembled the largest force ever to strike into Caledonian territory. He built a massive fort downstream by the Tay and marched though this valley once more. However, Severus died almost immediately and his sons hurried off to be at the centre of the ensuing political whirlwind in Rome. This was the last and shortest Roman incursion; nevertheless, for about 150 years there were few people in the valley who did not at some point in their lives have direct contact with men from many lands, all answerable to Rome.

Now historical darkness descends: ancient stones go silent and Roman writing stops. The circular homesteads remained occupied, but the valley economy drooped and some hill-forts were rebuilt to cope with intertribal skirmishes. However, the Romans left an unintentional, subtle and long-lasting two-part legacy.

First, opposition to the Romans had forced the tribes to unite; and this gave them a taste for how life in the highlands might be better-organized and better-governed. The different tribal units began to form themselves into something resembling a nation, with a clear hierarchy. One man, a Toiseach, controlled each local area.

There were probably five Toiseachs in the valley, in areas roughly corresponding to Fortingall, Dull, Weem, Grandtully and Logierait. Each family held land from their Toiseach. He ensured their security in return for payment in the form of cattle, corn, and services such as harvesting. He held considerable power, dispensing justice on his mote-hill and, if deemed necessary, executing people on his hanging-hill. These little hillocks have mostly disappeared, but in some cases the name lingers, as in Tomnacroich – Gallows Hill – at both Fortingall and Logierait.

The Toiseachs maintained peace locally and kept an ever-ready company of fighting men available for their direct superior, the Mormaer, who was based at Logierait and controlled the whole of Atholl. The Atholl Mormaer styled himself 'King', but was actually subject to the Pictish Over-King in his palace down at Forteviot near Perth.

This Over-King controlled a super-tribe, descendants of the Venicones conquered by the Romans. The people of Fortrenn, as they were called, were almost a nation; they dominated the area that now comprises Fife, Forfar, Perth and Kinross. To the west of Fortrenn lay the territory of the Scots. To the south, the Goddodin super-tribe was based on Edinburgh castle rock. Further south-west were the Britons of Strathclyde. And on the other side of the Grampians, another group of Picts controlled lands that stretched north as far as the Shetlands. The Forteviot Over-King was sometimes at war, sometimes at peace with any or all of these. Alliances were made though marriage; power was frequently exercised by use of high-born hostages.

The people of Fortrenn had several advantages. They had the extensive fertile fields of Strathearn that had originally attracted the Romans. They were wealthy and ready to trade. They had seen the benefits of strong Roman governance and had chosen to imitate it locally. And, during the later stages of Roman occupation, they had come into contact with the second part of the unintentional Roman legacy, Christianity.

Carrying a significance far beyond mere change of religion, Christian ethics reflected the requirements of increased wealth and trade. The simple belief that whatever one did to one's neighbour would be answerable before God, in an afterlife-court far higher than the local mote-hill, meant that entire communities could be more trusting. At almost exactly the same time as the last Roman units came through the valley in 208 AD, the Roman writer Tertullian claimed that Christ had succeeded in conquering parts of Britain that the legions had failed to take.

But the real impetus from Rome came a hundred or more years later via the tremendously dynamic church in Ireland. These men – and women: Saint Brigid, for example – were later pictured as dreamy Celts, but the Irish church was a powerhouse that sent and received churchmen from all over Europe. Although many of the monks came from aristocratic – and generally warlike – Irish families, many of them had visited Rome, or trained at the big Christian college at Auxerre, or carried out missionary work on the far side of the Danube. Initially they began to work among their Scots relatives over in Argyll (Ar-Gael, the land of the Gaels), but from soon after 400 AD they began to find their way up and over the Pass of Brander, along Loch Awe, through Glenorchy, along Loch Tay, or down Glenlyon, into the Aberfeldy valley. Their records are long-gone, but their legends are numerous. These men arrived, made their mark and travelled on.

Saint Palladius is reputed to have set up a cell in 469 AD, in the field immediately above the Crieff road where, now, the little bridge crosses the Moness burn. It used to be called the Feldy or Paldy burn. 'Aber' means 'the confluence of', and Aberfeldy is exactly at the confluence of the Tay and the Feldy/Paldy burn. 'Paldy' is the Celtic for Palladius. There is also a tale that Paldy was the name of a water-spirit that inhabited the burn, and there are several other examples of local saints being counter-interpreted as urisks, water-spirits.

After Saint Columba set up his monastery in Iona in 563 AD, the presence of saints in this area increased significantly. Columba's greatest disciple and biographer, Saint Adamnan, is reputed to have established the monastery at Dull, and his name remains in its Celtic 'Eonan' form in several local places.

Even if we choose to disregard all the tales told of saints in the valley, the sheer weight of names makes it impossible to deny their presence: Saint Ninian in Glenlyon, Saint Ciaran at Fearnan, Saint Dabhi and Saint Carmac on Loch Tay, Saint Muireach at Kenmore, Saints Cedd, Luag and Brandon at Fortingall, Saint Cuthbert at Weem and Saint Chadd at Logierait.

To the locals, these men might just as well have come from the moon. They had travelled vast distances to get here, and, like the Romans, they could read and write. They could handle the Celtic language sufficiently well to preach. They probably knew other tongues too – Saint Chadd and Saint Cedd were both Saxons – and they all certainly spoke the international lingua franca, Latin. They knew how to build labour-saving devices like watermills. In setting up monasteries they could mould entire communities into harmonious, self-sufficient profit-making units. They lived on nothing, they were made of iron and they preached faith, peace and love. Little wonder they made an impression.

The saints impressed not just the ordinary folk; they soon had the power-possessors on their knees, too. In the late 400s AD, the Over-King of the Picts provided these men with lands for their monasteries. Some historians argue that

Aerial photo of Fortingall monastery

powerful formerly-warlike families had found a new way to take control of territory, through prayer and writing, through farming and trade, rather than the sword.

Though much of what was written by the monks themselves has vanished, there are still traces of those early churchmen in our valley. Modern historians and archaeologists are convinced that the monasteries at Dull and Fortingall were exceptional. They were places of great influence throughout Pictland. Aerial photographs and archaeology have revealed substantial monastic buildings and enclosures, and from excavation work at another Columban site at Pormahomack, we now know how the monks lived.

Surrounding a typical monastery there was a ditch with banks both on the inside and on the outside to keep out wild animals and marauders. There was a church, a library, working and sleeping huts for the monks, a special hut for writing, accommodation for guests, a kitchen and a communal dining room; also a working area that included a smithy, and areas for woodwork, metalwork and leatherwork; and a cemetery. The buildings were constructed of timber, long since vanished. The monks brought with them heavy handbells and a taste for incising crosses onto great stone slabs. There are examples of these bells and stone slab crosses in Dull, Weem and Fortingall.

The new monasteries were often set up within sight of the old monuments. At Dull where the remains of the monastery look down on an ancient 'four-poster' setting of stones, the new priests chose not to have the old monument

Dull Church with the 1,400 year old cross, centre

removed. There is still a taboo connected with shifting these stones.

Rulers allowed priests to baptise them, and, perhaps more significantly, they accepted the Church's mediation between themselves and God. Coronations became acts involving kings, priests and the Trinity. The Church insisted that kings copy the biblical King David in having their eldest sons as their successors, thus creating peaceful transferences of power. Traditional death-of-king bloodbaths became outdated and unnecessary. The Church taught Celtic and Anglo-Saxon royal families and traders to read, write and communicate with each other in Latin, a powerful stimulant not only for trade but also for ideas, art and culture.

People in power acquired disposable wealth, used to promote specialists such as jewellers and sculptors. Much of the art produced was of course related to power: the inlaid brooches, elaborately chased buckles and silver sword hasps could be used in ceremonies. The gorgeous silver chains, necklaces and pendants could be given as gifts. Examples of breathtaking beauty and workmanship glow in the Royal Scottish Museum in Edinburgh.

Pictish sculptors soon began to produce much more intricately-carved stone crosses than those of the monks, and they carried them over long distances. There is one in Fortingall that was almost certainly made over in Strathmore. The sculptors produced the most extraordinarily vibrant, living carvings. To get an idea of their beauty and power, the best example is the Dunfallandy Stone, not far from Logierait. Its location can hardly be a coincidence as Logierait was the centre for Atholl, and these stones often lie close to similar centres across Pictland. Logierait itself has a Pictish cross and a serpent-sculpted cross-slab.

The carvings on the Pictish cross-slabs are an exciting, enigmatic testament from these now-silent people. The Dunfallandy stone has an elaborate cross on its front, but on the back, among other enigmatic symbols, there are two crescents with V-shaped rods across them, a double disc, and a weird long-snouted, curled-footed beast. These symbols – together with a comb, a mirror and a strange Z-rod device – occur again and again across Pictland, from Shetland to Fife. The fluidity and vigour in the depiction of people

Diagram of figures on the Pictish Dunfallandy stone, dating from about 700AD

and animals is stunning; but so far there has been no Rosetta Stone to unlock their meaning.

Atholl was in Pictland, but in fact the original word 'Athfotla' means 'New Ireland'. Somehow Pictish power hereabouts faded. Quite apart from the large number of Irish missionaries and monks sent from Iona to the local monasteries, Gaelic-speaking Scots had begun to migrate eastwards into the area. For example there was an outbreak of plague at the western end of the valley that decimated the inhabitants, and it was subsequently resettled by Scots incomers from Lorn and Oban in Argyllshire.

So the Scots began to move into the valley and, despite regular jockeying for power, the new Christian ethic shared between Picts and Scots meant that there was an increasing sense of unity and trust throughout the region, and an upsurge in trade and culture. It was too good to last.

Into the Mist

The days of the iron-hard saints were over. The Church's influence over kings waned. Here, the beginning of the decline was marked by the accidental drowning of a king at the west end of the valley; it ended with the forced drowning of another in the east.

In 647, Donald, King of the Argyll Scots was drowned in Loch Tay. No more is known of the accident, but it means that dark-haired, Gaelic-speaking Argyll Scots were certainly in the Aberfeldy valley by that time, sometimes fighting the fair-haired Picts, sometimes befriending them. With its fords over the Lyon, the Tay and the Tummel, the valley was on the main route between Argyll and Pictland. The 600s and 700s were a time of warfare between the two nations. It was not a simple two-sided conflict: Pictland itself was often divided and there were also battles with the Anglo-Saxons down in Lothian and the Britons over in Strathclyde.

During the same period, a rift grew between the Churches of Rome and Iona. The valley's trackways were the link between Iona and the rising, Rome-influenced monastic centres of Dunkeld, Scone and St. Andrews. Quite apart from the fact that Rome and Iona had different dates for Easter, and the monks at Dull and Fortingall wore their hair shaved at the front in the Ionan manner – those further east wore it with a tonsure – wealthy and powerful Rome perceived Iona's reputation for sincerity and simplicity as a threat. It acted. The Ionans were outnumbered and defeated in debate at Whitby in 664, but Saint Adamnan and Saint Cedd – names associated with Dull and Fortingall respectively – held out against the influence of Rome. They were powerful men. Cedd was Bishop of Iona. Adamnan had negotiated an international pact between the three kings of Pictland, Argyll and Ireland; it established that women, children and priests should not be harmed in warfare, Christian values that lasted until the Vikings came.

However, with the death of these saints, the Iona community finally accepted the dictates of Rome, and in 717, from his palace at Forteviot down near Perth, Nechtan, Over-King of the Picts, ordered Ionan monks to leave. The power of Dull and Fortingall waned. New crosses in the elaborate Pictish style were brought in, significantly from the east.

Potentates sometimes used the differences between Iona and Rome for their own purposes, as in the case of the second royal drowning, the one at the east end of the valley: Nechtan died at Forteviot, and in the ensuing struggle, a non-relative, Angus, forced his way to power. Talorgan, Nechtan's half-brother resisted him and tried to re-establish traditional Ionan influence. Like Atholl Mormaers before him, Talorgan styled himself 'King of Atholl' and his court was at Logierait. In 739, Angus defeated Talorgan, then forcibly drowned him. No one knows where the drowning was done or what sort of ritual was involved.

It was to be another hundred years before the Pictish control of this area completely evaporated, and by that time the Picts had dominated a substantial part of what was to become Scotland – including the Aberfeldy valley – for eight hundred years. Many of us must still carry their genes.

Into this relatively peaceful and prosperous land roared the first, piratical Vikings. Islands and ports suffered first. From 795AD, Iona, the mother-monastery of the Dull and Fortingall priests, was sacked three times in seven years. Each time, the surviving monks couldn't believe such horrors would be repeated and bent to their desks once more. These first Vikings – unlike their descendants – had no time for documents; what they wanted was gold, silver, jewels and slaves. As the raids continued, what was left of Iona's valuable library and its astonishing collection of religious artefacts and reliquaries was gradually divided up. Part of it was sent to Kells in Ireland, and the rest travelled down through Fortingall, Dull, Weem and Strathtay on its way to Dunkeld.

The helmeted, axe-wielding, Vikings strode straight into places that were held most sacred by Picts, Scots, Anglo-Saxons and Britons alike. The threat of the Norsemen forced the little kingdoms to unite, and it centralised the church. Only twenty years after the Vikings' first raid on Iona, Argyll and Pictland had one king over both nations: Constantine, based at Forteviot, near Perth. Initially the Pictish government with its system of raising men in arms stood up fairly well to the Vikings, but in 839 the Pictish army, led by its Over-King, its Mormaers and its Toiseachs, together with contingents from Argyll, gathered and attacked the invaders head-on. The Picts – including the men from this valley – were utterly destroyed.

The loss of so many Pictish leaders created a vacuum, and into it – in 842 – stepped the Gaelic-speaking Scot, Kenneth MacAlpin, the man generally recognised as the first proper king of Scotland. MacAlpin, being an Argyll Scot and a Gaelic-speaker, called the land he ruled by its Gaelic name, Alba, which remains the modern Gaelic word for Scotland. The word is hidden in Aberfeldy's 'Breadalbane Arms'. Initially his power base was Forteviot, the former Pictish administrative centre close to Perth. For the next hundred years, the three monasteries of Dunkeld, Scone – also close to Perth – and St Andrews, with their associated royal accommodation, were the key centres of power. One only had to walk to the Logierait Ferry and take a boat downstream to Dunkeld to find oneself at the apex of the triangular heart of Scottish religion and politics. But Kenneth MacAlpin's accession did not prevent disaster coming to the valley.

The dragon-shaped prows came nosing up the Tay past Dunkeld in 845. Dragging their longships through the shallows, their crews seized anything and anyone they fancied. Quite apart from the human cost, irreplaceable books and illuminated manuscripts in the monasteries at Dull and Fortingall went up in smoke. When Kenneth MacAlpin came closer, pushed back the Vikings, and made Dunkeld his capital, local people may have felt more secure. He brought a handful of Saint Columba's bones to the church there. The beautiful little church-shaped reliquary that contained Saint Columba's relics is in Royal Scottish Museum in Edinburgh. The delicate silver casket almost certainly passed down the Aberfeldy valley on its way from Iona to Dunkeld, pausing, with ceremonies, at the local monasteries en route.

Though Dunkeld's importance rose, the old monastery on Iona still held a powerful spell. Like so many Argyll kings before him, when Kenneth MacAlpin died in 858, his body was taken to Iona for burial and the Scottish kings who succeeded him were also buried there. And so from time to time, this valley witnessed the solemn progress of royal funeral cortéges as they passed through on their way to the west. The priests – now tonsured – would have rung the ancient handbells, and the singing of old songs would have awakened memories of the great days of the saints. Children would have been told of their miraculous deeds; of how, for example, as a plague raged through the valley, Saint Adamnan stopped the dreadful visitation in its tracks. Thus far, no further. Glenlyon children can still point to the spot, Saint Adamnan's Cross, up beside Craigianie today.

In 909, King Constantine II, at the head of the soldiers of the new nation of Scotland, finally stopped the Viking raids altogether and confined them to the land they already controlled. The Norsemen were to return to this valley later, in different guise. But, after a hundred years of attacks, the damage had been done. There are no records from the monasteries in the valley and from the moment the marauders appeared up the Tay from Dunkeld, the valley and its people disappear into mist. Though we know something of what was happening further downstream, Aberfeldy is shrouded in a historical fog that lingers for almost four hundred years and which does not begin to clear until, ironically, documents demanded by the descendants of the Vikings appear.

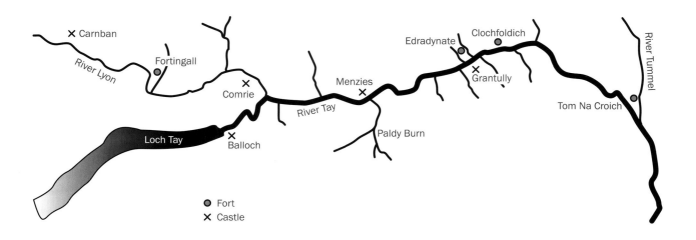

The Coming of Abyrpheallaidh

The first Vikings had no time for books and papers. Ironically it was their descendant's absolute reliance on legal paperwork that brings Aberfeldy out of the mist again. By the 1200s, the Anglo-Normans were in control of the southern part of Scotland. Their ancestors were the Norsemen who had landed in Normandy in 911, only two years after Constantine had united Scotland against them. These Anglo-Normans had great-grandfathers who had fought alongside William the Conqueror at Hastings and taken brutal control of as much of Britain as they could.

In the agricultural areas to the east and south of Scotland the feudal system took over from the old forms of government: all land was held directly or indirectly from the king, in return for military service. The King could and did grant lands to churches and to deserving nobles, who in turn could grant land to lesser men. Some Celtic chieftains integrated and 'Normanified', but in the highlands the tribal way of life generally remained.

Here by the Tay, on the cusp between highland and lowland, men still rendered goods and services to their lords and stood ready to fight if required, much as they had done for centuries. As before, there was a sense of being in between: no longer was the valley a hinterland between Argyll and Atholl, west and east; it had reverted to being close to the frontier between north and south, as in Roman times. In 1211, the last of the Celtic Earls of Atholl died and the final link with the Pictish Atholl Mormaers was broken. But the administrative area remained basically the same as in Pictish times. A handful of Anglo-Norman papers prove it.

In 1235, Weem Church is mentioned in a charter, at a time when the Chamberlain of Scotland was Sir Robert de Meyners (Menzies). Sir Robert was responsible for managing the entire Scottish exchequer and for ensuring the proper collection of all rents due to his king, Alexander II. Sir Robert was reappointed as Chamberlain when the eight-year old Alexander III came to the throne in 1249. Seventeen years later in 1266, we have the first actual evidence of the link between Weem and the Menzies family. Sir Robert's son, perhaps unsurprisingly named Alexander, was granted land around Weem. Like other grand families – the Bruces, the Balliols, the Fitzalans, the Grants, the Camerons, the Comyns – the de Meyners had come from France, from Mesnieres, and were now closely linked to the royal court in Edinburgh. The court itself was essentially similar to other European courts in culture and manners as well as arms and armour. The Normans had adapted well. Many now saw themselves as Scots and indeed were prepared to fight to keep Scotland as a separate nation, with its own king and its own feudal system.

Here, just inside the ring of the mountains, small pockets of gentility began to take hold. The former monasteries and religious communities metamorphosed into parishes run by priests answerable to bishops. Most of the area was controlled by the King or by the Earl of Atholl, or by men who held land from them. In general it was a reasonably peaceful self-contained interlocking structure but Scotland soon fell out with what was to become the traditional enemy. Kings based in London considered Scotland to be the northern part of their realm, just as they thought that lands as far south as Aquitaine were rightfully theirs. In 1296, after a shocking defeat at Dunbar, 2000 of the most influential Scots were forced to confirm their names on the Ragman Roll, a roll of fealty to King Edward 1, and the English army occupied huge areas of Scotland, including the Aberfeldy valley.

This is the moment when Aberfeldy itself first appears. One of the men who signed the oath of fealty to Edward 1 was John de Strathbogie, the Earl of Atholl. In the same year he signed a small charter: he granted about 1,500 acres in the valley – including two villages – to Sir Alexander Menzies; and the names of the two villages involved were Weem and 'Abyrpheallaidh'.

The Anglo-Norman occupation – and friction between warlords, like Robert Bruce and John Comyn, often prepared to fight for whichever side promised most – brought building developments to the valley in the form of defensive earthworks: mottes, which are mounds with timber palisades; ring-works which were similar but circular; and moated sites which are mounds with ditches or natural burns running round the sides. Archaeologists and historians cannot agree how military these sites were during their periods of use. Some prefer to call them mediaeval homesteads. Nevertheless, key sites in the Aberfeldy valley are strategically placed defendable installations even if they happen to have been later used as homesteads too.

If a map of the Roman forts in Scotland is laid on top of a map of the Anglo-Norman defensive sites, they correspond closely. But, unlike the Romans who paused on the other side of the hills at Fendoch, the Anglo-Normans built at least four forts in the Aberfeldy valley. They are still here. There are the remains of a fine one above Logierait overlooking the confluence of the Tummel and the Tay, built on top of a much earlier fortification. Another, carefully sited on the north bank of the Tay near Clochfoldich, makes use of two steep natural ditches as part of its defences. It was built by English soldiers in King Edward I's occupying army around 1296, so the story goes, and there were still two families called Mac-an-t'Sassunaich (sons of the Sassenachs) living in Strathtay in the 1600s. A third fort is on the east side of the Cluny burn, not far from Milton of Cluny. It is still known as Edradynate Castle and stands strategically above the point where the Tay narrows into a roaring torrent.

The fourth fort is at Fortingall, in the elbow of the River Lyon, guarding the approaches to the valley from Loch Tay and Glenlyon. It has a fine moat, fed by a small burn, and its fishpond – so important to mediaeval forts and monasteries – still ripples close by. There appear to be signs of outer banks, too, which resemble similar enclosures on sites in the south of England. Some experts have rendered the meaning of the word Fortingall as 'the fort of the foreigners', and not far northwestwards lies the significantly-named Glen Sassunn. The blows of Edward I, the 'Hammer of the Scots' rang out loudly in the Aberfeldy valley.

There were more forts: there is one half-way up Glenlyon, opposite Innerwick; and it is perfectly likely that the valley's four big castles, Grantully,

Weem, Taymouth and Meggernie now stand on what originally were simple defensive earthworks with timber palisades. Grantully stands opposite Edradynate Castle, for example, blocking the other side of the Tay. All this amounts to a serious occupation, although it was nothing compared to the number of Anglo-Norman military installations much further south: the whole of Scotland has less than 400 mottes, ring-works and moated sites, whereas in Essex alone there are 800.

Shortly after that first mention of Aberfeldy in 1296 came another charter. In 1301, the Earl of Atholl granted land to Alexander's son, Sir Robert Menzies. It is not clear whether this is more land or simply a change to the earlier charter; but it mentions 'Abyrfealdybeg'. 'Beg' means 'little' in Gaelic and it refers to the two groups of houses on the western side of the Feldy burn, called Upper Milton and Lower Milton, roughly above and below what is now Bank Street. It also implies that Aberfeldy proper, on the east side of the burn was larger. Together with Moness, these three villages remained more or less separate entities until the coming of General Wade's bridge in 1733. So by 1301 the Aberfeldy community was already laid out in a shape that, with its ford and ferry just upstream of the place where the Feldy burn flows into the Tay, was to last for the next four hundred years.

We can piece this together from Anglo-Norman papers. We would know very much more – not only about this period but also about the era which preceded it – had Edward I not taken cartloads of Scottish papers and records south from Perth and Edinburgh, along with the Stone of Scone. At some point someone down in London must have looked at the dusty records from up north, shrugged, and consigned them all to a bonfire; so much vital data about Scotland's transition from a collection of warring groups into a nation-state, so much about the valley too, up into the London air. A bonfire, lit by Anglo-Normans obsessive about paper, shrouded Aberfeldy's past in centuries of smoke.

*King Robert
Bruce (b1274
k:1306-1329)*

Six Men from Dusty Charters

Surviving Anglo-Norman charters first prove the existence of Aberfeldy around the time of the English occupation and the struggle for Scottish independence, but they also show what happened to people actually living here in that crucial period between 1286 and 1314.

Six men with swords, in chain-mail and heavy helmets, their shields bearing bright coats-of-arms, stride out from the musty local verbiage: John Comyn, Patrick le Grand, Hugo de Erthe, Alexander Menzies, John of Atholl, and William Oliphant. All six either lived here in the valley, or were paid from here, or controlled land here. All six were deeply involved in the fighting and were taken prisoner by the English after the Battle of Dunbar in 1296. All six would have heard of the construction of forts such as Clochfoldich in the valley. And their fates, recorded in the paperwork, serve to show what happened to hundreds more whose names will never be known.

Sir John Comyn, Earl of Badenoch was better known as 'The Red Comyn', perhaps because of the red background of his coat-of-arms, or his beard, or his temper. His family's power-base was further north, but the charters show that he controlled a large section of the Aberfeldy valley. When King Alexander III fell off his horse and was killed in 1286, the Red Comyn claimed the Scottish throne. Two other claimants were John Balliol and Robert Bruce. All three held lands in England from their liege-lord, King Edward I, who decided that Balliol, the weakest of the three, should be king.

King John Balliol promptly went to war against Edward to safeguard Scotland's independence. The Red Comyn joined the new Scots king and raised forces from all his highland fiefs; so local men who acknowledged Comyn as their liege-lord had to march south to join the Scots army. King Edward smashed the Scots at Dunbar, stripped Balliol of his kingship, and took the Red Comyn prisoner. Edward – who sometimes made use of hard, not entirely trustworthy men – pardoned and released him. He was to meet a worse fate: in 1306, in a church in Dumfries, Robert Bruce – who had until recently been fighting alongside Edward I – stabbed the Red Comyn, left him to die, then had himself crowned King of Scots.

The charters show that two of the Red Comyn's key men were also taken prisoner at Dunbar: Captain Patrick le Grand, commander of Cluny Castle in Fife; and the man who paid him, Baillie Hugo de Erthe, the Red Comyn's administrator for the extensive lands of the former monastery in Dull. Both men were never heard of again. There would have been scores of other local men captured too, not important enough to be recorded. Many families in Dull and Weem, and in Aberfeldy's hamlets, waited in vain for news of their husbands or sons who had marched away.

Earl John of Atholl was much more important. In order to obtain pardon he swore fealty to Edward and added his seal to the Ragman Roll. But he did not remain loyal to Edward for long, and when Robert Bruce was crowned with a golden circlet at Scone, Earl John was by his side. Shortly after, King Robert faced a joint force of English and MacDougalls in Rannoch, and Earl John was again beside him. The MacDougall chief was determined to avenge his father-in-law, the murdered Red Comyn. King Robert escaped – just – but Earl John was taken prisoner by the English once more; and this time they hanged him.

Sir Alexander Menzies was the man who had received land in the valley from Earl John in 1296. As Earl John's vassal, he had led his men south and was also captured. He was relatively small fry, a mere Scottish MP; he had to languish in an English gaol for a couple of years before finally talking himself free and returning to his wife Agnes and his new lands in Aberfeldy. When the English arrived here, they probably forced the locals to build their forts and they almost certainly acted with the ferocity recorded in other places. The Menzies chief may have submitted, but he bided his time. When fighting came to the valley, he and his men sided with King Robert Bruce. The King subsequently rewarded Sir Alexander with a considerable amount of land formerly controlled by the murdered Red Comyn. In addition to the Abthanage of Dull, he also received parts of Rannoch, Glendochart, Glenorchy, and even estates in the lowlands. His descendants were to remain major local landholders in this area for almost exactly six hundred years.

What of the sixth man? Of all six, Sir William Oliphant's career was perhaps the most extraordinary. He too was taken prisoner at Dunbar and locked away in an English prison in Devizes. Finally released, by 1304 he was in command of the Scots garrison in Stirling Castle when it was besieged by Edward I and eventually taken. Once again he was imprisoned, then pardoned. Edward placed him in charge of the English garrison in Perth. He was still in command there when King Robert and the Scots attacked and took the garrison in 1313. This was an ironic role-reversal as it had been Robert Bruce who had commanded Edward's English siege-engines at Stirling in 1304, when Sir William had commanded the Scots. This time Oliphant was sent to prison in the Hebrides, but he was released in time to change sides once more and fight beside King Robert at the triumphant Battle of Bannockburn.

In 1320 the nobles, clergy and commons sent a message to the Pope, the Declaration of Arbroath; they swore they would rather die than lose their liberty to the English. Perhaps recalling Bruce's earlier changes of heart, they added that if he himself broke the oath they would get rid of him. Sir William Oliphant was one of the signatories. And in 1328, just before Robert the Bruce died, the old king signed a charter granting lands in Glenlyon to his former twice-turned adversary, Sir William Oliphant.

Throughout Scotland, buried in dusty papers from this period, there are similar convoluted, life-or-death, snakes-and-ladders tales of local grandees. But how did the local people in the valley feel about these men, with their Anglo-Norman names, with their refined manners, with their talk of fealty and homage, with their murderous, sometimes utterly destructive power-struggles?

Grandees

As the nobles with their retinues and their Anglo-Norman names trotted past on their great war-horses, heading for or returning from far-off places, the local people must have felt these men were from some other world. Most folk never left the valley in their entire lives; their families had been rooted here for centuries. Generations of tenants, smallholders and labourers had worked together if not in harmony, at least in the same language and according to the same unwritten laws, laws meted out by the local Toiseach on his hanging-mound. Great men like Comyn, Atholl, Oliphant and – even Alexander Menzies and Hugo de Erthe – were very different.

The speed at which land began to change hands disturbed the locals, too. Immense swathes were granted out by the king to men he could trust, and when they turned against him, or when a new king came to power, the land often changed hands again. The Menzieses for example profited mightily from their support of Robert Bruce, but later lost some of their lands as the power of the Stewarts rose. Long before even the Romans arrived, people in the valley had expected their neighbours to keep their word, but these Anglo-Normans were modern men who believed in paper proof. That a piece of paper could be more important than a man's word would have been absolutely inconceivable to any highlander.

There was a change of emphasis, too. The stress shifted away from the character and loyalty of the people in the valley to how much the area might generate in terms of revenue and goods. There was no Scottish equivalent of William the Conqueror's Domesday Book, which assessed the value of every parish and estate in England, but many of the Anglo-Norman barons held land in both countries and certainly viewed their lands in Scotland in the same way as their English domains.

In 1305 Edward I insisted that the old Celtic laws be scrapped and replaced by feudal ones, and the Anglo-Norman Guardians – of whom was John Comyn was one – made no attempt to resist. All over Scotland local people began to feel disconnected from their rulers. But in highland areas, where the ancient Celtic traditions and way of life had continued relatively unchanged for a millennium, it was much more serious. Aberfeldy, though administratively 'lowland', was still essentially 'highland'.

So, as bands of soldiers under one flag or another came through the valley, seizing the locals' carefully-husbanded food supplies at sword-point, or as yet another non-Gaelic-speaking grandee took control of their lands and installed a new baillie, or as they discovered they were no longer able to settle their differences in the customary ways, there was growing resentment and occasional lawlessness. This was not simply another group of power-possessors taking over; it was an attack on the core beliefs that underpinned the whole of highland life. It was the complete sidelining of an ancient, tried-and-tested, much-loved, orally-based, traditional culture.

But these Anglo-Norman aristocrats proved they could be adaptable. Many of them – including Robert Bruce – spoke Gaelic, and many adopted the ancient custom of boarding out their sons with their senior tenants. These noble lads picked up an understanding and sympathy for local customs and traditions, and they learned details, gathered over centuries, of how best to farm, of the ways of fish and of the vagaries of the weather. They could see why most valley inhabitants moved up to the shielings with the cattle in the summer, and then returned to snug down in the wintertons against the snow and the long nights.

The Anglo-Norman families often replaced the local timber churches with stone-built ones, as the Menzieses did at Weem. Like many others across Scotland, the Menzies tenants could feel proud of their new building, where they could pray in comfort and hear the Word of God. Like other landholders, the Menzieses made sure that they themselves approved of the form in which the Word of God was delivered.

As the Stuart kings gained power, Stewart families were given lands first at the west end of the valley and then, replacing the de Bercleys, in the east. Menzies land stood between. There were other lesser lairds such as the Flemyngs in Moness above Aberfeldy. Ancient clans such as the MacDiarmids in Glenlyon and the MacNaughtons near Kenmore survived, and watched men like Sir William Oliphant come and go.

A new name appears: Campbell. The clan's origins are obscure; they may or may not have been a family with Celtic origins, but in any case they were quick to adapt and exploit Anglo-Norman ways. By the early 1300s they had developed a doubtful reputation, and gradually the power of the rapacious Campbells of Glenorchy began to spread eastwards. The Campbells were masters of the manipulation of paper proof. By its use they were able to take over control of lands previously in the hands of other clans, including the Menzieses and not least the MacGregors. The MacGregors reacted violently to what they saw as newfangled and underhanded methods and as a result later found themselves outlawed.

But as the Campbells moved east, it was a member of another grand family that attracted the most obloquy, a prince no less, a great grandson of King Robert the Bruce: Alexander Stewart. He had been kept on a tight leash – sometimes imprisoned – by his tough grandfather, King David II, but as soon as David died in 1371, Alexander began to work on the new king, his father, the weaker Robert II. In less than a year he was lord of most of the huge highland area of Badenoch. Two years later he got control of the ex-Comyn lands of Dull and not only stopped paying taxes, but seized those collected by other lairds. Seven years on, he married one of his sons to a Menzies heiress and so gained Fortingall.

By that time Alexander Stewart was already a middle-aged man, unmarried yet with a substantial clan of illegitimate children around him. His greatest coup was to court and marry a widow, Countess Euphemia of Ross, the most eligible heiress of the time. She brought with her vast tracts of land in Skye, Lewis, Caithness, Sutherland, Nairn, Inverness and Banff. Although he styled himself

Earl of Buchan, he is better-known as The Wolf of Badenoch. Within a year or so he deserted the Countess for his long-time mistress, Mariota. Rebuked by the Bishop of Murray and ordered to return to his wife, the Wolf responded by marching on Elgin cathedral and burning it down. The bishop himself only just escaped the flames.

Being a prince, the Wolf spent much time on the move. Kings and princes travelled constantly at that time for several reasons: to exert control, to honour their nobles with visits, to show their faces to their subjects, to vary their hunting, and to prevent supplies being exhausted in any given area. One of the Wolf's favourite castles was Garth, still a forbidding sight. It sits in the cleft of the Keltney Burn, frowning down on the valley between Dull and Fortingall, a walk up the hill track from General David Stewart's statue. Some absolutely rational locals insist it is haunted.

Later, Garth was the home of one of The Wolf's descendants, Neil 'Gointe' (Gaelic 'The Fated') Stewart, a man with a similar disregard for any authority. In 1502, he was enraged when James IV granted lands in Rannoch to his neighbour the peaceable and law-abiding Sir Robert Menzies, comfortably settled in his new castle at Weem. Neil, who considered Rannoch rightfully his, marched along to Weem, burned Sir Robert's castle, destroyed the family papers, and

Tomb of Alexander Stewart, Wolf of Badenoch (1343?-1405?) in Dunkeld Cathedral

took Sir Robert himself away to the dungeon below Garth. Partly because Neil was married to the daughter of the then Earl of Atholl, news of the business went to the highest level. King James had to visit the valley personally to sort matters out. The king rode into the valley from the Sheriff Court at Logierait and almost certainly stayed at Grantully.

The Stewarts at Grantully lived well. Their linen was soft and their plaids, silks and brocades were beautifully made and richly-coloured; they had red velvet bed curtains, embroidered with blue silk. Even the dogs had silk leashes and silver-studded collars. But a royal visit was something of a poisoned chalice: new beds, new bedcovers, new tapestries, new curtains. The Stewarts would have struggled to provide King James' idea of a banquet, which – quite apart from usual items like cream, milk, eggs, cheese, butter, oats and barley – might need two capons, two chickens, two sheep, a haunch of venison, a side of beef, a whole pig, three pheasants, three rabbits, five salmon, six partridges, a basket of eels; and a swan.

On separate sideboards, the King would expect such delicacies as bowls of almonds, hazels, figs, dates, raisins and olives. Cooking ingredients included olive oil, vinegar, salt, pepper, honey, sugar, cinnamon, cumin, nutmeg, mace, ginger, sage and rice; and two more, ginger-like galingale and balsam-scented spikenard; and mountains of wheaten bread loaves, a real rarity for ordinary people. There would also be wine: Gascon red, Malmsey, Muscadet and white Rhenish, some brought from the ice-house and the rest from cooling in the Tay. Beer, too, made with hops, unlike the barley-only ale drunk by ordinary people.

So, in contrast, what was life like for lesser folk?

Life for Ordinary People

By far the majority ordinary people were involved in the growing and the rearing of the food they ate. They went to local markets at Kenmore, Fortingall, Dull, Weem and Logierait to sell surpluses, and to buy items they themselves did not grow, or rear, or make. Down in Perth, the tanners, bakers, shoemakers, butchers, weavers, carpenters and wheelwrights were ready buyers of the valley's extra produce – if it could be got along what passed for roads. What concerned folk most was the weather and how it affected the land. Almost all food was grown locally. A bad harvest or an outbreak of animal disease signalled a serious survival struggle for almost everyone in the valley.

Most land was held by tenants in small parcels on yearly leases and was managed by the tenant's family and a handful of labourers. A lease that could be terminated after a year did not encourage tenants to build substantial houses, so most people lived in simple thatched, turf-built or wattle-walled homes. If they had regular employment, they might risk using stone, but there was the constant fear of what a rampaging army might do to a building of any size; or what they might do to crops. It was much easier to shift cattle and sheep out of the path of an oncoming army. In effect most people were barely a step away from slavery. Only when James IV came to power in 1488 did things begin to change. He had had a long exile in England. He brought English ideas and systems back with him, and encouraged his nobles and their baillies to rent larger areas of land for longer periods.

But it would be foolish to think that from the 1300s to the 1500s poor people's lives were constantly unhappy. People made the best of their lives; they played football, chess and an early form of golf. They attended weekly archery practice, as required by law. Some ministers permitted wrestling in their churchyards; others did not. Wednesdays, Fridays and Saturdays were fish days, no meat or dairy products; and, officially, no sex.

Weddings and funerals were great opportunities for getting together. In many cases, young couples received a very solid start when they wed. Friends and relations, depending on how well-set they themselves were, would bring eggs, butter, fat hens, mutton shoulders, kebbucks of cheese, linen sheets, blankets, bedcovers, possibly a couple of chairs, perhaps even a table. There would be a feast, with cnotan – a special barley broth – chicken and mutton to follow, and plenty of ale and whisky. Hats were passed round, usually one for the fiddler and one for the drink.

As for funerals, some of them were epic, especially when a laird died; there are stories of talk, games and drinking going on so long that people forgot all about the body. A week seems to have been the local record before everyone sobered up, remembered the corpse, and the priest was well enough again to perform the rites.

On the whole, priests seem to have been popular and well-respected. They knew their congregations extremely well. On occasion they were known to act swiftly and discreetly. One local minister is said to have found a couple in a hedge, the man naked, herself with no shoes on, and married them on the spot. Very aware of local superstition about fairies taking unbaptised children, priests would be quick to splash holy water on any weak-looking newborn. The formalities could come later if the child survived.

Most families lived in 'black houses'. The house would be literally black inside. A peat fire burned in the centre and the wafting smoke eventually found its way out through the thatched roof. The family shared their living space with their animals, for almost all had a least one cow and a few chickens. The small doorway might well be covered with a leather apron; wood was at a premium, used first for tools, and only secondarily for planks or window-frames. Chairs were rare, beds and tables even rarer. The commonest form of seating was a stool, carried to church on Sundays for the long sermons.

Imagine a sixty-year-old widow, living with her family in Easter Aberfeldy. Perhaps her husband had been a labourer, a cottar working for one of the Flemyng laird's tenants, a man at the bottom of the pile. Sixty was old; crippling arthritis was a common problem, but there were a few cases of folk who lived to over a hundred. There was no system of support for such people, although they might receive help from the local church's Poor Box if they were desperate, providing the parish itself was in funds.

Most important would be her relationship with her own family. The chances are that a sixty-year old would be a grandmother, possibly a great grandmother, and she'd have an important role to play in the household. She would care for young children while older ones worked alongside adults. She was a sort of moral compass, the bearer of family values and stories, the teller of wonderful tales in the long evenings. Her stories of good and bad years would be listened to carefully. The knowledge and experience of age was respected. Religion occupied an enormous part in mediaeval people's lives; the biblical commandment to 'honour thy father and mother' was closely adhered to.

If a visitor entered the widow's house on, say, a chilly late February day, she would probably blow the fire a little brighter, mutter the Gaelic blessing of the rekindling, and offer a bowl of broth. It was very important to be hospitable to strangers. Otherwise how could she be sure of her own folk's survival when they themselves had to travel? She would swing the kailpot from above the fire where it had been simmering, and ladle a little broth into a wooden bowl. Though thin, it would taste good, greenish from the kail and flavoured with barley, peas and perhaps a bit of dried mutton. Spring would bring young nettle-heads, another good ingredient. Above her, lit by the faint light of a crusie – a tallow lamp – the rafters would be hung with suet puddings, oatmeal bags, bunches of onions, kebbucks of cheese, and perhaps a half-leg of mutton. More mutton might be stored in crocks of brine. With stores like that and spring coming, clearly her family would have weathered the winter well. Some winters would have reduced them to tartan-purry, which is kail and oatmeal, or even drammock, plain oatmeal and water. Many houses kept stores of dried silverweed roots to eat in extremis. In such times of near starvation, it was not unknown to let a weakly child fade, just to keep the rest alive.

At the other end of the cottage, a cow would be standing in its stall, possibly bled a couple of times over the winter for black puddings. But she would be likely to come into milk again soon to supply plenty of milk, cream and butter. All being well, winter or summer, the widow and her family would eat porridge for breakfast, barley broth for midday, and brochan in the evening. Brochan is porridge oats with a bit of onion and cheese grated in. Teeth were cleaned with oak twigs.

Honey was used not only for sweetening but also for ailments and burns. Sage and thyme helped upset stomachs. Camomile calmed people and sent them off to sleep. Boiled violets eased fevers. Beeswax made excellent candles, although a household such is this would only use them for special occasions such as story-telling nights, when the tales were of Fingal, his wars, and his love for Grania; or long descriptions of past events, such as King James IV's visit, or the year of the battle of Flodden when so few came back, or of the Glenlyon McNab who demanded that his tenants' wives and daughters bring in the harvest naked, and whose horse stumbled and killed him the very same day.

The widow would know all the songs, songs for tending the kailyard, for milking the cow, for digging the peat in spring, for leading the women at the fulling of the tweed, and for working in the kailyard with a cascrom – a footplough. Or just for being by the fire, spinning wool with spindle and whorl. Knitting and darning for her family would have taken plenty of her time. She would know the secrets of dyeing wool, too, finding the raw materials, saffron or bog-myrtle for yellow, sundew for purple, iris for blue grey, and madder for red. She might get the madder from a pedlar, who would supply her with vital little items over the years: needles, thimbles, and scissors which he would sharpen again for her from time to time. She would get horn spoons, pots and pans from the tinkers, often dispossessed MacGregors from over in Rannoch.

Summer treats included nasturtiums cooked in butter, or a barley bannock topped with crowdie, which is crumbly white soft cheese. The old lady would still summer with the other women and children up at the sheilings in Glen Cochill, spinning and singing, caring for the cattle, making butter and cheese, keeping half an eye on the younger children while the older ones disappeared for the day to hunt and fish in the burns and lochans. While she was away in the hills, perhaps her sons would cut new sods for the cottage roof and give it a new coat of heather.

It is quite likely that some of her friends would have had children from liaisons with young masters, and then been married off to labourers. Being the mother of a noble's child was a sort of insurance policy, if you behaved yourself of course. Your sin would be forgiven by the local priest, himself appointed by the noble's family. Your labourer husband's chances of regular work and support for your subsequent family would be better than others. This was as true in the 1500s as it was in the 1300s. Often the grander the family, the more out-of-wedlock children they sired. The Wolf, a prince, supposedly sired thirteen sons and even more daughters; none were legitimate. Among others, the Stewarts of Crossmount, over in Rannoch, were proud to be his descendants.

Besides the daily routine to ensure survival, the most important thing for everyone in the Aberfeldy valley was how nobles and families and clans interacted. Peace was a fragile thing, easily fractured by pride and anger among the powerful, its loss sucking so many innocents into swordplay.

*Grantully Castle
in the 1900s*

Lairds, Castles and Clans

"The inconvenience of being stalked and shot down, like a mountain deer, by an unfriendly neighbour induced the Laird of Grantully to build another castle." This is how the *Red Book of Grantully* describes an incident in the early 1500s, when a member of the Grantully Steuart family was killed by an arrow fired from across the river, allegedly by the Laird of Clochfoldich. About a mile west of Grantully, just riverwards of the pretty track along the old railway line, there are the remains, not of a castle, but of a substantial estate house, within easy bowshot from the other side of the river. This presumably is the spot where the unfortunate Steuart met his end.

But the Steuarts' proper castle was exactly where Grantully Castle now stands. It looked similar to the square keep of Garth. Alexander, 7th Laird of Grantully modified the keep into a Z-plan in the 1520s. The new, grander, more defensible Grantully was the forerunner of a rash of castle-building and rebuilding in the valley.

Grey Colin Campbell, 6th laird of Glenorchy built Balloch – forerunner of Taymouth – in 1560. His land stretched westwards from Kenmore to the Atlantic. When asked why he was building his headquarters so close to the eastern border of his land, he remarked: "O, we maun just birze ayont", an unmistakable warning that the Campbells intended to continue their expansion eastwards, roughly translatable as: "We'll probably head on a bit yet". Other local lairds were not to be outdone on the matter of castles: Sir James Menzies rebuilt Weem in 1577, and in 1582 'Mad Colin' Campbell, 3rd Laird of Glenlyon built Meggernie.

So in the space of sixty years three of the valley's four key castles assumed a shape clearly recognizable today, over four hundred years later. The fourth, Balloch, later disappeared under a 'Scottish Baronial' extravaganza. They were built with considerably more comfort in mind than the old supposedly siege-proof square keeps they replaced, but the 1500s were still bloody and turbulent times. The French army was sometimes in Scotland; worse, there were the defeats of Flodden, Pinkie Cleugh, and Halidon Hill. Henry VIII and the English attacked and ravaged Fife, Dundee and the Stirling plain, places too close for comfort. Quite apart from the loss of men from the valley, these campaigns were good reasons to build with security in mind, and the thick walls, solid doors, iron-bar gates and musket- and cannon-ports of the buildings speak for themselves.

The valley's new castles indicated a shift in control. They were built as a result of the success of local lairds versus bigger more powerful aristocrats. The Stewart kings had realized the dangers of over-powerful barons and had broken up their enormous holdings, sometimes brutally. King James II, for example, personally stabbed the chief of the Douglas clan. Lands were given

*Castle Menzies
in the 1900s*

to less powerful lairds.

James III confirmed an area of lands in this valley to lesser gentry in the 1470s. The Steuarts took over lands in Grantully. The Flemyngs were granted an area in Aberfeldy. The Menzieses strengthened their control of Weem and land over in Rannoch. The Garth Stewarts were confirmed in the Abthanage of Dull. The Campbells took over large sections of former Menzies land and fortified Sybilla's Island in Loch Tay. And in 1488, after a bloodthirsty battle between the McDiarmid/Stewart and MacIvor clans in Glenlyon, Neil Stewart of Garth and Duncan Campbell, 2nd Laird of Glenorchy, feudal superiors of the respective clans, signed a peace pact. Though there was one more local convulsion to come, the valley was settling into an ownership format that would last for over two hundred years.

The Aberfeldy villages – Moness, Easter Aberfeldy, Upper and Lower Milton – were divided between several baronies. Alongside the eastern side of the Moness burn lay the land of the Flemyngs. Further east, the land of the Grantully Steuarts abutted that of the Flemyngs. To the west, the Garth Stewarts held Bolfracks, until they passed it to the Menzieses. The Menzieses themselves held the lands running down to the ferry and the boatlands, as they were called, and all of Weem across the river. And further west at Kenmore, ready to pounce, crouched the Campbells.

A new form of lifelong feu was introduced in the early 1500s, giving tenants much greater security. Lairds could either arrange these deals in a way that was mutually agreeable, or they could be very hard on tenants. They often demanded a substantial downpayment, which poorer tenants could not afford. Of course it offered good prospects for men with money, but it meant that some farmers were forced to become labourers, even to emigrate. Sometimes the Campbells and their factors drove over-hard bargains, yet another reason for their unpopularity.

For most people life continued very much as it always had done through the years. There were changes, though they were gradual and uneven. Bubonic plague, known as the Black Death, struck in 1349 and killed one in four of the Scottish population. There is still a plague mass-grave in the valley, opposite the Fortingall Hotel. Ironically so many deaths meant that labour became scarcer and employers were forced to pay higher wages but by the 1500s the balance had tipped the other way again.

Nevertheless, the local economy steadily began to improve. The Aberfeldy villages became places where specialists like blacksmiths, carpenters, shoemakers and millers worked full-time, each supported by a small plot close to their dwelling, and each with a cow in the byre. Close to the villages, in corduroy patterns along the lie of the land, lay the intermingled infield strips which belonged to the various local estates, rented out to husbandmen and tenants, some of whom worked as craftsmen in the villages. Further up the hill lay the outfields, less carefully manicured.

Apart from occasional violent events like the burning of Castle Menzies by Neil Stewart, and the battle between the McDiarmid/Stewarts and the McIvors, the local lairds rubbed along without too much friction, to the general satisfaction of most of the valley's inhabitants. There were, however, exceptions. The chief conflict came between the Campbells and the MacGregors, and as so often before, what happened here reflects life at the time elsewhere in Scotland. The Glenorchy Campbells were ambitious and hard-headed, prepared to use any tactic to further their aims, from manipulating papers to straightforward murder, whereas the MacGregors represented the old traditional highland ways. For them, clan loyalty was paramount. The smallest slight to any member the clan required swift response from other clan members. 'Honour' and 'Revenge' were vital concepts for them.

During the late 1400s, Campbells steadily acquired control of large tracts of land eastwards from their base around Loch Awe, gradually edging the MacGregors out of their lands in Glen Dochart and along Loch Tay. Through offers of money and preferment, the Campbells 'bought' small MacGregor lairds along Loch Tay, setting them against the traditional paternalistic

Meggernie Castle in the 1900s

OBIIT·ANo·DO 1583·SEPVLTVS IN FINLARG... Ætatis suæ 8...

control of their MacGregor chief. By the late 1400s many of the MacGregors had taken refuge in the lawless wastes of Rannoch, slipping over the Glengoulandie pass from time to time through the lands of the Garth Stewarts – who sometimes turned a blind eye – to lift a beast or two from the fat lands of Dull, Weem and Aberfeldy. This was a continual annoyance to the peaceable Menzieses who were supposedly responsible for the lands in Rannoch, but who had allowed the MacGregors to settle there.

These raids did not escape the eye of Grey Colin Campbell. When a child, Grey Colin had been boarded with a MacGregor family. Quite why he conceived a pathological hatred for the entire clan, no one knows. As a Member of Parliament he not only got them outlawed but also received permission to hunt them down. One June night in 1565, a group of his hired thugs went to Fortingall, set fire to the house of James MacGregor, the Dean of Lismore, and murdered his two sons.

A month later the MacGregor chief ambushed and killed the murderers, but such violence shocked the other lairds and prompted Mary Queen of Scots to visit the valley in order to see what was happening for herself. She immediately cancelled the order entitling Grey Colin to harry the MacGregors, and asked Alexander Menzies to allow the dispossessed clan to remain in peace up in Rannoch. Shortly after, Catholic Queen Mary was forced to abdicate by the all-powerful Protestant faction in Parliament and Grey Colin resumed his ferocious obsession.

Time and again, the MacGregors agreed to peace and pardon; time and again, they were forced by their sense of loyalty to stand by the actions of bloodier members of their clan. A MacGregor chief, Gregor Roy, fell in love with and married Campbell of Glenlyon's daughter but, after being insulted by Grey Colin and a consequent bout of raiding and plundering, he was caught and hanged in Kenmore, as his wife and his father-in-law watched.

After another series of raids and pardons, James VI's Scottish parliament – egged on by both the Glenorchy and the Argyll Campbells – passed a series of decrees: the clan was to be suppressed, anyone harbouring a MacGregor would be fined, and the name was never to be used by anyone ever again. The decree was only repealed in 1774.

However, on the horizon was an even bigger issue than the extermination of a clan. After Queen Mary's abdication, it was time for everyone to choose between remaining a Catholic or becoming a Protestant. For the people in the valley, in many cases this would be a choice between life and death.

Religion Splits the Valley

Up until the end of the 1500s, local people had essentially been affected only by local events. What mattered to them most of all was the annual rhythm of sowing, shieling and harvesting; and churchgoing, with its cycle of services throughout the year. There were excitements like the building and rebuilding of castles – a source of good employment – and bloodier episodes like the feud between the MacGregors and the Campbells. There were cattle-lifting raids from other clans within striking distance, for example the Macdonalds over in Lochaber, but the struggles between the English and the lowland Scots were mostly far away.

With the disintegration of the vast lowland monastic estates, the national changeover from Catholicism to Protestantism had been momentous further south, but here in the valley there was relatively little disturbance. Initially. Sir William Steuart at Grandtully and Grey Colin Campbell at Kenmore had both been MPs in the epoch-making Reformation Parliament in 1560 when Scotland changed from a Catholic country to a Protestant one. But, like other lairds, they had made sure that they themselves could still decide who should preach to their tenants on Sundays, and that the Kirk still had powerful bishops between the priesthood and God.

So the folk of the local parishes of Fortingall, Kenmore, Dull, Weem and Logierait generally listened to the minister who had been selected for them by the local Stewart, Campbell, or Menzies laird and generally formed their views accordingly. Come 1630, however, even the humblest were forced to think for themselves about their relationship with God, and to make decisions that would cost some of them their lives.

There were two groups inside the Kirk of Scotland. One group wanted to leave things as they were, with a Scots Kirk modelled along the lines of the Church of England, with the King as its divinely-appointed head, with bishops, and with ministers appointed by landowners. They were effectively Royalists. The other group wanted a more direct connection with God; they refused to accept the king as leader of the Kirk, they wanted to get rid of bishops and scrap lairds' patronage, and they insisted that congregations had the right to choose their own ministers. They often dominated the General Assembly of the Kirk of Scotland. They saw themselves as 'pro-Kirk'.

'Pro-Kirk' and 'Royalist' are simplistic labels, and some historians argue that this was as much an economic conflict as a religious one, with landlords supporting the quasi-feudal status quo – unless they stood to gain otherwise – and upcoming merchants and farmers demanding reforms in ownership and trading structures. Nevertheless, the labels 'pro-Kirk' and 'Royalist' will serve as guides through the upcoming mayhem.

In any case, here in the valley, congregations became discussion groups.

*St Mary's Church,
Grandtully built
in the 1600s*

The debates raged down to the smallest details. Should they stand or kneel to pray? What was the true significance of Holy Communion? What was acceptable behaviour on the Sabbath? In Weem, Fortingall and Kenmore, parishioners sometimes could not agree with their ministers. On one occasion at Kenmore, the entire congregation – except the schoolmaster – refused to attend the services of a new minister whose views did not coincide with their own. Local parishioners learned that the arguments further south between the pro-Kirk and the Royalist groups had begun to result in executions and murders.

Angry exchanges in church meant that even the humblest folk in the valley's five parishes had a fairly clear picture of what was happening in the wider world, probably more so than ever before. By 1630, Scots kings – James VI, then his son Charles I – had been based in London for twenty-seven years, so local people had become accustomed to the reality of a monarch almost inconceivably far away, and they had heard how the extremists in the pro-Kirk faction in the General Assembly of the Kirk in Edinburgh had taken advantage of this absence to increase their power. Compared to the highlands, Edinburgh had a much more vociferous merchant class, eager to sweep away feudal ideas such as bishops and patronage by landowners, but even here in all five valley parishes there was talk of a move towards a more fundamental form of worship.

Charles I was a devout Anglican, a follower of the Church of England. He wanted the Scots Kirk to be the same. He resisted pressure from the pro-Kirk General Assembly to remove bishops and simplify services. He went further and demanded that land in Scotland taken over from the Catholic church after the Reformation Parliament in the 1560s was to be handed back to him, or – a nasty sting – current owners could retain the land they had purchased on payment of a sum. Many lairds, whatever their religious attitudes, saw this as an attack on their wealth.

One of these was the powerful Archibald Campbell, Earl of Argyll, chief of Clan Campbell, a man with control over huge swathes of land in the highland west. Argyll really believed in pro-Kirk disciplinarian fundamentalism. His beliefs coincided perfectly with his own financial interests, but those beliefs – and those of his Campbell kinsmen here in the valley – were to have serious local consequences.

In the lowlands, when it came to religion and politics, ordinary people tended to make decisions closely aligned with those on whom their tenancies or labour depended. Further north and west, decisions were made in line with the attitude of the clan chief. The Aberfeldy valley, close to the highland border, was a mixture: some accepted – and often agreed with – the views of their landlords, others felt that clan loyalty over-rode everything else.

The two most powerful local lairds here took different sides. Sir Colin Campbell, 8th Laird of Glenorchy, Grey Colin's grandson, was related to the Earl of Argyll and shared his pro-Kirk views, although with not quite the same fervour. He had his main base near Kenmore at Balloch. At the eastern end of the valley, John Murray, 6th Earl of Atholl, was staunchly Royalist. His main castle was at Blair Atholl, but his tenants stretched from the Vale of Atholl to Fortingall and beyond.

King Charles insisted that a new Anglican-style Scots Prayer Book be introduced in every kirk. Here in the valley, all five congregations were in uproar; some parishioners accepted the new book, others saw it as a monstrosity, a return to superstition-laden – 'Popish' as they called it – mumbo-jumbo.

In 1638 matters came to a head. The majority pro-Kirk faction in the General Assembly set out a 'National Covenant' demanding the abolition of not only the new Prayer Book but also of bishops. A hefty piece of parchment was taken round hundreds of parishes and signed by thousands of people, many egged on by their radical ministers. The word 'Covenant' was to echo down the years.

Sir Colin Campbell, 8th Laird of Glenorchy

This Covenant was totally unacceptable to King Charles and in 1639, he raised an English army to retake control of Scotland. The Scottish Parliament supported the General Assembly of the Kirk and raised its own army against him. People here had to decide whose side they were on, and whether they should go to fight.

Either through clan loyalty or through tenancy obligations, a large number of Breadalbane men were led away south over the hills to join the 'Regiment of Perthshire Foot' in the pro-Kirk army, ready to fight against King Charles and the English. They were commanded by Colonel John Campbell, Sir Colin's nephew. The Scots troops invaded England and seized the coal towns of Newcastle and Durham. The effect on London was immediate; most of the coal burned in the city came from these two towns. More important for the people here, over two hundred of the local men who had marched away were killed during the fighting in England. Just as the harvest needed gathering in, a trickle of mutilated and dying men came home.

In late June the same year, the Royalist Earl of Atholl, called out nearly two thousand men in support of King Charles. But many of his tenants,

Ruined Fort on Sybilla's Island, Loch Tay, 1930s

including, for example, those at Fortingall, were very much pro-Kirk and in favour of the National Covenant.

Meanwhile Sir Colin Campbell had stayed at home. He expected trouble not only from Atholl in the east but also from the Macdonalds to the north and west. He fortified his castles at Balloch beside the Tay, Finlarig over at Killin, and Sybilla's Island, the little island in Loch Tay close to Kenmore Bridge. He was right to expect trouble from the Macdonalds, though it did not come quite yet.

When the Scottish Parliament heard that the Earl of Atholl had called out his men for King Charles, they ordered the Earl of Argyll and Sir Colin to march against him. Together, the two Campbell chiefs gathered four thousand men and prepared for battle. More than a few of the men were from their lands around Aberfeldy, Kenmore and Dull. Men from Strathtay, Ballechin and Grandtully stood against them.

In July 1639, the two armies met by the river Lyon at the ford near Comrie Castle, the square keep, almost hidden in a garden, close to where the green Comrie Bridge now stands. It must have been a very tense moment; so many men who had lived peaceably together for most of their lives had now been forced to take sides. As they faced each other across the shallows, perhaps wishing they had had time to practise more thoroughly with the weapons they now held, they would have been able to see faces of neighbours and friends among the enemy ranks.

Comrie Bridge and former ford, site of the 1639 confrontation between the armies of Sir Colin Campbell, 8th Laird of Glenorchy and John Murray, 6th Earl of Atholl

The Earl of Atholl moved his men back to Coshieville and risked fording the river with a handful of officers to parley. He found himself among sharp weapons and straight threats. The Campbells marched him off to Balloch Castle, and would not release him until he had agreed to accept the National Covenant. Until a short time before, the Earl and Sir Colin had been good friends; indeed the Earl was married to Sir Colin's sister, Jean. After a glass or two of claret perhaps, good sense was allowed to prevail over religious and political beliefs. Apart from a scuffle up the Glengoulandie road, there was no battle. But this was by no means the end.

Ruin, Occupation, Restoration

Three years after the stand-off between the Earl of Atholl and the Campbell chiefs at the Ford of Lyon, the Puritan English parliament declared war on King Charles because of his refusal to renounce his belief in his divine right to rule. It was called the English Civil War, but the effect on Scotland was enormous, and on this valley it was catastrophic.

Over a twelve-month period during 1644 and 1645, the valley was raided and plundered three times: cattle driven off, winter stores forcibly removed, houses robbed, thatch burned, dykes toppled, whole farms torn down. Quite apart from the shocking effect on ordinary folk, the old chief of Clan Menzies – neutral but attempting to protect his land – was captured and died a Royalist prisoner. The chief of the Grantully Stewarts had the axe of financial ruin suspended over his head, and Robert Campbell, the new laird at Balloch, lost goods to the value of £66,000 (today's equivalent would run into several millions). Worse, the entire valley fell under English occupation for virtually a decade.

The trouble began when the religious extremists in the pro-Kirk faction, who now had control of the Scottish Parliament, sided with their Puritan co-religionists in England and began to force their views on all Scots. Radical preachers insisted that using the Bible during funerals, communal saying of the Lord's Prayer, even celebrating Christmas and Easter, were all sinful. As a result, many more moderate churchgoers felt it was time to stand up for King Charles as leader and defender of the church. Why, local people asked, should May Days, miracle plays, feast days and masques be abolished? Why should the Sabbath become a day of absolute austerity? Or dancing be considered sinful? Or indeed any form of jollity be considered suspect?

Support for King Charles coalesced round Montrose (James Graham, Marquis of Montrose), a man who, like many others, had originally sided with the pro-Kirk faction; indeed he had led its army into England. But now he felt that things had gone too far. In August 1644, he raised the Royalist flag at the Earl of Atholl's base at Blair and highland clans began to join him. Men from throughout Atholl, from this valley, and from as far away as the west end of Glenlyon left their farms at harvest time. Clans from further west had to march down this valley to join Montrose. The Macdonalds – hereditary enemies of the Campbells – came from the glens and the Isles and brought their fearsome Irish relatives, the MacDonnells with them.

Sir Robert Campbell was as ostensibly pro-Kirk as his cousin, Argyll. He ordered his Campbell tenants and labourers to fortify their houses, hide their valuables and be prepared; but other clans and families were not expecting attack. The Macdonalds and the MacDonnells came east, ransacking the supposedly fair game of the Campbell lands. But they also stormed through the

James Graham, Marquis of Montrose 1612-1650

Royalist Robertson clachans around Fearnan, crossed the Lyon, robbed the farms of the Royalist Stewarts in Fortingall and rampaged on to Dull, Weem and down through Strathtay. The Stewarts and the Robertsons sent the Fiery Cross round their lands. The burning crucifix was an ancient and revered symbol: all clansmen must arm themselves and rally to their chief. Montrose only just prevented the two local clans from falling on their Royalist Macdonald 'allies'.

Sir Alexander, the seventy-eight year old chief of Clan Menzies who had managed to stay out of the conflict, was now forced to gather his clan. He watched his men die trying to drive the marauders off their territory and was himself wounded and captured. He died a prisoner of Montrose. The Macdonalds veered south across the river and began to pillage the little hamlets of Easter Aberfeldy, Moness, Over Milton and Nether Milton.

The MacDonnells were specialist warriors, experts in switching from patient guerrilla tactics to timing the perfect moment for the screaming, claymore-swinging charge. At Tippermuir, outside Perth, pro-Kirk lowland men met the wild swordsmen. The lowlanders, told by their own radical ministers that because it was the Sabbath, God would give them an easy victory against the heathen, died by the hundred. People said that you could have walked on dead bodies all the way from Tippermuir to Perth that evening.

With the earlier loss of pro-Kirk men in England, with the departure of many more to join Montrose's army, and now with the villages and fermtouns wrecked and robbed just as the harvest was being brought in, preparing for the winter in the valley was a serious problem. Worse was to come. In December, heading west to attack the Marquis of Argyll, Montrose brought his entire by-now-starving army to the valley. As they made their way along both sides of Loch Tay, everything connected with the Campbells that could not be lifted or burned was torn down. Every family lost their carefully-hoarded winter rations, lost their cow, lost their thatch and in most cases lost their cottage, too. Hundreds of Campbell families were left famished and homeless.

When the Macdonalds arrived in Kenmore, they broke into the church in search of the Poor Box, an iron-bound chest containing money ready for distribution. It had been hidden. Frustrated, they smashed up the church and made off with other items, including the baptismal cistern. The Poor Box was later returned to the church; where it remains.

From Glenlyon – which has a population of less than a hundred today – a thousand men had gone to support Montrose. As his army moved west the Royalist leader gave orders that Glenlyon should remain untouched, but the Macdonalds and the MacDonnells found the neat little farms and clachans too tempting. The damage caused in Glenlyon in those freezing weeks was not forgotten.

There were more bloody successes, but Montrose's royalist army was finally destroyed by the pro-Kirk Covenanters in September 1645. The few local royalists who managed to return to the valley in time to help with the harvest had witnessed appalling scenes: in Aberdeen they had seen swordsmen crazed with drink, raping women, butchering children, and stripping men – to ensure their clothes were free of blood – before killing them.

When the triumphant Puritan English Parliament executed King Charles I in 1649, most people were genuinely shocked. Royalists immediately hailed his son, away on the continent, as Charles II. He landed in Scotland in June 1650, promptly signed the National Covenant and gained the support of most Scots. General Cromwell and his English Ironside army marched north to attack, smashed Charles' army at Dunbar and, after another victory over a second Scots army at Worcester, sent Charles hurrying back to the continent. Like many others, William Menzies, son of Sir Alexander, was killed. Several local fighters, captured at Worcester, were sent to the West Indies plantations and sold as slaves.

Scotland came under English occupation for nearly a decade. The Scottish Parliament was dissolved. Cromwell – who was made Lord Protector of the whole of Britain – regarded Scotland as an important part of his Commonwealth, protected from insurrection by the firm hand of his well-trained troops. He made sure that previous restrictive trade barriers between the two countries were lifted. Commerce improved, and much of Scotland became considerably more peaceful than before. Proper schools were set up, at Kenmore and Dull for example. Likely troublemakers were bound over to pay heavy fines if they misbehaved. At Grantully, Sir Thomas Steuart, a known royalist sympathiser, had to stand a £5000 surety for a younger, wilder, royalist laird.

General George Monck, one of Cromwell's toughest generals and his close friend, became Governor of the North. Monck took Dundee and Stirling for the English and set both towns up as military bases. Colonel Daniel, one of Monck's officers, was sent with his dragoons to the valley. Though the local people strongly resented the presence of English soldiers and their use of kirk pews for firewood, the women in particular quickly took up the soldiers' habit of pipe-smoking.

The patrols came and went from their base at Perth, but Scots resistance leaders began to gather. They held their first secret meeting at Finlarig Castle at the other end of Loch Tay. Though the castle belonged to Sir Robert Campbell and several of the key men were his close relatives, Sir Robert himself cannily did not attend. Sir Duncan Menzies stayed away too, despite a personal letter from Charles II from his court at Chantilly.

The Finlarig meeting took place while Monck was at sea defeating the formidable Dutch fleet. On his return to Scotland, he immediately came up into the valley to deal with the troublemakers. Though they had occupied Castle Menzies, Garth Castle, Balloch and Blair Atholl, the royalist forces melted away. Monck placed garrisons at all the local strongpoints, and he himself took several squadrons to Sir Robert Campbell's castle at Balloch. The wily Campbell laird was ostensibly pro-Kirk, but Monck knew the views of his relatives.

On arrival at Balloch, the general noted that Sir Robert had called out his men; they were now gathered round the castle, glaring at Monck's Ironside troopers. Over a polite glass of wine, the general broke the news that he was going to have to occupy the place. Sir Robert said that was impossible, completely unacceptable. Monck put down his glass, walked out through the main door, turned to Sir Robert who had followed him out and said: 'Now, sir, you must look to your defences, for we are about to attack.' After a little face-saving, Sir Robert gave in. They dined together that evening.

One of the last royalist garrisons to hold out against Monck was the small fortress on Sybilla's Island in Loch Tay. Monck ignored a rude letter from its commander, prepared boats for an amphibious operation and waited. The fort gave up without a fight and the prisoners were treated with civility.

Six years later, after Cromwell's death, Monck was still Governor of the North, based in Edinburgh. In 1659, he rode south with a petition from the Scots Parliament for a permanent union of the two nations. Trade had thrived under the order imposed by the occupying army. Westminster rejected the petition.

And it was Monck, backed by his Edinburgh-based troops, who in 1660 oversaw the return of King Charles II and the restoration of all that had been

swept away during Cromwell's Commonwealth. All state-controlled religious fundamentalism was set aside: theatres reopened, the Scottish Parliament returned, and people could dance once more.

Soon after his London coronation, King Charles II, 'The Black Boy', with his dark curls, his charm, his roving eye, his intelligent curiosity, and his worldly humour appeared here in the valley. He paid a visit to Sir Duncan at Castle Menzies. Like everyone else, those that caught sight of him – as he rode his charger down though Easter Aberfeldy and splashed across the Tay – thought that his return was going to usher in a long period of peace and prosperity. They were seriously mistaken.

General George Monck 1608-1670

Pale John

One spring morning in 1658 – two years before Charles II's Restoration – as the days grew lighter and the snow eased, pale-faced twenty-three year old John Campbell came riding through Aberfeldy, back from a long stay in London. Watchers in doorways were astonished to see an expensively-cloaked woman seated behind Pale John, her arms clasped round his waist. Another pony trotted after them, laden with heavy leather bags. Word soon filtered out from Balloch that Pale John had brought home a wife. She was Lady Mary Rich, aristocratic widow and heiress. The pony's leather bags contained her ten-thousand pound inheritance. In gold.

The young man's father, Sir John, 10th Laird of Glenorchy, was a relatively mild man, but 'Pale John' – as he was already known locally – had been brought up by a tutor who had lived and learned in the times of his great grandfather, Black Duncan of the Cowl. Black Duncan had enormously increased the Campbell holdings in Breadalbane, especially along both sides of Loch Tay, and had confirmed the reputation of the Glenorchy Campbells as being men of unscrupulous ambition and intrigue. Pale John was to outdo them all.

Apart from the brief uprising, the English occupation during the last few years had been relatively peaceful. General Monck, Cromwell's Governor of Scotland was not a man to be meddled with, nor were his well-trained garrisons in Perth and Stirling, nor the buff-coated Ironside cavalry stationed in Weem, Grantully and at Pale John's own home, Balloch. Monck had met Pale John there four years earlier and had insisted on financial guarantees for the lad's good behaviour.

King Charles' Restoration in 1660 was a time of tremendous celebration. The new Scots Parliament immediately cancelled all the laws passed under the Commonwealth. Scotland was free again. Here in the valley, the ministers of all the kirks were sacked and had to re-apply to their local lairds for their jobs. Gone were the petty regulations on parishioners' behaviour – no dancing, no games on the Sabbath – exercised by the prurient snooping of self-elected groups of church elders. Pale John put his own minister, a relative, in at Kenmore. His father protested weakly to his son, and wrote wounded letters to other local lairds.

With the reinstatement of bishops over ministers, all the old arguments between Royalists and Covenanters reignited. Further south, radical ministers led their anti-bishop congregations out to pray in the hills. In Aberfeldy, there was little immediate trouble; the Campbells, the Stewarts, the Menzieses and the other lairds continued to meet, borrow money, lend horses, marry into each other's families and quarrel over their boundaries. Most ministers and elders reached a compromise with their consciences, accepted the wishes of their

DOMINVS DVNCANVS CAMPBEL DE GLEVRGVEA

OBIIT. ANᵒ. Dᵒ 1631. SEPVLTVS FINLARG

Ætatis suæ 65 Anno Dᵒ 1619

Sir Duncan
Campbell,
'Black Duncan'
7th Laird of
Glenorchy d1631

Right:
'Pale John'
Campbell,
1st Earl of
Breadalbane,
1635-1717

lairds and the control of their bishops, and fell into line.

Aberfeldy's ford, ferry and market became busier after Perth's bridge was swept away in 1661. In 1665, another local school, at Weem, was added to those at Dull and Kenmore. The valley was growing more prosperous; lairds and tenants were becoming less willing to upset the local economy for the sake of religious differences. Covenanting, they felt, was a thing for the lowlanders of the south-west. But the days of chiefs calling out their men were far from over, and the Aberfeldy valley was still highland in this respect.

Pale John began to run the vast Glenorchy and Breadalbane Campbell holdings and Lady Mary Rich bore her new husband two sons, then died in 1666. Local people gossiped that not only was he now a widower but also he had still not proved himself in battle; he soon tackled both.

Ever since the appalling destruction caused by Montrose's army in December 1644, the Breadalbane Campbell tenants and families had been living peacefully, gradually rebuilding their smashed properties. But in 1669, Pale John called his men out to help the government deal with a group of Sinclairs who had gone on the rampage in defiance of their chief, the Earl of Caithness. Pale John put down the rising. He spent time in the Earl's house and charmed Mary, the Countess. He quickly discovered that the Earl was not only unwell, but was also in serious debt, so Pale John used part of his previous wife's fortune to lend money to the impoverished man. In return for the loan he obtained an agreement that the Earl's lands and title should pass to him when the Earl died, which he conveniently did in 1676. Pale John promptly contacted Sir Thomas Steuart of Grantully, borrowed £10,000 to tide him over – the letters still exists to prove this astonishing figure – and became Earl of Caithness. Then he married the widowed Countess Mary.

Just before his marriage, Pale John called his men out again. He himself stayed at home but 1,500 Breadalbane men marched away from Aberfeldy, Kenmore and Lochtayside over the track to Amulree to join 'The Highland Host'. 8000 highlanders gathered on government orders and marched south to deal with the rebellious, bishop-hating Covenanters. Men from throughout the valley tramped down to Glasgow and on into Ayrshire. Sir Thomas Steuart's son John was among the officers. Empty of men from end to end, the valley must have been unnaturally quiet during the snowy February days.

This attempt by the Government to have highlanders do their dirty work failed. Apart from ransacking south-western farms and towns, the highlanders did little, and soon returned north. The lowland Covenanters immediately rose again and went to their open-air services with muskets and swords; they bloodily defeated Government dragoons sent against them.

While burns ran red in Ayrshire, by contrast here in the valley Countess Mary wrote from Balloch to Sir Thomas Steuart at Grantully. She sent him a few of her largest apricots and complained that some of the best had been plucked without her permission. Her servant also brought Sir Thomas a home made beeswax candle with the offer of more if he liked it, once the bees were drowned.

hn Earl of Breadalbane Anᵒ 1696
rried first Lady Mary Rich
ughter of Henry Earl of Hol:
nd, Secondly Lady Mary
mpbell Daughter of Archibald
rquis of Argyll Countess Dowager
Caithnes.

17

Excess swarms were either smoked or drowned in those days. Drowning in pure Tay water was preferable because the honey remained untainted.

The *Red Book of Grantully* refers to Sir Thomas as: "Grim of visage, but of gorgeous apparel". He was one of the few lairds who had been able to stay afloat – just – in the choppy waters of the mid1600s. During Cromwell's Commonwealth he had been suspected of being a royalist, and placed under serious financial constraint. Then, at the Restoration, the King's men had found a letter from one of Monck's officers, offering Sir Thomas reparation for any damage caused to his property by English soldiers; he was once again threatened with fines. Despite suspicion from both sides he was able to protect his relatives and tenants, and retained his wealth. Not only did he lend money to Pale John – all Pale John's letters to Sir Thomas are about money, the borrowing of it, and the reasons for delaying its return – he also possessed English money which was asked for by another local countess. When Pale John heard of this, he naturally asked Sir Thomas for English money too.

The men of the valley came back from Ayrshire unscathed and booty-laden, but the Campbells were out two years later, back up to Caithness to strike once more at the Sinclairs, now deeply resentful of Pale John's grasp of their hereditary earldom. Many of the men who marched north would have been to Caithness twelve years before, and down to Ayrshire in the meantime. Being called out by your chief was certainly a way to see the world. This time the Campbell force, aided by Government troops, was led by Pale John's cousin, Robert Campbell of Glenlyon. The Sinclairs were pacified, Pale John swapped his title and became Earl of Breadalbane, and Robert Campbell returned home victorious. But his name – and that of Pale John – can never be dissociated from what was to happen twelve years later.

Sir Thomas Steuart, 12th Laird of Grantully 1605?-1688

The Work of a Winter Dawn

Robert Campbell, chief of the Campbells in Glenlyon, a drinker and gambler, found that King Charles' Restoration in 1660 offered ample opportunities for every sort of extravagance for wealthy young lairds like him. He soon found himself in serious financial trouble. He was the despair of his cousin, Pale John, who clung on to money, preferably other people's. No amount of loyal loans from tenants – many of whom were descended from MacGregors who had controlled the glen before the Campbells and had adopted different surnames – saved Robert Campbell. He had to sell the timber from the forests of his glen. The men who bought his trees and sent their sawn work downstream, inadvertently choked both the Lyon and the Tay with floating trunks and ruined the salmon fishing. Robert petulantly used this as an excuse to wreck the foresters' sawmill. He was finally forced to sell off most of his land in Glenlyon, some to Pale John, most to the Atholls.

The way that Robert Campbell's tenants reacted to the sale and transfer of these Glenlyon lands is a local example of the essential difference between lowland and highland life. The sale went against the whole concept of 'duthchas', an almost untranslatable Gaelic word; it signifies the essential responsibility of a chief to protect his clan and ensure their continued possession of their time-honoured landholdings. Robert's tenants simply could not understand how mere money and documents could transfer their land and their loyalty. The entire clan system was rooted in ancient Celtic traditions, in lineages, in loyalties and in unwritten trust. For them it was beyond belief that they should suddenly be expected to behave towards the Atholls in the same way as they had behaved towards Robert Campbell, their 6th Laird. How could they see the distant Atholl family – sometimes up at Blair, sometimes down at Dunkeld, often away in London or Bath – in the context of the glen's traditions and lineage? How could they trust them not to sell them on? Which in fact they did, to a Menzies, only a few years later. Others had taken control of the glen before, an understandable if sometimes unpleasant part of highland life; but a cash sale?

While Glenlyon men gritted their teeth and spoke politely to Atholl's agents, Pale John's wife Countess Mary wrote once more to Sir Thomas Steuart, this time to thank him for the present of a box of oysters. She loved oysters beyond measure, she said, but had never expected to be able to have them at Balloch. But it was a series of much more peremptory letters that set the valley astir again.

In 1685, the Marquess of Atholl, writing on behalf of the Government, ordered local clans to gather and fall on the lands of the Covenanting Archibald, Earl of Argyll who had rebelled against the re-imposition of bishops. Chieftains called out their men and set off for Argyll. Amid the violence and the smoke of

Robert Campbell, 6th Laird of Glenlyon, 1632-1696

burning buildings, hundreds of ordinary men and women, along with seventeen Argyll lairds, were hanged. The men from the Aberfeldy valley were as cruel as the rest, but of all the clans that invaded Argyll, the Macdonalds of Glencoe behaved very much the worst. Their viciousness embarrassed the Scottish Government but did not surprise folk here. Over the previous fifty years, the Glencoe Macdonalds had attacked and raided the Campbells at the west end of the Aberfeldy valley four times; and they were not finished.

The attack on Argyll had been ordered by the Scottish Government, but it had been sanctioned by the new king, James VII and II. Unlike his elder brother Charles, from the very start James managed to alienate almost everyone because of his insistent Catholicism. As far as most Protestants were concerned, it pervaded his every judgement and appointment; and when William of Orange invaded England in 1688, he received so much support that King James was forced to flee abroad.

Though a Dutchman, William was hardly an outsider; he was James's nephew, and his wife Mary was James's daughter. After consideration, the Scottish Government accepted William and Mary as their sovereigns. Many highlanders did not, and in 1689, their leader, James Graham of Claverhouse gathered the clans of the north-west. The rebels called themselves Jacobites, after 'Jacobus', the Latin for 'James' and they nicknamed Claverhouse 'Bonnie Dundee'. He had previously been given another nickname by the Covenanters of the south-west when he had ridden against them at head of his Government dragoons: 'Bluidy Clavers'

Local loyalties were split. Sir Archibald Menzies sided with the Government and sent his sons Robert and James – and 100 well-trained Menzies musket-men – to join General Hugh Mackay and his Government troops as they closed for battle with Claverhouse in the Pass of Killiecrankie on the evening of July 27th. For generations, the Menzies family had tended to adhere to the views of whoever was in government. By following the Government line, the Menzieses were able to protect their people from a great deal of trouble, though not all. Indeed, some Menzies clansmen ignored the advice of their chief, sided with Claverhouse, and when the battle began, charged down on the redcoats – and their own relatives.

Several local chiefs called out their men for the Jacobites: Patrick Stewart of Ballechin and his ferocious little clan – hereditary bodyguards to the Atholl family – fought alongside Claverhouse. So did their local minister from Logierait, who got so blood-crazed his fingers became locked in his claymore; they had to prize the hilt from his hand after the battle. And it is possible that the horse Claverhouse was riding when he was shot had been given to him by John Steuart of Grantully. Steuart had collected fifty men for the rising.

Others were looking for ways to stay out of trouble. In Parliament, the Marquess of Atholl had voted in favour of King William, then discreetly retired to take the waters at Bath. In the meantime his men had rallied to Claverhouse.

At the other end of the valley, Pale John Campbell, still a force to be reckoned with, had also voted for King William, but everyone expected him to join Claverhouse and the Jacobites. Never a man for loyalty except to his own interests, at the last moment Pale John carefully failed to commit himself and his men. Robert Campbell of Glenlyon, Pale John's cousin, followed his example and stayed at home in his glen. But Robert Campbell knew that many a highlander had not forgotten that, like Mackay, he too had led government troops against clansmen. So he contacted Claverhouse and tried to protect himself with paperwork.

The result of the battle was a disaster for the Government, and early the following morning, General Mackay rode rapidly through Weem towards Castle Menzies. Behind him tramped four hundred bedraggled Government soldiers, their shoes still sodden from fording the Tummel at Fonab, their eyes red-rimmed from a sleepless night spent in Edradynate Wood, close to Easter Cluny. They had left two thousand of their companions dead up at Killiecrankie. The Government men had been defeated by a bloodily successful claymore charge, and the Glencoe Macdonalds had been among the wildest of the clans that evening.

Though the Jacobites were victorious at Killiecrankie, Claverhouse was killed, most likely by a Menzies musket. His death meant that the clan federation fell apart and they began to drift westwards again. But King William was a warrior from the battlefields of the Continent, not accustomed to hearing of his men being beaten. He decided to make sure it would not happen again. Another battle would not be necessary; he would talk to his Scottish ministers; they would know of a clan who might be made into a brutal example for the others; and they would know of someone, some insignificant army officer, who might lead a unit for such brutality. He would leave it to them to ensure that any action would not be traced back to him. There was no rush.

Before the battle, Robert Campbell had succeeded in obtaining what he wanted, a letter from Claverhouse guaranteeing that his Glenlyon property would not be touched. But as they returned westwards, the Glencoe Macdonalds ignored it. What was a piece of paper, after all, compared to the centuries old feud between themselves and the Campbells? They promptly wrecked what little property Robert Campbell had not sold and took anything they could. Robert himself lost over two hundred cattle, all his sheep, all his goats, all ten of his horses, a stag, and the entire contents of his kitchen. Glenlyon tenants suffered as badly. In one case, a Macdonald rolled a baby out of her cradle, pulled off the blanket and left the child naked on the floor. Middle-aged men and women in the glen, who had been children when Montrose's Macdonalds had come through in 1645, had seen it all before.

In the subsequent assessment it was calculated that Robert and his tenants had lost goods to the value of £7,500. Now aged 59, the impoverished laird was forced to find a way to keep himself afloat. He became an officer in the Regiment of Foot that was being raised for King William by the new Earl of Argyll. The Argyll Regiment's clansmen-soldiers were the very men whose land had been wrecked and whose relatives had been killed by the Glencoe Macdonalds.

Like other clan chiefs, moustachioed old Alasdair Maclain, the Macdonald clan chief of Glencoe, was ordered to sign an oath of loyalty to King William. Maclain played dilatory games – as did several other chiefs – and missed the deadline by only a few hours; but King William's Scottish ministers had already decided which clan was to be the brutal example for the rest.

The ministers, aided by senior officers in King William's army, cynically manoeuvred the pawns most likely to carry out the task into place: two companies of the Earl of Argyll's regiment of Foot, men with a real grudge against the Macdonalds. And, from the same regiment, they chose their officer: Captain Robert Campbell of Glenlyon, the man whose horses were now stabled in Glencoe.

When Robert Campbell's two companies were quartered on the Macdonalds in Glencoe in February 1692, Campbell himself was under the impression that because Maclain had finally sworn the oath of loyalty, the old chieftain had been forgiven. But his powerful cousins, Pale John and the Earl of Argyll knew something grimmer was on the cards, as did Sir Archibald Menzies. Perhaps they were unsure precisely what King William and the Scottish Government had in mind – or chose not to ask obvious questions – but it is certain that all three agreed to block the passes leading from Glencoe. An incriminating letter still exists.

It seems Robert Campbell knew nothing of the government plans for the massacre until he received the written government order immediately beforehand: either carry out an act of genocide or be seen as a traitor to the government. That he executed his orders does not exonerate him. Nor does the fact that three hundred Macdonalds survived – or were allowed to survive – and only forty or so were killed. Two Argyll Regiment officers broke their swords rather than obey the command to kill women and children; and, so they say, a Macdonald child was killed pleading for mercy as he hung on to Robert Campbell's leg.

Even today, a stillness lingers around the ruined moss-covered walls of Robert Campbell's home in Glenlyon. He died, penniless, with his regiment in Flanders four years after the massacre, the work of one winter dawn etched on his face.

Rebellion and Change

Seven years of bad harvests followed the 1692 Glencoe Massacre. Lean years reduced many families to near-starvation, even to eating seedcorn, the basis for next year's crop. People looked for something to blame for their troubles. Local Jacobites spread the word that all of it was God's judgement on a people who had forsaken their true king.

Pale John, ageing now, knew that eighty years ago his grandfather had bought and supplied fresh seedcorn to his tenants after Montrose's men raped the valley. When the wretched rain-filled gales began to blow for the seventh winter running, and the Tay and the Lyon roared into spate once more, and ferry jetties were again swept away, and fords were impassable, and fields flooded, and the waterfalls above Aberfeldy excelled themselves, local people began to think that linking with a fatter country might help.

The Union with England and the disappearance of the Scottish Parliament took place in 1707. It made no immediate difference here. Pale John refrained from voting and John Murray, the Duke of Atholl voted against the union until the Scots got better terms. However, some locals took the view that it was time to bring the Stuarts home again. Soon after George I became king in 1714, the London Government decided to tax the Scots on essentials like salt, malt, beer, linen and soap. It was a direct contravention of what had been agreed in the Act of Union only seven years before and the smouldering resentment against London burst into flames.

On a mid-September day in 1715, villagers in Weem watched kilted, armed men march through. Robert Campbell's son John was leading his Glenlyon tenants to join the Jacobite revolt against King George. The standard of James Edward Stuart had been raised at Moulinearn near Logierait. Not that James Edward was there; he was still in France. King George's supporters called the would-be Jacobite king 'The Pretender'. The Glenlyon men were on their way to link with the formidable Stewarts of Ballechin, to be part of James Edward's Atholl Brigade.

There were more bands of men on the march through Weem. There were Menzies clansmen from Culdares, Bolfracks and Glenquaich. Very nearly the entire clan was going, in spite of the pro-Government views of Captain James, the man at Castle Menzies. The Captain was great-uncle and tutor to the nine-year-old, lame clan chief. As Menzies clansmen tramped past, Captain James – who had fifteen children of his own – spirited the hirpling young chief away to save him being used as a clan mascot.

Over at Kenmore, Pale John sent a letter to the Government men in Edinburgh, pleading illness and infirmity and regretting his inability to help. He then climbed into his coach, trundled the length of the valley to Logierait and stepped nimbly off the ferry to confer with the Jacobite commander, the Earl of

The Weem Hotel in the 1950s. Wade lodged in the smaller, original inn at the far end of the building

Mar. The Government heard about it and did not forget.

News spread about Pale John's two sons: the elder, whom their father maintained was an imbecile and had disinherited – but whom the locals knew to be a man with his own mind – was leading the Breadalbane men out for the Jacobites. Pale John's younger son had decided to remain on the Government side. He allowed himself to be imprisoned for the duration and as a result later became the 2nd Earl of Breadalbane. The Duke of Atholl was also imprisoned to stop him causing trouble. Like Pale John, John Steuart at Grantully was too old; he sent his men out commanded by a cousin.

A section of the Jacobite force headed into England. They were caught at Preston and forced to surrender. Menzies and Stewart clansmen were imprisoned in London and Carlisle. But the main government and Jacobite armies met each other at Sherrifmuir, near Perth. Men from the Aberfeldy valley distinguished themselves at the battle, but it decided nothing. Soon after, James Edward himself arrived from France. His cold manner did a great deal to dampen enthusiasm for him, but John Steuart of Grantully welcomed him into his house in Dundee. 'The Pretender' was crowned at Scone but, miserably aware of his failure to raise support, sailed away again shortly after.

On the way home from Sherrifmuir, John Campbell of Glenlyon and his men, finding Castle Menzies unguarded, occupied it and helped themselves to whatever they fancied. Captain James gathered a small force, surrounded the castle and starved the raiders out; it was another black mark for the Glenlyon Campbells.

The London government re-established control and acted relatively leniently, much more so than it was to do thirty years later. Prisoners returned home and those under sentence of death were reprieved. In the spring of 1716, government soldiers came through the valley, disarmed the local men and searched houses for weapons. The loss of swords and muskets made it hard for local people to defend themselves from increasing numbers of lawless gangs, so Pale John, John Murray and Captain James set up local militias, forerunners of the Black Watch.

John Steuart was fined £10,000 for his hospitality to James Edward in Dundee. His cousin, the man who had led the Grantully men out for the Jacobites, forfeited his entire property, as did the Robertson laird of Fearnan. John Campbell of Glenlyon fled abroad, but his tenants continued to pay their rents to his wife and children. And Pale John had his last bed-ridden hurrah: when a government officer came to arrest him with the words: "Sir, you are my prisoner", Pale John replied: "Your prisoner! I am the prisoner of God Almighty, and eighty-one years of age. Duncan, take that poor man away and get him out of the country before my people get to hear of the insult he has offered me."

Things began to change. Lairds and tenants in the valley began to see that the old run-rig system of farming was inefficient. The centuries-old system of everyone having a strip of land, just enough to eke out a living – with an outfield, a little infield, a kailyard and a cow – was no way for the community to grow. Almost every family still had a cow of course, but the land round Aberfeldy and Weem was now run by bigger tenants with broader fields, much more productive. Though many cottage folk resented what they viewed as a loss of freedom and independence, the regular pay they now received as labourers meant they lived a little better and healthier, and it enabled their children to stay longer in school. Parents began to see the importance of their children learning to read, and even to write. In the little villages of Aberfeldy, though the details are now lost, 'dame' schools – women teaching in their homes – and 'adventure' – small fee-paying– schools sprang up.

A formal society for improving agriculture was set up in Edinburgh, joined by many lairds keen to improve their lands. Forests were planted. Captain Menzies of Culdares, on a visit to the Austrian Tyrol, spotted the value of larches; he brought back seedlings and gave some to a fellow tree-enthusiast, the Duke of Atholl. Potatoes were now being grown all along the valley, an excellent and easy source of food. In the little plots behind the cottages, 'London Lady' was a favourite.

Trade began to grow. The business of rearing and driving the shaggy, big-horned black cattle to the October trysts at Crieff and Falkirk steadily increased. By the 1720s, 30,000 head of cattle were coming south across the Tay yearly.

The demand for linen and spun wool was opening up. Flax was first grown on the Breadalbane estate in 1725. Kenmore was still the main market, but with the construction of General Wade's Tay Bridge in 1733 – and another over the Moness/Paldy burn, properly linking the four original hamlets – Aberfeldy was beginning to compete.

General George Wade, a tall impressive Irishman, stayed months at the Weem Inn completing his survey of possible routes through the highlands. Aberfeldy was on his route from Crieff in the south to Dalnacardoch in the north. Kenmore was not. For cattle heading to Crieff from the north and north-west, the track from Aberfeldy up past Loch-na-Craig was far easier than the old rustlers' path from Kenmore over into Glen Quaich.

General Wade's bridge was the key to Aberfeldy's expansion. Designed by William Adam, it was built of chlorite schist, stone that hardens with exposure to air. Brought from not far away, each

Field Marshal George Wade, 1673-1748

piece was hewn into its pre-ordained shape up at the Bolfracks quarry. Hardly a chisel was used at the riverside. Once it was finished and opened in 1733, General Wade placed a stone memorial on the parapet. It states that the bridge was built "for the safe and easy communication between the highlands and the trading towns in the low country." It makes no mention that these roads facilitated the rapid movement of troops, baggage wagons and horse-drawn artillery trains. Wade would never have dreamed of the weights and speeds it takes today.

Cattle-lifting between clans had always been regarded as not too much of a crime, but perhaps because of the general improvements, lawlessness now seemed more noticeable and less acceptable. In 1729, Wade, as Commander-in-chief of all troops in Scotland, re-organized the local lairds' militias into six official Independent Companies. There were a hundred men in each company and they were nicknamed 'The Black Watch' because their dark tartan contrasted with the red uniforms of the regular army.

Black Watch soldier, original uniform 1742

A private of the XLIII (Highland) Regiment 1742
From a sketch in "Illustrations of the Clothing of the British Army" A Volume prepared by order of George II

In 1739, George II authorised the Black Watch to be formed into a regular unit of the British Army. In May 1740, 'The Watch', newly increased to ten companies, gathered on the flat land just to the north of Wade's bridge and formally mustered as the '43rd Regiment of Foot'. Kilted highlanders outfitted in scarlet tunics, a thousand of them, wore Black Watch tartan and red-and-white Menzies tartan stockings. Their Colonel and their Commanding Officer, in their gold-laced coats and tricorne hats, rode proudly through the ranks. Many of the ordinary soldiers were sons of lairds and well-to-do tenants; they had brought their servants and gillies with them. The gillies stood to the side of the parade, blethering, the occasional bottle passing discreetly from hand to hand. Rotten harvests a year or two earlier had meant that a law had been passed outlawing the malting of grain for alcoholic drink.

Less than three years later, the Black Watch soldiers were marched to London against their will. They were under the impression that they had been formed specifically to police the highlands, but now they discovered they were to be sent abroad like any other regiment. So, soon after they arrived at Finchley, they marched north again, without their officers but in good order. In Northamptonshire they were surrounded by General Wade's own regiment of dragoons. Marched back to London, they were charged with mutiny and three of the men were shot. All suspected barrack-room lawyers were dispersed to other regiments, and the Black Watch was shipped to the war in Flanders. They rapidly gained a reputation as a phenomenal fighting regiment, but there were families here that were left very angry about the whole affair. And in August 1745, real trouble came. Had 'The Watch' remained at home, it might not have been so serious.

In August 1745, Prince Charles Edward Stuart, son of James Edward Stuart, landed at Arisaig. Had the Black Watch stayed in the highlands, 'Bonnie Prince Charlie' – as some called him – might well have had a shorter stay. Most who heard the news knew all the old bitternesses would spill out again. There had been four monarchs on the throne in London since the last one acceptable to the Jacobites. The House of Stewart had been in exile for nearly sixty years, and Scotland had been united with England for nearly forty.

Within a week of Prince Charles' landing, a squadron of scarlet-coated Government dragoons came galloping down the Crieff Road and halted at the Aberfeldy bridge. They were a reconnaissance party for an entire Government army coming along Wade's road from the south. This was exactly what the road had been built for, and soon columns of cavalry, grenadiers, infantrymen and light artillery came drumming over the bridge. Weem villagers saw General Sir John Cope himself, in his wolfskin coat and gold chain, step out of his coach near the inn.

By nightfall, the whole army was camped in white tents, between the village and the bridge. They made no demands on the local people, many of whom had soldier sons away with the Black Watch on the continent. Sir John was a guest of lame Sir Robert, now 39, at Menzies Castle. A day or so later, the army moved on along General Wade's road, past Dull and Coshieville, over Glengoulandie, across the Tummel, up to Dalnacardoch, northwards.

Only a week or so after Cope and his troops marched away, Prince Charles and his highland soldiers – plus contingents of French and Irish – came down from Corryarack and raised the standard at Blair Castle, over in Atholl. Hundreds of men went off along Strathtay to join him. Once again families and clans were split between supporting the Government and rallying to the Prince. Here, the most dramatic example of a divided family was the Garth Stewarts, three pocket lairds, each with a little land between Dull and Fortingall: Patrick of Drumcharry was pro-government, William of Garth was a Jacobite and marched away with his men to Blair; and Charles of Inchgarth, though fit enough himself, stayed at home and sent his son to join Prince Charles.

Other Stewart families from over the hill in Rannoch, from Tullochcroish, Kynachan and Tempar also marched out for Prince Charles, as did the Steuarts of Grantully and the Atholl bodyguard Stewarts of Ballechin further east. The Rannoch Stewarts were used to long treks; during the summers, many of them would rise at four o'clock of a Sunday morning to attend the big congregations at their church in Dull, a long haul over the Glengoulandie pass.

John Campbell of Glenlyon's younger son, Archie Roy, a boy of fifteen, led the glen's men out for Prince Charles as his father had done for James Edward. His elder brother was an officer in the Black Watch, and Fergus Ferguson, his minister at Fortingall had been preaching pro-Government sermons for weeks. Another pro-Government minister, John Douglas of Kenmore, was tipped into the Tay by the mothers of the Jacobite boys who went from Fearnan. Alan Stewart from Woodend marched away with Archie Roy. Men from Dull went, too. The Rannoch Robertsons to the north came out, wild, lawless men, always siding with those up to most mischief. Men from Grandtully were recruited into the Edinburgh Brigade but their laird went abroad

As before, there were Menzieses on both sides: Menzies of Comrie was pro-government while Menzies of Culdares sent a horse to Prince Charles. A Fiery Cross was sent round the Menzies lands of Glenquaich, Bolfracks, Rannoch and Dull. Immediately downstream of Wade's bridge on the left bank, the Laird of Killiechassie called out his handful of men and set off eastwards. Almost all the men who went to Blair Castle, including those from Killiechassie, were organized into the First Battalion of the Atholl Brigade.

However, most of the Campbell tenants of the 2nd Earl of Breadalbane in the west of the valley stayed at home. In some cases they joined the Argyll Militia, a body of highlanders who supported King George, or, more correctly, did whatever the Campbell aristocracy considered best.

A few weeks later, Sir John Cope's coach reappeared from the south, surrounded by laughing and cheering Rannoch Robertsons. Inside sat Alexander Robertson of Struan, their chief, wearing Sir John's wolfskin coat and gold chain. They had captured the coach after charging and scattering English redcoats. Cope had sailed south from Aberdeen to Leith, with his artillery – and coach – then been defeated at Prestonpans in a matter of minutes. The victorious Prince Charles was now in Edinburgh. Significantly the Robertsons had left the Prince because it was time to get the harvest in and to make ready for winter, and, over the next few weeks, many more highlanders headed home over Wade's bridge for the same reason.

Aberfeldy first caught sight of the Prince's troops the following February as, amid the skirl of pipes, the highland units came marching down to Wade's bridge. The cavalry, artillery and lowlanders were going separately up through Atholl. This army had never lost a battle: they had smashed the government troops at Prestonpans, Clifton and Falkirk. Ahead of his men, mounted on a fine horse, surrounded by a small troop of lifeguards, was Prince Charles Edward Stuart, in a waterfall of lace, tight-fitting trews and glittering boots. The Prince's army camped between the bridge and Weem, in the same place as Cope's had so recently, but the Prince's highlanders lacked the rigid discipline of the redcoats. No doubt local men such as those from Killiechassie stole home to family and friends.

The following day, a Fiery Cross was run around the north side of valley, relayed from hand to hand. Jacobite "Duke" William of Atholl was calling out his men. More ominously, Jacobite press gangs appeared, mainly Rannochmen and Macphersons, who hovered flaming torches close to thatch and took any able-bodied man they found.

Three days after the highland army marched off to Blair, King George's forces arrived once more, the pipeclayed North British Fusiliers and the Argyll Militia. Methodically, they set about garrisoning Menzies Castle. Some of the Fusilier officers were highly experienced in dealing with what they called 'irregular warfare'; they were recently back from fighting the Maroons in

Jamaica. A detachment of King George's German Hessians, in immaculate uniforms and tasselled boots, set up a checkpoint by Wade's bridge.

Up at Tighnalechan, where Wade's road headed off towards Crieff, a thirsty Fusilier officer on patrol gratefully took a drink of warm milk from a young wife; he was unaware that her husband was away with the Jacobite army. Another Fiery Cross appeared, this time coming up from Kenmore into Aberfeldy. The lairds of Glen Quaich and men of Glenlyon were trying to raise more support for the Jacobites. The cross made its way round the thirty-two miles of the Loch Tay shoreline in three hours, but attracted few recruits.

On Sunday, the 26th of June, 1746, in Kenmore and west at Killin – two places where the men didn't march out for Prince Charles – there were Thanksgiving Services that the rebellion was finally over. Though summer had arrived, the valley was full of sadness. April had brought the news of Culloden. Many locals may have been pleased that the government had won, but too many from the valley had died.

Most of the local men had been in Lord Nairn's battalion. Along with the rest of the Atholl Brigade they had been on the right of the Jacobite line. Nairn's highlanders had led the first terrifying, bloodcurdling charge, but they had been caught in crossfire from the Argyll Militia, then shot down by the ranked muskets of red-coated Government infantry regiments. The Duke of Cumberland had trained his men carefully; he wanted no repetition of Prestonpans or Falkirk. The redcoats stood their ground and fired volley after volley. Only twelve men from Lord Nairn's entire battalion remained uninjured.

Tighnalechan, on the Old Crieff Road. The house stood on the track of General Wade's road, above the Cottage Hospital

Immediately after the battle, Cumberland ordered all wounded Jacobite soldiers to be killed. Other prisoners were transported across the Atlantic; and a new law forbade anyone in Scotland to carry arms or even to wear their kilts, the beginning of a brutal and relentless programme designed to destroy highland culture and customs.

Alan Stewart from Woodend, who had fought alongside Archie Roy, walked back to Glenlyon from Culloden, dodging dragoon patrols by nimbling across bogs. He picked up his scythe and got to work, ready to vanish at a moment's notice. He was never caught.

Downstream at Killiechassie, the widows and children were hit especially hard. On that grey day at Culloden, the Laird of Killiechassie and his little band had led Lord Nairn's battalion in the charge, at the very front of the entire highland army. The laird was killed and of the thirty-four Killiechassie men that marched away, there were only four survivors. All four were now in hiding in the valley with a price on their heads. Not a soul revealed their whereabouts.

The woman from Tighnalechan who had given the milk to the Fusilier officer was one of the few lucky ones. She heard that her husband had been taken to Carlisle Castle. She walked the whole way there, and in the street below the castle, the very same officer recognized her and asked why she was there. He arranged for her man's release.

Profit Comes to the Valley

In 1749, three years after Culloden, Captain Hughes, in red coat and tricorne hat, reported that a party of fully-armed highlanders had plundered cattle at Killiekrankie, and that he and his soldiers had chased them as far as Aberfeldy. He had appealed for help from the villagers but no one had come forward, and the gang escaped. They were risking execution: carrying any form of weapon was a capital offence. Wearing a kilt was a crime. Bagpipes, too, were forbidden.

Laws such as these won the redcoats no sympathy among people whose relatives had been killed, or transported, or were still in hiding. Aberfeldy was seething with resentment towards the government in London, towards the occupying army, and towards the Commissioners for the Forfeited Estates, as the administrators who took control of land that had been owned by rebel Jacobite chieftains were called. Soldiers hunted for fugitives such as the four men from Killiechassie. Archie Roy, now sixteen and squirreled away below Schiehallion was almost – but significantly not quite – caught near the Finduie burn above Fortingall by his own brother, a lieutenant in the Black Watch.

The Government in London, determined to wipe out the old Celtic way of life, introduced measures designed to smash the old patriarchal power of chieftains over their clans. They abolished the clan chiefs' hereditary right to administer justice. In Logierait, the enormous Hall of the Court of Regality, from which the Atholls had dispensed judgement for centuries, fell into disuse. Only a few stones of its prison survive in the hotel yard.

Though some chiefs took care to maintain their fatherly role over their clans, most adopted 'southern' ways, spent more time in Edinburgh and London, and started to view their properties as sources of income and their people as rent-providers. And, though most people in the valley continued to speak Gaelic, English began to be used more and more. A good command of English was becoming essential for getting on in the world.

Down in the Central Belt, cotton mills were being built. Scottish exports were increasing, especially from Glasgow. The new industrial towns needed food and the numbers of black cattle coming down over General Wade's bridge on their way to the October trysts at Crieff and Falkirk steadily increased. Even before the 'Forty-Five', several landowners hereabouts had begun to develop new ways of farming. Lint mills – such as the one at Invervar in Glenlyon – had already been built, and now business started to pick up. Spotting a technological opportunity, John Campbell, the 2nd Earl, brought wool-workers from England to teach his tenants new spinning and weaving techniques, and by 1734, local people were using the Kenmore market days to sell lint yarn and bales of tweed to dealers from the ports of Perth and Glasgow.

Spinning wheels began to replace the old-fashioned ways of hand spinning.

Benevolent lairds gave the wheels as rewards for good tenancy and soon the familiar creak-and-whirr was heard from many an open cottage door. By 1769 there was a watermill close to Kenmore that could card and spin wool as well as dress and dye cloth. Twenty years later, its tenant was a MacNaughton, a name still familiar in the local tweed and tartan world. The tradition of village women gathering to 'walk the cloth' with their feet began to fade; the accompanying songs went, too. But there was more money to be made at home than ever before, a significant amount of it made by women.

Small watermills that could shell barley in substantial quantities were also built locally; they replaced the thumping of old-fashioned family mortar stones, querns. Sacks of profitable barley were soon on their way out of the district. There was competition for labour between local landowners and mill managers in Glasgow and Paisley; but when labourers heard of the working conditions in some of the mills, they were often happy to stay here and work for someone they knew.

After the 'Forty-Five', the shift in farming from subsistence towards being a profit-making, labour-employing industry accelerated. Some parts of the valley still were stuck in the old system of run-rig, with the tenants on yearly verbal leases and with no incentive to improve the land. But in other parts local lairds noted what was happening in England, examined their properties carefully and re-organized their estates into larger more manageable farms, rented to tenants with fifteen-year leases. They created more employment on modern farms such as Achloa and Acharn, Croftmoraig and Stix. Further east, new farm buildings replaced old fermtouns, even quite high up the hillsides, at Tominteold, Rawer and Glassie for example, and along the north slopes of Strathtay. Sturdy little highland ponies were at work ploughing the land east of the top of the Birks and in similar places above the valley, right up to a height of 450 metres.

Farmers erected dykes to enclose their fields and mark their boundaries. Whenever they could find sufficient wood to fire up their kilns, they limed their land. There is an example of a lime-kiln up by Loch Kinardochy, another at Margmore above the Birks, and yet another at Tominteold on the other side of the valley.

Enlightened lairds sent their tenants' sons to Norfolk and Leicestershire to learn the new farming techniques. They stopped leaving fields fallow and began to rotate them annually through turnips, sown grass and barley, effectively adding a third to their farms' profit-making area. A smaller number of people was needed to work the land than before, but the quantity of grain grown in the valley almost doubled. As land values increased, so rents rose. And though the fewer labourers were better paid, it meant that many folk had no work. In this valley, the clearance that was chiefly responsible for so many youngsters heading south was more subtle than burning thatch; it took the form of farming rationalizations and scarcity of jobs. As a local minister wrote: "It is almost incredible to tell what swarms leave the country every year and go south for service."

There were forced clearances too: the Commissioners for the Forfeited Estates led the way in modernising the lands taken over from the Jacobite lairds. Unencumbered by what they considered sentiment and tradition, they cleared estates of what they calculated to be idle labour, and turned farms into profit-centres. They then used the money made to build better roads and bridges. But, for example, they removed 195 tenants and 95 cottagers from the parish of Fortingall, and in some parts only one family remained where previously there had been four or five.

There were more clearances from the valley, rarely as brutal as those carried out further north, but grim nevertheless. In the 1780s and 1790s both the Earl of Breadalbane and the Duke of Atholl cleared families from their estates; and became angry with lesser lairds when they refused to do the same. Robert Stewart, Laird of Garth, lost his job as factor for the Duke because he simply could not bring himself to rationalize his own land and send away Stewart people whom he considered to be members of his extended family.

Landowners cut back on black cattle – others could rear them well enough in the harder lands further north – and experimented with different breeds of sheep, Cheviots, black-faced Lintons, Lammermoors and Leicesters. Sheep cropped the grass round the deserted sheilings. By 1790, when there were 24,000 sheep in the parish of Logierait alone, Duncan Mc'Ara, Minister of Fortingall commented: 'Crofters, cottagers and day labourers, who can earn no bread at home, set out for the great towns to get employment. Our extensive sheepwalks are certainly, in that respect, a loss.'

For some of those that had to move, the opportunities were good. Archie Roy joined the 75th Regiment of Foot, whose tiger of a colonel had been, like him, a Jacobite; its ranks were crammed with former rebels. Together, they fought with distinction against the French in Canada. There was also the East India Company, already a discreet Scottish 'mafia'.

Some young families found they enjoyed the freedom, open space and challenges of Canada, but many had to confront the realities of commerce and manufacturing in Scotland's Central Belt. Families and single mothers with three or more children aged seven or over, fit for work, could obtain contracts, with housing provided, in the massive mills such as New Lanark, or closer to home at Stanley near Perth. There was other work down in Perth, too, at the printing works, the shoe factories, the paper mills and the port. In 1791, James McDiarmid, Minister of Weem stated: "Whole troops of boys and girls go annually to the low countries for service, and of late to the cotton works, many of whom settle there."

More than merely a refuge for Jacobites, the army became an important employer, highly appreciative of the hardiness and courage of highlanders. For many a young clansman, the British Army provided a respectable outlet for energies that might otherwise have been directed towards members of other clans, or cattle-lifting. In 1775, the Black Watch came home, now numbered as the 42nd and already legendary as the 'Forty-Twa'. They had been away on service for over thirty years. During that period, men had come back to the valley with tales of conflicts in Flanders, New York, Montreal, Havana and the West Indies. Only in Ireland had their time been peaceful. They were off again a year later in 1776 to fight the colonists in America. They acquitted themselves well in a war about which few felt comfortable. They even put George Washington to flight in a little place called Brooklyn. They did not come home again until 1789, and in 1792 they were used to control unrest up in Ross as landed proprietors cleared tenants from their cottages.

One of the regiment's lieutenants sent to Ross was young David Stewart,

Robert of Garth's son. He had already seen the struggles over clearances between his father and the Duke of Atholl, and though he later became a distinguished general, he never forgot what he witnessed in Ross, as thatch was set on fire and weeping families were driven from their homes. He became a fearless critic of highland clearances. He spoke out even though it affected his own career opportunities, and he made sure such brutality did not happen on his own estate here. He was often seen in Aberfeldy, seated on his old grey charger, chatting in Gaelic to the locals. Historians still turn to his book, 'Sketches of the Highlanders', for an understanding of highlanders in the eighteenth century, their customs and codes, their weaknesses and their very considerable strengths. His statue stands proudly beside the bridge at Keltneyburn.

The valley was enjoying something of a golden age. The highland staples of linen, wool, barley, mutton and beef were all in demand. Whisky

Statue of General David Stewart of Garth, 1768-1829, at Keltneyburn, newly erected in 1925

was now being exported, especially from the eastern end of the valley. Salmon was being sent from the Tay as far as London. Up in the hills, people continued to haul stones on sledges and carry peat on their backs in creels, but down in the valley roads and bridges were being constructed. The bridge at the Ford of Lyon for example was built in 1793. The number of carts increased: in the parish of Logierait there were 50 carts in 1760; by 1790 there were 400.

The road along the north side of the Tay was still 'deep and miry,' carts often sinking up to their axles, but along the south side the route was much better. Every week, even in winter, half a dozen big four-wheeled carts left Weem and trundled over General Wade's bridge, down through Grantully and Balnaguard to Perth. As they hauled away the valley's exports, they returned with salt, iron and tar, and extra supplies of essentials like butter and cheese. Suffolk cheese was the most popular.

By 1800, local people's lives had improved dramatically. Thanks to the efforts of local elders and the Scottish Society for the Propagation of Christian Knowledge (SSPCK), there were more schools. Most children were better educated, although many were absent during summer farming and autumn harvesting. Jaundice had mysteriously appeared – no one understood viral infections in those days – but inoculation had cleared the valley of a greater threat, smallpox. There was now a full-time surgeon in Dull. Despite rheumatism, pleurisy and whooping cough, many people lived to impressive ages. As the Rev. Duncan McAra of Fortingall noted in 1794: "In general, the people are pretty long-lived. Many are between 80 and 90, some between 90 and 100. A few live beyond that age. There is at present a gentleman living, and still healthy and strong, aged 103. We have also a woman born the same year with him." Another local man, Donald Cameron, lived to an alleged 127.

The standard local diet of organically-grown oatmeal, barley, potatoes, turnips, cheese, butter, milk, eggs and ale is now recognized as a major contributor to the general health and longevity of people in the valley at that time; that, and jobs involving steady exercise. However, little double-edged luxuries like tea and sugar were beginning to appear.

With all the local spinning and weaving, clothing was cheaper. The availability of linen for underclothes led to greater cleanliness and a reduction in disease. The potato had solved winter starvation and cut the need to import extra oatmeal by 75 per cent in under thirty years. Better diet and improved health brought a significant increase in the number and size of families in the tiny fermtouns throughout the valley. More people meant greater strain on the crops from the little infields and outfields. The old system could not cope with anything other than the subsistence of a small number of people; yet another reason for people to move away.

Substantial farmhouses were now being built. The Flemyngs had already erected their big mansion at Moness in 1758, the oldest dated house in Aberfeldy. Significantly not designed to be defended, its date-stone is still high up on the south gable. There was more business for local tradesmen. Many a farmer and craftsman now had a grandfather clock ticking in his hallway. Apart from people being pestered by what a local minister referred to as 'sturdy beggars from the north' attempting to find an easy life, and trying to avoid being sucked into the mills further south, life was generally much better in the valley. In the 1790s Aberfeldy began to coalesce into a town.

*Moness House,
built 1758,
looking towards
Schiehallion,
before timeshare
properties
were built on
adjoining fields*

The Town Takes Shape

Aberfeldy took shape as a town in the 1790s. Though this was certainly helped by the relative peace after the 'Forty-Five', the town's growth was almost entirely due to one family: the Campbells at Balloch, the descendants of Grey John, the man who had built his new castle meaningfully close to the eastern edge of his enormous lands. The Breadalbane Campbells may not have been popular but they provided substantial employment and opportunities for less wealthy men to develop businesses in the area.

Pale John's grandson, yet another John Campbell, the 3rd Earl of Breadalbane, began the process. In 1767 the Commissioners for the Forfeited Estates sold him the lands around Fearnan that had belonged to the old chieftain Struan Robertson. (It was Struan who had 'lifted' General Cope's coach and brought it back over Wade's bridge). With the purchase of Fearnan, Earl John Campbell's hold of both sides of Loch Tay, running west from Kenmore, was now secure.

More significantly however, the Earl had designs on land further east, especially the villages grouped on the south side of Wade's bridge. In 1771, he bought Aberfeldybeg (Little Aberfeldy) from the Menzieses. Aberfeldybeg was really two hamlets, both on the west side of the Moness – then still called the Paldy – burn: Over Milton, a group of about ten houses on the higher, south side of what is now Bank Street; and Nether Milton, another ten houses trailing towards the Tay along the lower edge of the burn. The Menzieses also sold the larger village of Easter Aberfeldy to Earl John, fifty houses grouped around the area to the north-east of what is now the Square. So the Earl came to own most of what we now know as Aberfeldy, with its population at that time of about 350 people.

However, lying between Easter Aberfeldy and Aberfeldybeg was a piece of land that cut a broad swathe between his new purchases: the Moness Estate, owned for the last three hundred years by the Flemyngs. In addition to land up around Moness House and the little village of Moness strung along the foot of the Old Crieff Road, the property ran down the east side of the Paldy burn, including where The Square now is, and on northwards down Burnside and Chapel Street. Like the Paldy burn, these two streets still retained older names: Burnside was known as Black Street, possibly because it was a long line of rather decrepit, heather-thatched, 'black' houses; and Chapel Street was known as Factory Street because it led towards a lace and muslin factory erected by the Flemyngs in 1772. The Factory remained in use until the 1950s, for some time as a dance hall and then as housing. With its neat stone spiral outside staircases, had it lasted another twenty years it would surely have been preserved. There was an inn down there, too, nearer the river.

On the eastern side of Factory Street lay a time-honoured jigsaw of small

*Fearnan in the
early 1900s*

plots held by various tenants of both the Earl himself and the Flemyngs. Plots held by Borlick were jumbled into those of West Strade, Mid Strade, Dundai and Croft Dow. (See the 1753 map, p78). Each tenant had a degree of independence, enabling him to scrape by with his plot, his black house and his cow. But the whole area could support only a handful of people. Earl John and his factor could see the obvious advantages of sweeping this mediaeval muddle away and of setting up a small town in its place.

Earl John wanted a place to service the needs of his ever-expanding estate, a town with a decent, modern market square and which, unlike Kenmore, would be ideally positioned to take advantage of increasing trade moving up and down General Wade's roads and over the bridge. The Earl was convinced that Aberfeldy, at a suitable yet convenient distance from his eastern gates, would also bring him profit from rents and a steady supply of estate employees.

Not that Earl John ignored Kenmore, so close to his castle at Balloch. In 1760 he had begun to convert Kenmore from a small bustling market into an English-style estate village able to accommodate staff that worked in the castle and its grounds. He also remodelled the church. In 1774, with finance from the Commissioners for the Forfeited Estates, he built Kenmore Bridge, giving access to the new road along to Killin. Kenmore's conversion took a while: even thirty years later, the place still had 63 weavers, 38 tailors, 36 wrights, 26 shoemakers, 20 flax-dressers, 10 smiths, nine masons, eight coopers, four hosiers, and a dyer.

Earl John noted that the Duke of Atholl had distributed flax seeds to his tenants to encourage linen production, so he went a step further and erected a long row of thatched cottages at the west end of Aberfeldy – along what is now Kenmore Street – to accommodate flax spinners. Almost entirely women, these spinners took locally-grown flax, which they soaked in well-pits till the stalks disintegrated. They then removed and cleaned the flax, and took it along to the lint mill by the burn for processing. Once processing was complete, the women collected the flax and spun it on their spinning wheels. In good weather they met and worked together outside. They wove the yarn into cloth on handlooms before taking it up to the bleachfields above Bank Street. Once bleached, the cloth was ready for making into shirts and sheets, or for selling in the market. The work brought the women a certain independence, which was not to last.

Old Earl John may well have smiled at the success of the flax-spinners, but two things stood in the way of his grander plans for the town: his own age, and the wedge of land owned by the Flemyngs of Moness. He knew the Flemyng family well, and he knew their chances of a male heir were slim. It was a matter he was only too conscious of, having lost his only son. In 1782, aged 87, Earl John died. It was left to his successor, his third cousin, another John Campbell, to become 4th Earl and to wait for the old Flemyng laird to pass away; in 1787, he duly did.

The Moness Estate came on the market later that year and the 25 year-old Earl bought it. Moness was an attractive property encompassing Aberfeldy's famous walks and waterfalls. Just as it changed hands, Robert Burns visited and wrote his famous poem *The Birks o' Aberfeldy*:

(*Chorus*)
Bonnie lassie, will ye go
Will ye go, will ye go
Bonnie lassie, will ye go
To the Birks o' Aberfeldy?

Now simmer blinks on flow'ry braes
And o'er the crystal streamlet plays
Come let us spend the lightsome days
In the Birks o' Aberfeldy
(*Four more verses follow*)

Map of east end of the Earl of Breadalbane's Estate, showing the Moness 'wedge'

The young earl immediately put his predecessor's plans into action. It took a while for old leases to fall due – and not be renewed – and for new 99-year building leases to be issued. But within two years, Aberfeldy's Market Square was taking shape and a Post Office was established. And, within ten, there were two watermills, one for meal, and one for lint, both not far from where the existing watermill now stands; old cottages were pulled down; in Dunkeld Street, new stone-built houses were erected; a school was set up by the SSPCK, boasting 107 pupils; trees were planted in the Den of Moness; the banks of the Moness burn were strengthened; and the little bridge above Moness was built, bringing a new easier road downhill from Loch na Craig.

Kenmore was still bigger in terms of population. In a 1798 census there were 646 men between the ages of 15 and 60 in the Kenmore area and only 168 in Aberfeldy. But, while Kenmore was commercially on its way down, Aberfeldy was swiftly moving up. Under the control of the Earl and his factor, Aberfeldy was becoming a fledgling town. Some its inhabitants, making a good living, conversant with Scottish Enlightenment literature, and aware through increasing numbers of papers and journals of more revolutionary French ideas, felt it was time to shed old-fashioned deferential ways.

Burnside, Aberfeldy, formerly known as Black Street, in the late 1800s, little changed from previous centuries

An Independent Congregation began to meet, initially in a private house, then in a chapel in what is still called Chapel Street. The chapel itself has gone now, marked only by a plaque, but it was the first sign of a religious movement that would split the valley fifty years later. This little group, like so many before them, felt that lairds had no right to appoint ministers and that no one should stand between a man and his God. The Church of Scotland minister of Weem, eyeing the chapel in Aberfeldy, gleefully noted that none of his own parishioners had seceded from his church, and none were of the 'speculative, disputatious kind'. Apart from the 'Seceders' in their Aberfeldy chapel, there were only a handful of Episcopalians and even fewer Roman Catholics, but if the minister had known what was coming, he might not have been quite so smug.

Aberfeldy's inhabitants were still almost entirely Gaelic-speakers, Menzieses, Campbells, Camerons, MacGregors, MacLeans and MacFarlanes. These names show that Aberfeldy had been a place of refuge for different clans, often with long histories of hatred for each other, but here they were, living together as a community, a community whose living standards were steadily improving. Many young men now sported watches and most women had cotton gowns. Kilts had been officially permitted again since 1781; though they were still regularly worn in other parts of the valley, there was only one resident of Aberfeldy who regularly went about kilted, a carpenter-roofer called MacIntyre – frequently working up ladders.

Almost every household had a cow. The herd-boy blew his horn in the Square in the morning, and the cows came out of their own accord from the byres behind the houses, then wandered away to their designated cow-parks – one of which now forms

Right: 1753 map, showing jumble of plots

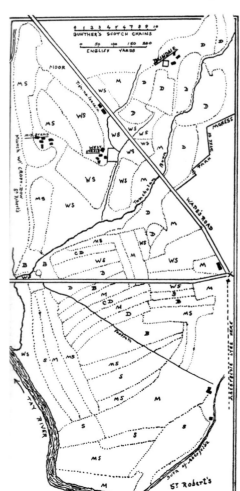

A PLAN OF THE HAUGH OF ABERFELDIE ETC. AS RAVELD IN PROPERTY BETWEEN SR. ROBERT MENZIES AND THE LAIRD OF MONESS.

A. WINTER *fecit* 1753.

LANDS :

B. - BORLIG (as spelt on the original Plan).

C.D.-CROFT DOW

D. - DUNDAIE

M.S.-MID STRADE (or Straid)

M. - MONESS

S. - MR SPALDING

W.S.-WEST STRADE

X————X

This shows the line of the old road to the east from a point corresponding to what is now the south-east corner of THE SQUARE.

the Golf Course – to be brought home again in the evening.

Why had Aberfeldy not grown before? In earlier centuries the parish had been the basic component of local government. Before the agricultural and industrial revolutions introduced greater market demands, greater movement of people and greater religious independence, each parish in Scotland was virtually a ministate. The Minister was appointed by the local laird, and the Kirk Session – a group of elders – was elected for life. They were far more important in most local people's lives than distant politicians in Edinburgh. The elders controlled their parishioners' education, social security and local discipline. They used the Poor Box as form of micro-bank, and at times of shortage even bought products in bulk, oatmeal for example, to sell on to their people at lower-than-market prices. They supervised respect for the Sabbath, and officiated at fairs and market days. They oversaw parish morality – sometimes through ill-concealed snooping – and backsliding was met with public penances and fines.

Aberfeldy lay where three enormous parishes met in a tangle of boundaries. A map drawn as late as 1862 makes this instantly clear. East of the burn lay land in the parishes of Dull, Weem, then Dull again. Unbelievably, the land west of the burn was an outlier of the valley's easternmost parish, Logierait, a leftover from its time in the ownership of the Atholls. On the other side of the river, the land was divided between Weem, Dull and Logierait. A forty-minute walk could take you across seven parish boundaries.

Each of the five parishes in the valley was jealous of its own interests. As well as the busy market-villages at Kenmore and Fortingall, there were others at Dull, Weem and Logierait. Even after General Wade built his bridge in 1733, there was no obvious reason for the local lairds or the elders of the different parish Kirk Sessions to develop anything at Aberfeldy. It was the commercially-minded Campbell Earl John who saw things differently. He would certainly have studied Adam Smith's *The Wealth of Nations*, published in 1776. The book went on to have a major influence on the development of national economics, but it was based on

Aerial view of Kenmore, showing the Earl of Breadalbane's 1774 bridge and model village

1880s photograph of the Birks of Aberfeldy.

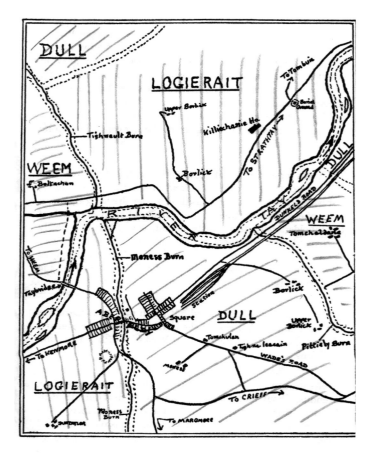

Chart, from an 1862 Survey, showing old Parish Boundaries.

Scale: 3" to the Mile.

1862 Map, showing how it was possible to cross seven parish boundaries within forty minutes.

practical observations of Scottish estates, and Earl John's was one of the largest.

The same year that the Aberfeldy Post Office was established – 1789 – brought the French Revolution. Though lairds became very concerned either that the French might invade, or that revolution might happen here, many Scots who had sympathised with the American colonists during the War of Independence now looked south with interest. The number of papers and journals had more than doubled in the last few years, many of them supporting such dangerous topics as parliamentary reform, even republicanism. It still took a week for letters and newspapers to reach places like Fortingall, but it was now much easier to receive information and opinion from the outside world. The pulpit now had competition, and interest in politics was becoming widespread.

Britain declared war on the French revolutionaries in 1793. The war sparked an even bigger demand for products from the valley estates, grain and mutton to feed the troops, wool and cloth for their uniforms and equipment, and of course highland soldiers. It soon became clear that the Government was considering conscription, and intended to use the age data contained in parish registers. Whilst it was honourable for a highlander to join the army voluntarily, the idea of being forced to was anathema.

Newspapers stirred up hysteria. A crowd of old men and angry women stormed down Glengoulandie from Rannoch to seize the registers from their parish church at Fortingall. They attacked Butters, the lame schoolmaster-registrar, then confronted David Stewart of Garth's elder brother William. William, a JP, held the registers aloft and dared the crowd to take them from him. They promptly flung a plaid over his head and made off with the books, found later in a ditch, rain-soaked. William took no action against the rioters, which, in view of what was to happen to him four years later, was perhaps just as well.

Nevertheless, in the same year, the Earl of Breadalbane raised over two thousand men to fight the French: the Breadalbane Fencibles. The Earl took the opportunity to clear out forty-odd tenants who refused to join his regiment. Parading proudly at Taymouth, the ranks were given commands in Gaelic by Lieutenant-Colonel Francis MacNab of MacNab, aged sixty and allegedly father of thirty-two illegitimate children. But the Fencibles followed in the dangerous footsteps of the Black Watch: when one of them was given an unjust punishment by an officer while in Glasgow in 1795, they too mutinied and, in an echo of 1743, one of them was shot.

There was more serious unrest nearer home two years later. The weather in 1797 had resulted in a shockingly bad harvest. The price of wheat shot up; the war was going badly; Ireland was in turmoil; and the Royal Navy had to cope with two mutinies. To cap it all, the Government showed its hand about conscription and introduced the Militia Act requiring a quota of men from each parish. As a result, in August and September, there were riots all over Scotland.

On Sunday, September 3rd, the Duke of Atholl found himself besieged by his tenants at Blair and was forced to sign an agreement to abolish the Militia Act. That same day, after the church service at Dull, a full-scale uprising began. Men and women from throughout the valley gathered, led by two men from Weem, members of a radical group called the Friends of the People of Scotland. This group wanted the vote for all adult males – at a time when only 0.2% of the entire population could vote. They also wanted peace with France, and this chimed neatly with the angry parishioners. Swords, scythes and hayforks appeared. The Dull Kirk registers were seized, and Frazer, the local schoolmaster-registrar was tied up and taken on horseback into Aberfeldy.

With more folk coming in from other parishes all the time, the noisy crowd then collected the Rev Menzies of Dull and the Rev MacDiarmid of Weem – and William Stewart JP once more – and marched on Sir John Menzies in his castle. Surrounded by what was now a vast mob reportedly several thousand strong, William Stewart and Sir John were forced to do the same as the Duke. The petitioners then rampaged through the valley insisting other lairds sign similar agreements. Lairds and ministers had never been so collectively buffeted before.

From Kenmore to Logierait the valley was in uproar until, at dawn on Thursday 14th, a small detachment of dragoons rode into Weem, seized the two ringleaders, forced their way past an angry crowd swiftly gathering on Wade's bridge and packed the prisoners off to Edinburgh. Matters quietened down with the appearance of more dragoon squadrons from the south; but the lairds had had a real fright. It was less than ten years since many of their counterparts in France had gone to the guillotine. Even if tenants

An Aberfeldy herd-boy

Horn used by herd-boy

1856 drawing of original 1790 Chapel in Chapel Street, now gone. Note gasworks chimney, erected that year and still extant

1856 drawing of the north-west corner of Aberfeldy Square, before the Congregational Church was built

in the valley had not actually read Tom Paine's *The Age of Reason*, many certainly knew about it, and it was no coincidence that the unrest at this time was focussed on fairness and individual rights: soldiers reacted to unfair punishment, mothers reacted to unfair conscription of their children, political activists spoke up against the unfair voting system; and, as so often before, parishioners reacted to priests imposed on them by lairds.

Despite the communal civil disobedience in 1797, for fifty years after the 'Forty-Five', there was relative peace in the valley; and in any case, by 1800, the whole status of the valley and its significance in national affairs had begun to change. Scotland had been made wealthy by the agricultural and industrial revolutions, by trade, and by embryonic capitalism. As a consequence of the Scottish Enlightenment, it had also become more rational, better able to avoid differences of opinion automatically slipping into open conflict. The ideas of freedom and individual liberty that had led to the war for American Independence and the French Revolution had brought wider questions about how communities should be governed, and about lairdism and parochialism, particularly where such issues hindered newly-developing trade.

The days of benevolent despotisms, both local and national, were numbered. The valley was still an important power-base for two influential nobles, the Duke of Atholl and the Earl of Breadalbane, but this was becoming less significant. As the Minister of Fortingall remarked in his 1791 Statistical Account of his parish: "Attachment to chieftains and lairds is dying away." Power was moving south. As the industrial revolution gathered pace there was more money further south for grand buildings and fine furniture, and there was more time to consider higher things such as economy, finance, philosophy and art. The valley was becoming a backwater.

Walter Scott wrote: "There is no European nation which in the course of half a century or a little more, has undergone so complete a change as the Kingdom of Scotland," and, backwater or not, this was certainly true of the Aberfeldy valley. It was a time of steady improvement in people's standard of living. For the first time, some women had gained real earning-power. Though most people still lived 'in the abode of their forefathers' as the Minister of Kenmore put it, there were new possibilities: besides flax-spinning, there was weaving, whisky-making, work on the new farms. But religious argument was soon to divide the valley once again.

The Early 1800s

In June 1838, the Rev David Duff completed his long and detailed Statistical Account for the Parish of Kenmore. The four other ministers, at Fortingall, Dull, Weem and Logierait had yet to finish theirs. Though the interior of Duff's church still had 'a cold, damp, chilling appearance', nevertheless it was a 'handsome substantial edifice, in one of the finest conceivable situations'. And, since its renovation, his manse was now much more comfortable.

By December 1842 the Statistical Accounts for all five parishes had been completed. They provide a series of snapshots of the valley at the time, but they also reveal the attitude of Duff and his fellow ministers. There is an aloofness about their observations, as if they are looking down upon their parishioners from their manses – all five of which had either been recently built new, or substantially refurbished. Extra servants' accommodation and offices had been provided.

The first set of Statistical Accounts had been written in the 1790s by the predecessors of Duff and his colleagues. They described vast, jumbled, disjointed parishes, but these had since been rationalised, with the more distant parts – Rannoch for example – being handed over to other parishes or divided into smaller, more manageable ones. Ministers were no longer required to make immense Sunday hikes to outlying parts of their domains, walks that had turned some of their predecessors into community heroes.

These five ministers were 'all right': this was an upper-class euphemism for moderate churchmen, on the side of the gentry, not affected by the current craze for evangelism that once again seemed to be gaining the upper hand in the General Assembly of the Church of Scotland. Though these ministers saw themselves as tolerant, they had a strong dislike of weeping and wailing congregations and of mass conversions. In their Accounts, they maintained that the number of 'Dissenters' in their own parishes was not increasing. By 'Dissenters' they meant non-Catholic Christian evangelical congregations who refused to accept the authority of the Church of Scotland because of its connection with the state and its acceptance of lairdly control of priests' appointments. However, despite the ministers' claims, the spirit of evangelism was creeping into their own congregations.

They also turned a blind eye to the sudden religious 'happenings' led by preachers in Glenlyon and on Lochtayside, and to the steadily-increasing number of the dissenting Congregationalists in Aberfeldy. This group, founded in the 1790s had had their own chapel for twenty years now. After Edinburgh, it was the oldest Congregational chapel in Scotland, which is why its plaque in Chapel Street is so significant. There were no churches at all in Aberfeldy at this time; the nearest was over the bridge at Weem, where a substantial new church was under construction. It was as if the Church of Scotland wanted

Logierait Church and Manse

little to do with Aberfeldy and its 'mission folk', despite the obvious fact that there were more people in Aberfeldy than Weem, and the place was far busier.

It had been a difficult time for the whole valley after the end of the Napoleonic war in 1815. The need for the valley's exports, linen, wool, beef, grain and soldiers suddenly dropped. The two Black Watch battalions – the 42nd and the 73rd – had fought magnificently at Waterloo but now had little requirement for new recruits. Men who wanted to fight had to go further afield. Piper John McGregor left Dull soon after the war finished, and twenty years later became part of American folklore: at the siege of the Alamo in 1836, he and fiddler Davy Crockett took turns to keep up the spirits of the 200 Texan defenders. They held out for 13 days, finally overcome by 5000 Mexican soldiers.

Cotton, imported from America and made up in the big mills around Glasgow, began to replace the local product, linen. Then, in the 1820s, lowland manufacturers worked out how to spin flax using steam power. The lint mills and spinning wheels here in the valley began to slow. The Glasgow dealers who had been such regular customers at Kenmore market gradually stopped coming, and by the early 1840s no linen was leaving the valley. Though there was still a demand for woollen items – many women changed to knitting woollen stockings – nevertheless, for every stocking-knitter and tweed weaver here, there were six women working the machines in the lowland cotton mills.

The engineer and bridge-builder Thomas Telford and the poet Robert Southey had visited the area in 1819 and had not been impressed. Southey wrote: "Aberfeldy is a place which might properly be called Aberfilthy, for marvellously foul it is. You enter through a beggarly street and arrive at a dirty inn." He reluctantly acknowledged the Marquess of Breadalbane's efforts to improve the place: "A sort of market place or square has lately been built so that, mean as the village or townlet is, it appears to be thriving." And he was very scathing about Wade's bridge: "It makes a wretched appearance on close inspection. The foundations are very insecure." Southey and Telford would gasp were they to see fully laden tri-axle trailer trucks rumbling over it nearly two hundred years later.

Chapel Street in the 1870s

Lairds were hit by the downturn, too. The Stewart families at Garth and Ballechin found themselves in debt. Estates began to change hands. Writing in 1842, the minister in Dull noted that 13 out of the 15 estates in his parish had changed ownership within the last 50 years. In the 1840s, with the advent of train travel, percussion cap shotguns, shooting parties and driven shoots, landlords began to rent their houses to English sportsmen.

As peace continued and trade stabilised,

conditions gradually improved and the middle class started to expand and assert itself. An Atholl Wrights' Brotherly Society was set up, along with the Strathtay Farmers Friendly Society. These organizations provided help for injured members, and for members' widows. Local ploughing matches began, a tradition that the Atholl and Breadalbane Ploughing Society continues today. There were very few tenants still using the old run-rig system.

As Duff walked about his parish, he could see that the planting of turnips had become the norm. West Highland and Ayrshire cattle remained the favourites, and local men preferred black-faced Linton sheep though they tried other breeds. Barley yields rose dramatically; much was turned into whisky. There were small distilleries in every parish, and some larger ones: between them Blackhill and Pitilie alone turned out 20,000 gallons a year, most – but not all – of which had duty paid on it.

Since the 1790s there had been two small water mills in Aberfeldy. But in the 1820s the Moness burn was harnessed much more effectively by the construction of a substantial wheel-driven meal mill. The Watermill bears the date 1826, making it one of the oldest dated buildings in the town; its long lade still runs down from below the Moness bridge and under Bank Street. The lint mill at the bottom of Mill Street was also modernized. The Flemyngs' lace factory at the foot of Chapel Street had been converted into housing, but a dye mill had been erected a little further downstream. It was run by the same

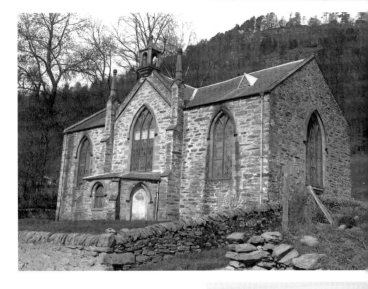

Weem Church, built 1839, now completely rebuilt as a private house

A ploughing match at Weem

*Camserney
Mill Pond*

*Camserney,
from the south*

company that operated the two Breadalbane woollen mills on the west side of the burn. The lower still manufactures tweed.

There was more industry in the valley as a whole. At Camserney, the Menzieses had effectively created an industrial area: there was a carpet mill – with 30 employees – plus a meal mill and two saw-mills, one specialising in bobbins, the other in wheels. There was a carding mill at Kenmore and a sawmill at Pitilie.

Gaelic was still the predominant language – Duff spoke it fluently – and old customs such as Beltane Day at the beginning of May were still celebrated. Almost everyone in the valley was much better dressed. As Duff wrote: "A single instance of the kilt is scarcely to be seen from one end of the parish to the other." Most of the young men wore suits of West of England cloth, with hats, stocks and bright silk handkerchiefs. Duff's colleague, the minister of Dull frowned that the women were now "gaudily dressed in fashionable prints." They wore silk and cloth pelisses over their shoulders. In the old days, he said, umbrellas and beribboned bonnets were rare, but "now the meanest serving maid cannot appear without being provided with both." As an example of the quality of life, the minister of Logierait noted that, unlike in the past, nowadays "the rarity would be to find a house without a clock, and a young man without a watch."

In 1832, as a result of the Scottish Reform Bill, the number of voters in Scotland shot up from 4,500 to 65,000. Local farmers and others began to take an even greater interest in politics and to feel a little more in control of their valley. But, that same year, disaster struck Aberfeldy. A cholera outbreak began to spread from the east. There may well have been one – possibly two – surgeons in the town but no one knew how the disease was transmitted or how to cure it. The street gutters were regularly used as common drains. Within thirteen days of its arrival in Aberfeldy, 54 of the 800 townspeople were dead. Duff and his congregation at Kenmore remained unscathed.

Despite such ghastly visitations, a few people continued to live to a great age. In 1838, eight women in Kenmore had an average age of 85. In Dull, Lilias Clark lived to 107. In Aberfeldy, 'The Colonel' – a tinker – managed an alleged 112. People in general seemed to be better behaved. At funerals and weddings, wrote the Rev Robert Macdonald, Minister of Fortingall, there were "no more unseemly scenes and riots. Propriety and decorum now prevail."

Salmon was cheap, and most people still relied on the traditional foods: oatmeal, barley, potatoes, kale, turnips, cheese, butter, eggs and milk. There was, however, a significant change in the diet of the local folk. Even the humblest houses now enjoyed so-called 'dainties'. Duff noted that in his parish there were "ten small retail shops where such articles as tea, sugar, tobacco, snuff, oil, cutlery, woollen, linen and even silk stuffs may at any time be procured. And as if all this were not enough, two rival bakers from Aberfeldie penetrate twice a week upon average a considerable way into the parish with well-stored carts, to supplant our oaten cakes by the substitution of the luxury of wheaten bread."

Dull Village

In spite of emigrations, modernizations and moves away from run-rig, most people were able to remain in their family homes. In Glenlyon, many families were still making the annual trek up to the shielings. But there were some harsh rationalizations: Sir Neil Menzies cleared clansmen from crofts and small farms dotted throughout his estate, driving Menzieses to Australia and New Zealand and replacing them with sheep. In 1834, the new 2nd Marquess of Breadalbane – yet another John Campbell – cleared about five hundred families from his properties further west in Morenish, Kiltyrie, Cloichran, in Glen Quaich and in Glenlyon. Eight families were cleared from Duntuim, the farm at the west end of Aberfeldy. As soon as the little groups were out of their cottages, the Marquess's men, under orders from John Wylie his factor, tore the thatch from each roof and burned it to prevent any attempts to return.

John Campbell, 5th Earl and 2nd Marquess of Breadalbane (1796-1862)

Though there was no physical resistance, a detailed, angry pamphlet was published. R. Alister's *The Extermination of the Scottish Peasantry* exposed the Marquess's activities: "On the Braes of Taymouth, at the back of Drummond Hill, and at Tullochyoule, some forty or fifty families formerly resided, where there is not one now!" The Marquess promptly ordered his men to buy up all the copies they could find. And an angry poem was written about the 2nd Marquess by an evicted tenant. The historian Archie McKerracher found a copy. Its second verse reads:-

The fish that swim, the birds that skim,
The fir, the ash, the birk is his;
The castle ha' sae big and braw,
Yon diamond crusted dirk is his;
The roofless hame, a burning shame,
The factor's dirty work is his;
The poor folk vexed, the lawyer's text,
Yon smirking legal shark is his;
Fra Kenmore tae Benmore
The warld is a' the Marquess's.

Local people could not bring themselves to feel affection for the 2nd Marquess. Unlike his father he was a distant, private person, occasionally spotted on hillsides, geological hammer in hand, dogs round his feet, obsessing about finding minerals. Nor did his passion for reintroducing the capercaillie, for copper mining and for sending round farming advice to his tenants strike any chords.

No apology has been or can be made for clearances such as that at the little clachan at Duntuim farm. None of the local ministers, including David Duff, intervened. But these former tenants went to on lead fulfilled lives in Perth County, Ontario; and in some dusty drawer may lie the answer as to who paid for their six-week passages to Canada. The expense was almost certainly met by the Marquess, possibly with help from the Government. But, new opportunities aside, his tenants were being moved inconceivably far from their homeland, and with their departure a whole culture was being cleared, too. Nevertheless, the fate of the enforced emigrants was very different from Donald McDonald of Fortingall, aged 55, who, for non-payment of rent, was turned off the farm that his family had held for generations, with his wife and six children, and who died a pauper in Perth.

Not only on the Marquess's land but also throughout the valley, the road system had vastly improved since the 'deep and miry' days of the 1750s. There was a turnpike from Killin, along the north side of Loch Tay, over the Kenmore bridge, through Aberfeldy to Dunkeld; and another from Dalnacardoch via Coshieville through Weem and down Strathtay. The toll-house still stands at the west end of Kenmore Street, and there is another opposite the Ailean Chraggan hotel. Many other roads were now properly surfaced, or 'macadamised'. Farmers, distillers and manufacturers could export more easily, and coal could be brought in to augment the ever-decreasing stocks of peat. Coal was strictly for the middle classes, so for poorer folk the annual peat-cutting trek into the hills was still vital.

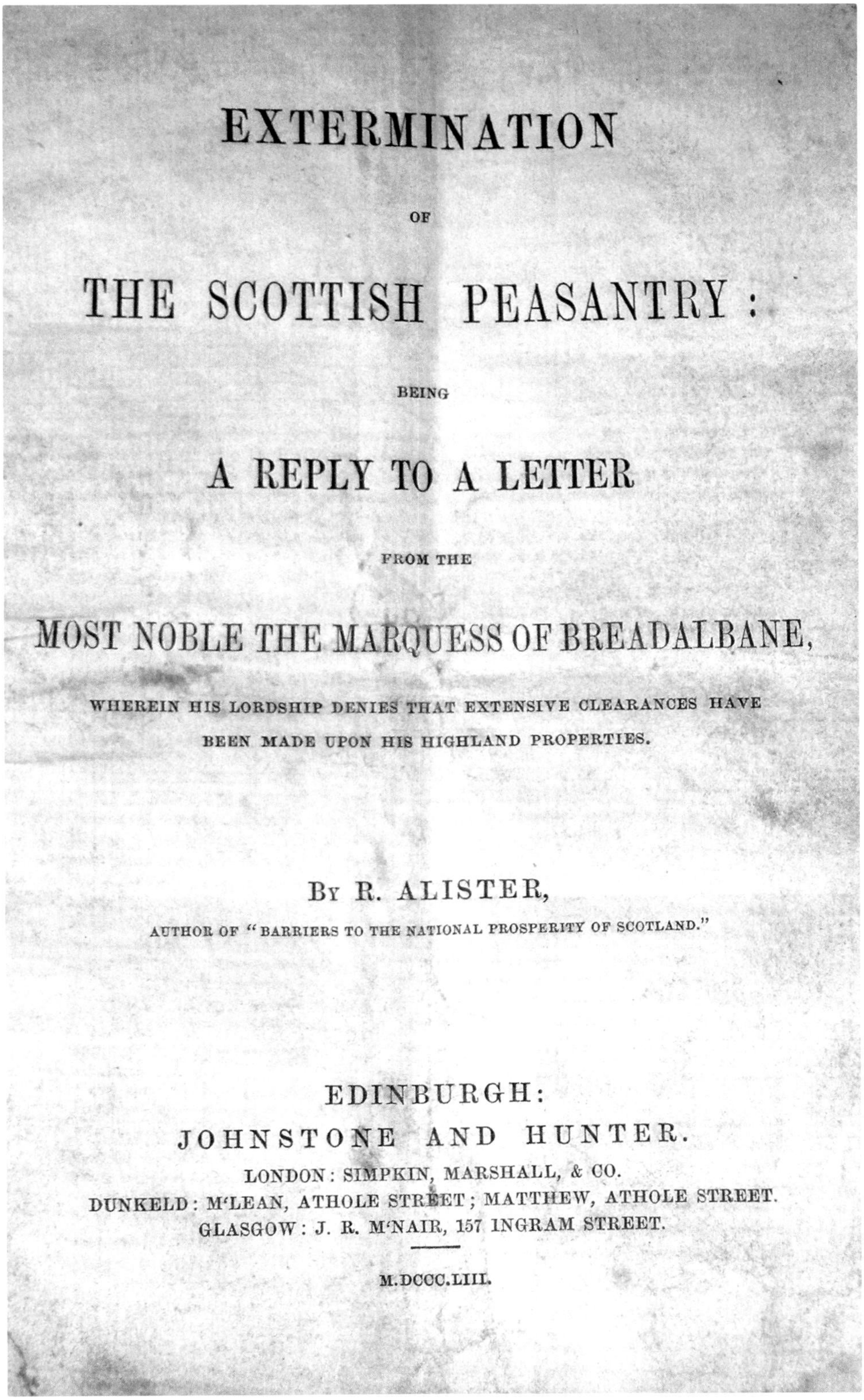

EXTERMINATION

OF

THE SCOTTISH PEASANTRY:

BEING

A REPLY TO A LETTER

FROM THE

MOST NOBLE THE MARQUESS OF BREADALBANE,

WHEREIN HIS LORDSHIP DENIES THAT EXTENSIVE CLEARANCES HAVE BEEN MADE UPON HIS HIGHLAND PROPERTIES.

BY R. ALISTER,

AUTHOR OF "BARRIERS TO THE NATIONAL PROSPERITY OF SCOTLAND."

EDINBURGH:
JOHNSTONE AND HUNTER.
LONDON: SIMPKIN, MARSHALL, & CO.
DUNKELD: M'LEAN, ATHOLE STREET; MATTHEW, ATHOLE STREET.
GLASGOW: J. R. M'NAIR, 157 INGRAM STREET.

M.DCCC.LIII.

Front cover of R. Alister's 1853 Extermination pamphlet-letter to the 2nd Marquess

Mail Coaches outside the Breadalbane Arms

Education was very much better. There were schools in all the parishes. High up on the north side of the valley, Daniel Stewart's Free School provided excellent teaching for 200 crammed-in children; having to climb to such a height every schoolday must have been excellent exercise. The school building is still there, a fine uphill walk from Clochfoldich. As for exotic fauna, if a mother wanted to show her child an emu, or a buffalo, or a bison, they had only to walk to the grounds of Taymouth Castle and peep over the wall.

At Weem, Logierait, Fortingall, Dull and Kenmore, fairs and markets were dwindling. Aberfeldy sported six fairs to Fortingall's three. Duff and the other four ministers all seemed a little reluctant to accept the fact that Aberfeldy now far surpassed any of their respective villages. The Minister of Dull wistfully noted that, unlike Dull, "all the necessaries and even some of the luxuries of life can be easily and moderately obtained at the village of Aberfeldy." And the Minister of Logierait added that, unlike his own village, "Wester Aberfeldy is improved with a number of excellent new houses and shops." The eastern end of the central block of shops in Bank Street bears the date 1838, and the buildings in Kenmore Street were also put up around this time.

By 1840, a branch of the Central Bank had been established with 154 depositors. Rebuilt in 1905, it is currently the town ironmonger's shop. The Penny Post had arrived. There was a Masonic Lodge, a Debating Society and two libraries. The Breadalbane Hotel – from which stagecoaches now ran to Perth – was described as 'a very tolerable Christian-like inn.' There was a mail coach to Dunkeld daily, another to Kenmore, and 'another conveyance of an inferior description' to Fortingall.

Besides all its other inhabitants, Aberfeldy now boasted two surgeons, two midwives, six grocers, four haberdashers, three milliners, two clothiers, two dressmakers, two shoemakers, two bakers, two butchers, two auctioneers, two blacksmiths, two coppersmiths, a constable, a sheriff-officer at the Sheriff's Court, a notary public, a hardware store, a saddler, a chandler and a printer-cum-stationer-cum-bookbinder. Whatever the parish ministers called it, this was surely a town.

Royalty and Disruption

On Wednesday, 7th September 1842, Aberfeldy was a town ablaze with flags and bunting. From the moment the twenty-three year olds, Queen Victoria and Prince Albert, paused to change horses at the Balnaguard Inn – where a young girl from Logierait offered the Queen a posy – the valley was in a buzz. The next stop was in freshly whitewashed Aberfeldy to change horses at the Breadalbane Arms, where 200 townsfolk greeted the Queen, and, armed with glasses of whisky, drank a toast to her.

The royal couple travelled on along the turnpike to Taymouth Castle. The 2nd Marquess had only just completed the building in time. His father had begun it in 1801 and for forty years its construction had provided good employment in the area. It was built from the same chlorite stone and from the same Bolfracks quarry as General Wade's bridge. That evening, forty or so titled personages and politicians, the cream of Scottish society, sat down to dinner in the Baron's Hall, in use for the first time. The hall was but one of a series of eye-wateringly lavish rooms. The diners ate from gold plates in gothic splendour, surrounded by suits of armour, shields, halberds, and old masters lit by enormous golden lanterns. Today, though there are hopes of its revival, Taymouth stands empty. Very few people have seen the astonishingly grandiose interior whose craftsmanship – according to cognoscenti – rivals anything else in Europe.

When the dinner was over, a cannon fired from the little fort up the hill and the guests moved to the windows. They were treated to what was to be the Breadalbane's most spectacular moment. For an hour fireworks blasted into the sky, 50,000 lanterns glowed, a series of glittering tableaux and flaming arches came and went, the fort turned red then green, and the whole hillside to the south was covered in bonfires. Then a hundred highlanders gathered with blazing torches to light up three large raised platforms, on which dancers performed reels and sword-dances.

On the Thursday and the Friday, both maddeningly dreich days, Prince Albert went shooting above Bolfracks and then on Drummond Hill, his prey driven towards him by 300 beaters. The Prince was supposedly the first person ever to bag a pair of the recently reintroduced capercaillie. On the Friday evening, there was a grand ball to which the ministers of the five parishes were invited. Taymouth being in his Kenmore parish, David Duff naturally attended, although he disapproved of the Marquess's religious views. Almost alone among the aristocracy, the Marquess favoured the evangelical group in the Church of Scotland. For the last ten years there had been increasing bitterness inside the Church; on one side were those that wished to retain the close connection between the government in Westminster, the local landowners and the church; on the other were the evangelicals who wanted the church to stand separately.

TAYMOUTH CASTLE

HYDRO HOTEL LTD.

GOLFING
TENNIS
FISHING
SHOOTING

Centrally situated at Kenmore end of Loch Tay — amidst the most Beautiful Scenery in the Highlands

STATION - ABERFELDY, PERTHSHIRE, L.M.& S. RAILWAY.

LMS Poster of Taymouth Castle Hotel, opened 1923

Effectively the old argument about laird's patronage of parishes and the independence of the church had resurfaced. The evangelicals saw themselves as the successors of the old Covenanters. This time they had much more money. They were supported by a wealthy, growing middle class, with a strong egalitarian element, often deeply resentful of the hereditary rights of lairds. The lairds – and David Duff – would have been horrified to know that the Queen herself sympathised with the Marquess's evangelical views.

But the glitter and luxury of Queen Victoria's Taymouth Castle Ball was not the place for arguments about church patronage. The whole visit was a stunning success. As the royal party rowed off up Loch Tay in three gilded barges on the Saturday morning, they were accompanied by pipers and singers – Gaelic ballads, naturally – and played off by a band aboard a 'wherry' moored by Kenmore pier.

The Marquess could feel relieved and satisfied, and his factor could pay off the hundreds of locals involved in the whole business: the craftsmen, the suppliers, the pipers, the dancers, the singers, Mr Fogle and the band, the fireworks operators, the lamp-lighters, the torch-holders, the beaters, not to mention squads of extra staff in their new uniforms both inside and outside the castle. But there would have been no question of paying Sir Neil Menzies and his company of Menzies Highlanders who had paraded at attention in Aberfeldy for the Queen's arrival, and replaced the horses to haul her carriage for part of the way. Sir Neil had just built a fine new wing to his own castle at Weem.

However, as the sound of the pipes died away up the loch, the old troubles returned. Duff began once again to consider the problems in his parish, in particular the fact that there were just too many people for the space, food and standards now expected. Like the other ministers in the valley, sitting in their comfortable manses, and under the unspoken protection of their lairds, he could afford to take a lofty view. He wrote it was "the duty of the young to betake themselves to other scenes where their industry and talents would be abundantly in demand." His colleague, the Rev Cameron at Logierait added: "I am however no friend to the expulsion of any part of the community. The remedy I should hope may in part be left with themselves." Neither man seemed committed to helping their parishioners personally. Coupled with their refusal to countenance the more 'modern' evangelical needs of their congregations, it was this aloofness that brought trouble.

The Banner Hall,
Taymouth Castle

In any case, even before the Church of Scotland wrenched itself apart, David Duff was in for a shock. As winter erased the cheerful memories of the royal visit and the spring of 1843 came round, a rumour reached his manse that evangelical speakers were coming to Kenmore. When they arrived to address his people he refused to hand over the keys of the church, saying that such preachers would cause "a disturbance among the congregation." The Marquess heard of this and promptly sent a message to Duff saying that, though Duff had the right to refuse any preacher he pleased on the Sabbath, he, the Marquess had the right as patron to choose whomsoever he wanted on other days. On the following Saturday the church was crammed to hear the evangelical men. Duff did not attend.

Only a month later, on Thursday 18th May, a national event took place that many at the time considered to be one of the most socially divisive in the whole of Scots history: the Disruption. At a meeting of the General Assembly of the Church of Scotland in St Andrews Church in Edinburgh, the church community split in two. Well over a third of the ministers walked out intent on setting up their own Free Church, free that is from governmental and lairdly interference. The rebels already had plans – and funds – in place for the construction of their own churches, their own manses, their own schools and the payment of their own salaries. Aberfeldy was to play a highly significant part.

Here in the valley, congregations split, as they did everywhere else;

The Library,
Taymouth Castle

separate chapels were set up. Every churchgoer had to ask themselves what to do. Should they stay with their existing minister, under the wing of the Established Church and be smiled upon by the laird, often their landlord? Or should they follow their conscience and allow nothing between themselves and their God?

That the Disruption was even more significant here than in other parts of Scotland was primarily due to the Campbell laird at Taymouth. The 2nd Marquess was never popular, never forgiven for his clearances; yet his dissenting views set him apart from other grandees. Immediately before the Disruption, evangelicals both locally and in the General Assembly of the Church of Scotland were overjoyed to have his support. His speeches on their behalf in the House of Lords may well have given them the courage to make the final break.

The Marquess's support is still visible today in Aberfeldy. In November 1843, he laid the foundation stone of the first proper church in the town. It was of course a Free Church. It drew its enthusiastic new congregation not only from Aberfeldy but also from Grandtully, Dull and Weem. As the church took shape, its people met meanwhile in a field to the south-west, praying sometimes in the open air, sometimes in the marquee supplied from headquarters in Edinburgh.

At the east end of the valley, supporters of the Free Church built a chapel in

Strathtay, since demolished. As for Fortingall in the west, the Rev Donald Stewart, a local man, was new and very popular; only a handful of his parishioners left his congregation. Those that did were supplied with a marquee that they set up close to the Plague Stone. When the laird at Glenlyon House heard of this, he ordered the tent off his land. The Free Church group dismantled it and, singing hymns, carried it shoulder high over the Bridge of Lyon and onto the Marquess's land. The Marquess then talked the tenant of a field a little nearer Fortingall into allowing the Free Church to have a tiny plot beside the bridge, and provided timber for its construction.

There was a sequel: thirteen years later, when the Rev Donald Stewart died, Sir Neil Menzies, Fortingall's patron, forced an unacceptable minister on the congregation. Almost all of them decamped to the Free Church and raised enough money to build a bigger chapel nearer the village, close to the old school, but since demolished and replaced by a modern house. The original timber chapel had in the meantime been rebuilt in stone. It survives, connected to a larger, much more recent extension.

David Duff at Kenmore was shocked to discover that the Marquess intended to build a new Free Church a couple of minutes' walk from his own. This time the Marchioness laid the first stone. The church is now a tearoom and gift shop. In 1842, before the Disruption, David Duff counted 323 communicants at his services. In 1843, by his own generous reckoning, that number had dropped to 107. There was a saying at the time that David Duff would have preferred to forget: as people passed his fine church on its promontory, they would mutter: 'The auld kirk, the cauld kirk, the kirk wi'oot the people.'

Breadalbane Free Church, Aberfeldy, erected in 1843 under the auspices of the 2nd Marquess.

Fortingall old church, demolished 1901

Drawing of Queen Victoria's departure from Kenmore, 1842

Threat of Famine; Fear of France

Following the 1843 Disruption, the valley settled into two separate religious communities. Religion remained a key factor in people's lives, but the old, life-or-death choices between Kirk and King had gone. However, in the autumn of 1846, trouble of a different sort appeared: after a shockingly wet summer, farmers and gardeners lifted their potato crops to find them ruined. For over a year, the newspapers had been reporting the Irish potato blight. Anyone with an imagination could read between the lines and picture the thousands of men, women and children driven mad with starvation, and the shrivelled corpses in the village streets. Now the blight was here.

In some cases, tenants and cottagers whose potato crops failed got little sympathy from their landlords. That year, John Wyllie, factor for the Marquess of Breadalbane, wrote to one of his Ground Officers that in his view some of the tenants "did not now have a claim on the private charity of the Proprietor." However, the new Free Church leaders reacted immediately and began to deliver oatmeal not just to their own parishioners but to anyone in trouble. Further west and in the Hebrides, there were desperate shortages. The newly-built Free Church schooner *Breadalbane* – judging by her name, the Marquess may have paid for her – sailed from island to island, bringing food and prayer to the little ports, often with Aberfeldy's Free Church Rev Donald Clarke aboard.

But here, what with the Aberfeldy bakers' vans travelling regularly along the turnpikes and up into the glens, there was less dependence on the potato, and consequently less need for the oatmeal handouts that the government finally organized. As David Duff of Kenmore remarked: "Irish-like indeed, we use a vast deal of potatoes, but we manage to season these roots with a due mixture of beef, mutton and pork; not to speak of the milk, cheese and butter with which we are supplied from our dairies." But the status of Duff himself was fading, along with the other Established Church ministers and Church Elders. Their power was sapped as responsibility for the desperately poor was transferred to locally-elected boards, and the Free Church set up its own schools.

Communication, urbanisation and recreation became significant for Aberfeldy inhabitants: regular daily mailcarts began to run to outlying areas, and in 1856 the Aberfeldy Gaslight Company was set up. The crenellated baronial chimney of the local gasworks still stands, at the bottom of Chapel Street. There are two similar chimneys for Taymouth Castle, close to 'The Courtyard' at Kenmore. The Aberfeldy gasworks was built on land sold to the company by the 2nd Marquess. He put in Wylie, his unpopular factor, as one of the directors. But the Marquess knew that decent street lighting and a gas supply to shops, mills and houses would be profitable steps forward. Rents would increase; and he of course owned most of the town. A veteran from the Battle of Waterloo,

Carmichael, took a newly-created post: town lamplighter.

Aberfeldy Curling Club was founded in 1853; they first met at Duntuim, the farm cleared by the 2nd Marquess a few years earlier. Later they moved up to Pitilie. A severe frost would provide the perfect excuse for a bonspiel; four gallons of whisky was the usual amount brought up from the distillery below, ready for curlers and spectators.

There were the usual dramas: on the 5th July 1859, Aberfeldy's Dr Thomson got home at ten-fifteen in the evening, exhausted after his day's visits. His last call had been at Crachan Farm in Camserney. He was no sooner through his door than Margaret, daughter of the Andersons up at Margmore, came knocking. Her mother was taken bad. Could he come? Dr Thomson seized his bag and set off on the mile-and-a-half slog uphill to the farm. He found Mrs Anderson, already well advanced in her tenth pregnancy, lying in bed, very seriously ill. She'd taken what she thought was a dose of magnesia powder for her heartburn. Dr Thomson examined the powder and found it was arsenic. The two extant copies of his report are both tantalisingly unfinished. Mrs Anderson's fate remains a mystery.

Over the centuries leading up to 1860, there had been remarkably little gunfire in the valley. Most local bloodshed had taken place at close quarters with fist and knife, sword and shield. Cattle-lifters had carried pistols and the occasional long gun; there had been the ghastly time when Montrose marched through with his army and there had also been skirmishes during the Cromwellian occupation. Shooting as a sport had put food on the grander family tables for many years, and the poacher's occasional moonlit gunshot had done the same for lesser folk, but compared to many other valleys in Scotland, the crash of mass muskets and cannons had scarcely been heard; there had been a pattern of marching away to battles.

In 1854, Black Watch recruiting sergeants arrived in Aberfeldy's Square to drum up young men for the Crimean War. Compared to the old days, they met with little success; most youngsters were either at work on local farms, or had already migrated south. Unlike his Campbell predecessors, the 2nd Marquess could hardly raise a man. As the fearless pamphleteer Alister wrote to him: "You must be aware that your late father raised 2,300 men during the last war and 1,600 of that number were from the Breadalbane Estates. My statement is that 150 could not now be raised, and not one of them unless they could not possibly do otherwise." Clan loyalty and local tenancy agreements no longer stretched to the old lengths. The days of the Fiery Cross had long gone. For the first time the Black Watch was forced to find men outwith Perthshire, even Englishmen, though there were of course local men in its ranks.

The Black Watch in India, 1860. Note the different orders of dress

The regiment fought with distinction at the Alma, and most survived the grim days of siege that followed. Scarcely had peace been declared in 1856 before they were shipped off to deal with the Indian Mutiny. Men returned to the valley with tales of starving through months of freezing cold at Sebastopol, and fighting mutineers in the sweltering heat of Cawnpore.

But as fear of Russians died away and the horrors of the Indian Mutiny faded, the newspapers began to fill with the threat of invasion from France, a rumour that Napoleon III did nothing to discourage. The Westminster Government ordered up a vast force of local volunteers but this time they took care to avoid conscription. As a result, the men of the valley responded splendidly. This was a national appeal, not a local laird-driven one, though of course lairds were often in charge. By 1861, there were units in Pitnacree, Strathtay, Grandtully, Killiechassie, Aberfeldy and Kenmore. Over 400 men met for drill at early morning parades and evening meetings. At a time when there were only 1,145 people in Aberfeldy town, this represented a substantial number of the valley's male population.

The Perthshire Rifle Volunteers had to buy their own uniforms, but this did not stop them kitting themselves out in extremely smart outfits. There were variations between companies but most units wore smart grey doublets with red facings and silver piping, kilts of Black Watch tartan, and black glengarries. The officers – farmers, shopkeepers and teachers as well as lairds – wore

neater-tailored doublets, blackcock feathers in their glengarries and fancier sporrans.

Though grandees such as Sir Robert Menzies and the Marquess of Breadalbane were successively Colonels of the '5th Volunteer Battalion, Royal Highlanders' – as they became in 1887 – the men who stood in its ranks were solid examples of the steadily-expanding Victorian middle class, from both sides of the religious divide. The early morning drilling, the digging of ranges, the target practice, the summer camps, the outlay on uniforms, all these cut through the sharp divisions of the Disruption, uniting members of the Established Church and the Free Church. For nearly forty years, the drill hall behind the tollhouse in Aberfeldy rang to the commands of burly, pigeon-breasted sergeants. The sound of shooting came from ranges at Edradynate, Pitcairn, Kenmore and Aberfeldy. Gunfire helped to bring the community together again.

Stationmaster Fyfe

On the 3rd of July 1865, Aberfeldy station welcomed its first train, a dark yellow tank engine hauling a rake of green four-wheeled coaches. In it sat the town's new stationmaster, thirty-nine year old Thomas Fyfe, a man of medium height and sharp eyes. His wife Helen and their four children sat beside him. Thomas Fyfe had had a meteoric career, first up, now down.

At twenty-five, newly married to Helen, he had given up his job as a handloom weaver and joined the railway in Dundee. He had watched the machinations of the different railway companies as they tried to find ways to reach Inverness, and noted the development of one line in particular, the Perth and Dunkeld Railway. At Taymouth, the 2nd Marquess of Breadalbane had been one of the original promoters of this line. He was keen on railways and had been trying to arrange a line to Aberfeldy for twenty years. Over at Weem, Sir Robert Menzies also threw his weight behind the Aberfeldy Branch plan.

Two other major local landowners, the Duke of Atholl at Blair and Sir William Steuart of Grandtully had played for time with the company and demanded special terms. But, despite a court case, the 'P&D' had negotiated successfully and had begun running from Perth up to Dunkeld in 1856. The Marquess immediately inserted a clause in local Breadalbane Estate tenants' leases: each tenant had to provide a man with horse and cart to bring coals from the Dunkeld station to Taymouth Castle once a year. Pressure for a line to Aberfeldy naturally grew.

Fyfe had decided that the 'P&D' was a company worth joining, and by 1858, aged only thirty-three, he had been appointed Secretary and General Manager of the Perth and Dunkeld Railway at a salary of £100 a year. Two years later, the directors announced they would have to make cuts. They said they could only afford a General Manager at £60 a year. Desperate to keep his job – by now he and Helen had three children – Fyfe had offered to stay on at the lower salary. Fortunately, Fyfe found he was back up to £100 the following year; but there was trouble ahead.

It soon became clear that, as Fyfe had guessed, the 'P&D' terminus at Dunkeld would be the jumping-off point for the line northwards. By September 1863, trains began to run from Dunkeld right through to Inverness. At the same time, work began on the branch line from Ballinluig to Aberfeldy. But, unfortunately for Fyfe, the Perth and Dunkeld Railway was one of a number of lines absorbed into the newly-formed Highland Railway, and in 1864 he lost his precious job. There was of course no safety net for the unemployed. He would have been only too aware that the Cuil-an-Daraich Poorhouse at Logierait, not far from the new line, had just opened. It catered for the destitute and infirm of eleven parishes. Fyfe immediately applied for the new post of stationmaster at Aberfeldy. It was a step down but a good position nevertheless.

Thomas Fyfe,
Aberfeldy's first
stationmaster
Note wall-niche
to his right for
station hand-bell

There had been efforts to get a railway line to Aberfeldy long before 1865. In 1845, when 'Railway Mania' was sweeping the country, the Aberfeldy Debating Society had carried a motion that a line to the town was a necessity. And in 1846, well before other lines reached the area, Parliament passed a bill for the grandly-named 'Strathtay and Breadalbane Railway'. But even with the Marquess of Breadalbane behind the scheme, not enough money could be raised.

The branch line to Aberfeldy had presented several headaches for its engineers. The track had to cross the Tummel and the Tay and there were forty-three other bridges besides. There were to be intermediate stations at Balnaguard and Grandtully; and a never-used platform area at Lagg, handy for the Cluny Ferry and the Grantully Distillery, all three now vanished. But the work, including the line's ferociously-expensive, backbreaking number of cuttings and embankments had been completed in less than two years. Many of the navvies were from Ireland, though several of the more experienced foremen were former crofters from the West Highlands and Islands, forced to find a new trade after the terrible potato famine of seven years before.

As the first train stood at the platform, its safety valves lifted with a roar and a column of steam shot into the air. On the platform stood the local lamplighter, Carmichael. He had been lighting lamps for nine years, ever since the Aberfeldy Gaslight Company had been set up. As other spectators shied away from the hissing monster, Carmichael stood unafraid, shouting over the din; a local journalist broadly interpreted his words as: "It's only the iron horse breathing."

As Thomas Fyfe stepped onto the Aberfeldy platform, instantly he saw how far he had come down in the world from his fine office in Perth. The station building was a wooden affair, second-hand, from Rafford up near Forres. Nor was the rolling stock up to much; unless you travelled in the plush comfort of First Class, there were only wooden seats, no corridors, no toilets and no catering. Separate compartments were reserved for smokers.

Sketch of Aberfeldy in 1868, looking west, three years after the railway arrived

Fyfe had seen what railways had done to other towns. He knew that the American Civil War had stopped the supply of cotton to Glasgow and had forced Scots factories to diversify into heavy industry. So Glasgow-produced items like harrows and ploughs could be brought into the valley on railway wagons. Farmers could export goods and animals in much greater quantities. His railway trucks could supply local shops in bulk. That most desirable of items, sugar, could suddenly become easily available. A whole series of trades would no longer be required in the valley: no need, for example, for all eight shoemakers in Grandtully – with a 'd', as the Highland Railway chose to spell it on their new station nameboards.

The railway would bring a new class of inhabitant to the area. The wealthy merchants from Perth, the jute barons from Dundee – men whom Fyfe knew – would be attracted to the delightful little estates along the north side of Strathtay. Large new houses would be erected. Killiechassie, for example, was built that same year, 1865. Edradynate, Cloichfoldich and the astonishing pile of Derculich were soon to follow. In terms of civic importance, Weem, Dull, Kenmore, Fortingall and Logierait would be forever left behind.

Aberfeldy became a very busy station: cattle, sheep, potatoes, oats and whisky going away, everything from shoes to typewriters arriving, and a constant flow of tourists, shooting parties and families with second homes in the area. Fyfe had been in post less than year before Queen Victoria passed through. She did not use the train; indeed she was upset that the line, still bare and brown, its embankments and cuttings scarring the countryside, spoiled happy memories of her previous trip down the valley. She was travelling incognito with the Duchess of Atholl. They passed through Kenmore – still a busy place – on a bustling Fair Day. They kept away from Taymouth Castle. The 2nd Marquess had been dead for four years, and the court case as to who should succeed him in the ownership of the vast Breadalbane estates was dragging on.

Gavin Campbell of Glenfalloch, the future 3rd Marquess of Breadalbane, 1851-1922

In 1867, the case was decided in favour of forty-three year old Gavin Campbell, the dead Marquess's original choice. The new Earl turned out to be a humane man; he curbed the power of Wylie the factor, though he left him in his big house at Bolfracks. Though the Earl had waited for five years while the courts debated, he only lived for another four. His twenty-year-old son – another Gavin Campbell – then became the 7th Earl.

Young Gavin had been brought up at Moness House, just up the hill from the station. When Fyfe's train had rumbled in, the future earl had only been fourteen. Gavin liked trains; he was probably standing on the Aberfeldy platform that day, and would have shaken hands with the new stationmaster. Gavin Campbell was soon to share Fyfe's vision of how Aberfeldy could grow. As the years went by, both men, in their very different and separate spheres, noted and respected each other's work. Later, Gavin, by then a Marquess and man with considerable railway interests, was to do something quite exceptional for Aberfeldy's first stationmaster.

Fyfe's management of the railway station ensured the free flow of goods and passengers into and out of the town. He instituted a tradition that would last almost a hundred years; a porter would ring the station hand-bell just before any passenger train was about to depart. People in the Public Bar of the Station Hotel had time to down their pints and get across the road. Fyfe turned a blind eye when engine drivers, having set off, spotted latecomers and reversed smartly back into the platform.

From his station office – and from his house in Dunkeld Street – Fyfe could observe much that occurred in the town during the next thirty odd years. But it was Gavin Campbell who was in a position actively to influence what happened in the place. After all, he still owned most of it. In 1869 he began to lease many more properties for longer periods. He also set up the Breadalbane Cricket Club; at twenty-two, he was a confident cricketer. Two years later, after graduating from St Andrews and whilst on holiday on the Isle of Wight, he met and married eighteen-year-old Alma, daughter of the Duke of Montrose, whose ancestor had wreaked such havoc on the Breadalbane estates in 1645.

Soon after they were married, Gavin had a yacht – *Alma* – brought up from the Isle of Wight. Towed by a traction engine through the town, it crashed through the mill lade under Bank Street. During its rescue, a tree-trunk tripod was set up to lift it clear. One of the trunks snapped, shot into the air and smashed through the window of a local shop. Mr Robertson, the owner, was fortunately bending down behind the counter as the massive baulk flew over his head.

Yacht Alma *aground in Bank Street, Aberfeldy, 1872*

In the 1870s Aberfeldy was on the cusp of serious change. By now there were over 1,200 people in the town. The gasworks and the railway – even the postal telegraph – were well established. Fyfe's eldest boy, also called Thomas, was now an apprentice Station Clerk. But the old ways had not disappeared. There were still cows in byres behind Kenmore Street. Dunkeld Street was not entirely free of ducks or pigs. The local herdboy was still a fixture. Quarter days like Beltane and Halloween were still celebrated. And for poorer folk, there was still the May trek into the hills to gather peat.

Farmers and lairds were astonishingly mobile; they used the train for trips to Inverness, Edinburgh and Falkirk, but their horses and pony-traps were constantly in action for shorter journeys. In February 1877, Duncan McDiarmid of Glengoulandie – his 'machine' freshly back from the smith's – was at Perth Sales on Monday 12th, met his uncle at Fortingall on the Tuesday, watched the Forteviot Ploughing Match on the Wednesday, examined tups at Larbert on the Thursday, met men at Tummel Bridge and Aberfeldy on Friday, and sat on the Agricultural Association Committee at Dull on the Saturday.

Meanwhile, the education war between the Established Church of Scotland and the Free Church continued. The Church of Scotland controlled Weem School, set up back in 1665. In Aberfeldy itself, the Free Church managed the school originally organized by the SSPCK in 1796. The Free Church had taken it over in 1846 and named it Breadalbane Academy in honour of their greatest supporter, the 2nd Marquess. But the influence of the churches waned further when the Education Act was passed in 1872. It set up local School Boards and enforced universal fee-paying education for children between five and thirteen. People who couldn't pay were helped by the Poor Law scheme. The changes reached Aberfeldy a year later.

Thomas Fyfe's younger son James was eleven. He and the other 180

Early road locomotive in Bank Street, Aberfeldy, 1872. Note the Watermill in the background

pupils moved to new school premises in 1887. An Infants' Department was set up in the Lesser Town Hall, run by Miss Clark, the first teacher in Aberfeldy to hold a proper Teaching Certificate. The school's name was altered to 'Aberfeldy Public School'. It reverted to 'Breadalbane Academy' early in the 1920s.

The Education Act put a number of smaller establishments out of business, including Dominie Maclean's in Black Street, now Burnside, Miss Macdonald's in Dunkeld Street and Miss Malloch's Infant School in the close behind No.14 Kenmore Street. But there were two other schools in that same close that provided further education and they did well from the new arrangement. Mr Gow ran a very successful Secondary School; its impressive list of alumni still exists. And it is quite possible that Helen Fyfe, now seventeen, who had left Breadalbane Academy two years before, was attending the third school in the close, Miss Smith's Young Ladies Institute. On the other hand, she may have attended the rival Young Ladies Institute run by Miss Scott in Taybridge Road.

The original school at Weem continued, and several Established Church parents who lived in Aberfeldy, reluctant to accept change, sent their children trudging over Wade's bridge to Weem daily. But downstream, Daniel Stewart's Free School, high on the hill above Clochfoldich, finally closed.

In 1874, Thomas Fyfe and his station-clerk son whistled Black Watch soldiers away, heading for the Ashanti wars. The soldiers were equipped with khaki trousers, more suitable than kilts for tropical jungle. The regiment performed with courage and distinction, astonishing its commanders with its ability to withstand the sweltering humid conditions.

By that time a building boom was under way in the town, and a sewage scheme was duly set up with filter beds, thoughtfully to the east. Many of the villas in Taybridge Road date from the late 1870s. And in 1878, nearly

Peter Fegan

a hundred years after they had set up their small congregation in Aberfeldy, the dissenting Congregationalists held a last service in their old chapel in Chapel Street and moved into a new Congregational Church in the Square. It is now the Tourist Information Centre.

That same year was a memorable one for Thomas Fyfe. For some time, amid protests, he had been allowing a beggar to sell postcards on the station platform. Peter Fegan was no ordinary beggar; he was rumoured to have been a body-snatcher. Early in 1878 the old man died, allegedly aged 107. Almost immediately after Fegan's death, the station burned to the ground. It was rapidly replaced with a fine stone-built, crow-stepped one, just in time for the visit of the Liberal politician, WE Gladstone, in December. Gladstone, a once and future prime minister, was on his way to visit Gavin Campbell, now a Liberal peer. Fyfe made sure the station had extra lighting and arranged a dais so that Gladstone could address the people of Aberfeldy.

The great man was well received. He and his Liberal Party were very popular locally; he championed the labouring classes, the trade-unions, free education, and votes for all adult males. In April the following year he was re-elected Prime Minister. Sir Donald Currie, already a favourite in the area, was elected as the local Liberal MP. In the blaze of election night excitement and Liberal success, several windows belonging to prominent local Tories were smashed. Sir Robert Menzies, a strong Tory, remained discreetly at home in his castle at Weem.

In a disturbing development for railwayman Fyfe, tolls were abolished and all roads came under local government control. The tollhouse at the west end

of the town became the headquarters of the Aberfeldy Rifle Volunteers; their drill hall still stands behind it. Fyfe had by now become a pillar of the community. Known as a man who cared about the poor and elderly, he was one of the organizers of a proper hospital-cum-care home, in Home Street, as it is now called, just round the corner from his own home.

The big annual event in the Aberfeldy calendar was the October Feeing Market. When these days were on, Thomas Fyfe might stop by Cooper's Pump at the top of Chapel Street for a blether, then take a wander round the booths that filled the Square, spilled down Dunkeld Street and even stretched up and over the bridge along Bank Street. There were coconut shies, shooting galleries and mountains of gimcrack goods on offer. There was an organ-grinder with a monkey, and a dancing bear. So-called 'German Bands' would go blaring through the streets in their blue uniforms. Fyfe might listen to a new device called a phonograph.

The chief reason for these Feeing Market Days was that they provided an opportunity for farm labourers to offer themselves for the following year's work. They walked up and down among the local farmers and struck a deal, often settled in the Breadalbane Arms or the Station Hotel. For example, Angus MacLellan from South Uist, a former soldier, did two and a half years

Sir Robert Menzies, 7th Baronet, 1817-1903

labouring at Tirinie Farm, followed by further 'terms' at Borenich, Dalmally and Rowardennan. Each time the arrangement was sealed with half a crown's payment in advance.

By the late 1870s the number of agricultural labourers who continued to work in this annual itinerant way was gradually dwindling. Many opted for permanent employment on the farm of their choice. Others took their pay, salted it away in one of Aberfeldy's three banks – the Commercial, the Union, or the Bank of Scotland – and then used it to go abroad where pay and prospects were more attractive.

Besides, young men were better educated now and the prospect of farm work was less appealing. Up at Tirinie, there was never a day in all of Angus MacLellan's two and a half years when James Menzies, the grieve – the foreman – kept him and his mates indoors. Angus spent one winter fattening cattle; each time he had about eight beasts ready, he would drive them the four miles to Aberfeldy station, helped by his dog. He was up at four in the morning and not finished until eight at night. Instead of such ninety-hour weeks on the farm with few holidays, men could work on the railways or the police force or in a shipping office in Dundee with greater job security and much more free time.

Similarly, young women could live easier lives as domestic servants. For women as a whole in the valley, the days of earning money through work on linen or wool had gone; they were less independent than they had been. Poorer girls were expected to go into service and then marry.

Dunkeld Street in the 1880s, with the Station Hotel (now The Schiehallion) on the right, and entrance to station on the left

Aberfeldy Public School, erected 1887, demolished 2008

It was different for middle class girls: the Fyfe daughters, Elizabeth and Helen, simply stayed at home once they left school. Not many occupations were open to them. They might have found work as nurses or midwives. Really determined women, like Miss Clark up at the Infants Department of Aberfeldy Public School, could become Certified Teachers – at half the pay of their male colleagues. It was not until 1892 that women were permitted to enter universities, by which time it was too late for the Fyfe girls. Elizabeth was 41 and Helen was 36.

Washing day, in Aberfeldy

Logierait Ferry,
6th May 1896.
An artist selects
her viewpoint

For all women in the valley, finding a husband was not easy; many more young men than girls went south or abroad. As for married women, they were expected to stay at home and care for their wage-earning men and their children. Even among poorer families, going out to work when married or even doing piece-work at home was now considered slightly shameful.

Elizabeth and Helen Fyfe remained at home, unmarried, for the rest of their lives. From their father's seven-roomed house in Dunkeld Street, close to the Station Hotel, they watched Aberfeldy grow.

Logierait Hotel,
1890s

Bank Street,
looking east.
Note absence of
McKerchar and
MacNaughton
building

Aberfeldy from the North, with several 1880s villas yet to built

Congregational Church in the Square, Aberfeldy, built 1878. Bank Buildings erected 1886

A Real Town

By 1882, Thomas Fyfe's station was handling 13,000 tons of outgoing and 14,000 tons of incoming goods annually, including increasing numbers of trains loaded with cheaper coal. That year, once more, he supervised the departure of contingents of the Black Watch. In kilts and khaki topees, they boarded trains on their way to join the Highland Brigade, first in Egypt and later in Sudan. The Watch distinguished themselves in a risky frontal assault on the Egyptian army.

As Fyfe busied himself with arrivals and departures, he and his family witnessed a transformation in the town. Buildings, larger and grander than anything before, began to mark the skyline. In 1884, the Established Church reacted to the presence of both Congregational and Free Churches in Aberfeldy and erected its first church in the town, the imposing St Andrew's Church in the Crieff Road. Empty for years, it is now set to become apartments. Not to be left behind, the Roman Catholics put up a corrugated iron building in Home Street a year later; it has recently been replaced by a smart modern church and the original 'tin church' has moved to the hillside at Dull.

In 1886 the fine red stone Commercial Bank buildings – now RBS – were erected in the Square. As the Square increasingly became the focus for trade in the town, the Thursday cattle sales began to get in the way, so the market moved to a new Auction Mart at the bottom of Home Street, convenient for the station. P&J Haggart took over the woollen mills, at the bottom of Mill Street, still there. Haggart's mill had formerly been out at Keltneyburn; now they needed to be in the town, nearer the station.

There were other developments. The town's Football Club was set up, replacing shinty as the most popular sport. A Masonic Lodge began to meet in an upper room of the Breadalbane Hotel. Aberfeldy gained its first uniformed postman, a significant step: the increasing use of regular posts and telegrams brought a nineteenth century information revolution. The speed of commercial transactions leaped forward. In many ways this helped, but it also meant that current prices elsewhere were instantly available for comparison. Imported barley, oats, meat and dairy products were sometimes cheaper. Farmers had to work harder and watch labour costs carefully.

In 1883, aged thirty-six, Gavin Campbell launched the Loch Tay Steamboat Company. As a result, more traffic appeared in the streets, as a steady stream of coaches came and went from Aberfeldy to the boats at Kenmore. Two passenger steamers headed a fleet of five vessels that plied up and down the loch. It soon became fashionable to travel by train from Glasgow and Edinburgh to Killin Pier, to sail on *The Lady of the Lake* down the loch to Kenmore, then take coach-and-horses to Aberfeldy station, and finally speed away home down the valley on the train. The little lochside villages were glad of coal deliveries and

Private owner wagon

the hundreds of other items brought in by the smaller freighters. Thomas Fyfe, who, along with thousands of other householders, had proudly exercised his new right to vote a year earlier, oversaw the comings and goings of the horse-drawn charabancs and goods carts at the railway station.

Between them, Gavin Campbell and Donald Currie owned most of the west end of the valley. In 1885, Sir Donald bought the huge estates of Garth, Fortingall and Chesthill, formerly Stewart, Menzies and Campbell lands. Other wealthy men had bought up smaller estates in Strathtay before this, but here was a magnate purchasing a massive piece of the valley. Sir Donald had started as a clerk in a shipping office in Belfast, had set up his own Castle Shipping Line. Closely involved in the development of the Cape Colony in South Africa, he was known for his outspoken demands for fair treatment of the Boers. 1885 was a turning point for him: in that year, disagreeing with Home Rule for Ireland, he deserted the Liberals and was elected as Conservative MP for West Perthshire. Gavin Campbell – the 3rd Marquess, as he'd now become – remained a Liberal. In the years ahead, Aberfeldy was to benefit from their friendly rivalry.

In October 1887, Queen Victoria's Jubilee year, Aberfeldy officially became a Burgh. A Provost, a Town Clerk, two Baillies and six Commissioners were elected. The Council had the power to raise rates from the townsfolk to get the town properly paved, properly lit, properly cleaned – 'scavenged', as it was called – and to ensure a night watch was kept throughout the town. The Council immediately set about laying pavements and covering open drains. The Aberfeldy Public School – now with 219 children – moved into new buildings. Work began on the fine villas in Taybridge Drive.

In November, the town celebrated its new status in style. Early in the morning of the 14th, a cold dry day, Thomas Fyfe supervised the arrival of a series of special trains from Edinburgh, Glasgow and Perth. Literally thousands of people began to flood into the town, and a procession began to assemble at the new Auction Mart in Market Street. Gavin Campbell was to unveil the Black Watch Memorial, erected to commemorate the first muster of the Black Watch back in 1740. The proud figure on top, still drawing his claymore, is Farquar Shaw, ironically one of the men shot by the Government in London in 1743. The Watch had in fact originally mustered on the other side of General Wade's bridge, on the watery Boltachan land still in Menzies hands that day, but Gavin Campbell had given land for the memorial's construction on the higher, dryer, town side of the river.

The owner of Boltachan, Sir Robert Menzies, was a powerful local figure,

Aberfeldy Distillery, erected 1898. Note railway sidings

prominent on several local committees. His ancestor had raised the first local Independent Company and there had been more than a few Menzieses in the Watch's first muster. He was Colonel of the 2nd Perthshire Rifle Volunteers who were to feature prominently in the day's events. One summer morning a year or two earlier, the irascible old chieftain had woken his volunteers when they were in camp at Bolfracks by firing off a twelve-pounder cannon beside their tents.

Headed by their regimental band, the Aberfeldy Company of the 2nd Perthshires – soon to become the '5th Volunteer Battalion Royal Highlanders' – nearly a hundred strong, led the parade. In their grey doublets and Black Watch kilts, they contrasted nicely with the scarlet tunics of the regular Black Watch contingent marching behind them. Four more volunteer units followed, from Edinburgh, Glasgow, Forfar and Fife. The Fife Light Horse nearly stole the show, riding on nutbrown chargers, in their bright red coats, white-plumed silver helmets and glittering black boots.

Then, triumphantly, came Provost Forbes, the two Baillies and the Commissioners of the new Burgh of Aberfeldy. They were followed by a procession of worthy representatives of the Burgh's associations, societies, masonic lodges and temperance groups. The crowd gathered at the Monument and the speeches began. Douglas MacKay, a youngster who was there, felt they were almost endless; he was later to join his father as a doctor in the town. The pubs were busy for the rest of the day.

The new Council members settled into their regular meetings, but the shadow of Gavin Campbell hung over them in the form of his factor, ever-present, often taking time on details of feus, and regularly having to refer matters to the Marquess before they could proceed. The Marquess still owned most of the town, but he gave land on the Crieff Road for the construction

St Andrew's Church, Crieff Road, 1884. Note absence of villas built soon after

of the Town Hall. Sir Donald Currie laid the foundation stone of the Hall in 1889. He made a substantial donation towards it and chose James Maclaren to design it. Maclaren – now considered to be a forerunner of Charles Rennie Macintosh – was Sir Donald's favourite architect; it was he and his partners who effectively rebuilt Fortingall, and their distinctive work is still there.

The weekly *Atholl and Breadalbane Times* proudly published lists of people coming and going from the rented villas overlooking the Tay. The paper also noted the names of the shooting party guests on the various estates. Most came by train. Thomas Fyfe set out attractive train fares for groups and excursions. Angus MacLellan and his fellow farm labourer, Donald, took a young lady by train to watch the Highland Games and Military Display at Birnam. The three of them were amazed by the Fife Light Horse with their lances and their tent-pegging skills. Angus and Donald both had their own allocated pairs of horses up at Tirinie for ploughing, carting and so on, but they had never seen animals ridden like that before.

Close to the station a new road, Moness Terrace, was built uphill; and on the corner, Haggarts erected their fine red stone emporium, still there, still selling tweed. In 1896, Haggarts, proudly sporting a 'By Appointment' sign, were advertising their Royal Sandringham tweeds in the *Atholl and Breadalbane Times*. Other advertisers included McLaren, the Bookseller ("Hymn books, Bibles, Violins, Melodeons and Grate Ornaments"), Dawson's the Chemist ("Surgeon-Dentist attending on alternate Thursdays") and Campbell's in the Square ("Corsets! Corsets! Corsets!").

That year was a busy one for the valley. The little green bridge at Comrie was opened by the tall figure of Alma, Marchioness of Breadalbane. People had been campaigning for it for sixty years. With the permission of her husband the Marquess, the Golf Club set about erecting a fine Clubhouse. Thomas Fyfe organized reduced train fares for golfers coming from over five miles away. The course ran through one of the town's cow parks and for more than forty years golfers had to contend with cattle – and cow-pats.

Two years later, Fyfe attended the funeral of James MacKerchar, the town's second Provost. It was a big affair. MacKerchar had also been the Agent for the Bank of Scotland, although Donald McDiarmaid, also at the funeral, had taken his place some time before. The current Provost, Peter Campbell was there, as was Dr Haggart who had taken care of MacKerchar during his last illness. They all contributed to a fund for the installation of the clock on the tower of the Breadalbane Free Church, still there. On his way to the funeral, at the top of his street, Fyfe would have passed the new Post Office under construction, with two new shops alongside. There would soon be four post deliveries a day.

Dewar's new, high-output Aberfeldy Distillery opened that year, too, replacing the Pitilie distillery further up the hill. Fyfe would have overseen its rail connection and its sidings. Almost all Aberfeldy whisky left by train. There was increased rail traffic for the Logierait Agricultural Show and the Breadlabane Highland gathering. The line's favourite tank engine had been renamed *Aberfeldy* and repainted pea green. Its former name, *Breadalbane*, had been transferred to a bigger, newer, main line engine.

Fyfe began to receive written complaints about train times. The last one south left at 4.45pm; he got the departure time altered. On one occasion, he also had to deal with a wayward flock of sheep being herded to the station: they filed into MacGregor's the butcher's, caught sight of their likely fate, went

Breadalbane Football Club, around 1910

berserk and escaped by smashing through the 7'x6' front window.

The editorials in the local newspapers were, if anything, even more outspoken than papers nowadays. In the 1890s, while the Westminster government and the political parties in London argued over Home Rule for Ireland, the *A&B Times* was arguing vociferously for Home Rule for Scotland. It was preaching to the converted: Scotland was Liberal, and Home Rule was a Liberal policy; but England was Tory, and the Tories were in power. Pressure for self-government built up steadily; it was to reach a vital point in 1914.

In 1899, full-scale war broke out with the Boers in South Africa. Yet again Fyfe and the townspeople waved Black Watch soldiers off. At Magersfontein in December, the Watch were caught on barbed wire and slaughtered by accurate Boer firepower, part of what the newspapers dubbed 'Black Week', a jolting series of unthinkable British defeats.

The Aberfeldy townsfolk were shocked: self-government for Scotland

Garth House, Fortingall, home of Sir Donald Currie

was one thing, but a setback for the British Empire was quite another. Though foreigners sometimes mistakenly referred to England when they meant Britain, they only ever called the Empire 'The British Empire'. Indeed, most Scots saw Scotland as an equal partner with England in the Empire. The Scots nation was acknowledged worldwide as excelling in engineering skills, and in the export of ships, machinery and locomotives. Scotland punched far above its weight at Westminster. The local MP, Sir Donald Currie, lived in the valley, and local people were proud of the valley's contribution to the British Army. Quite apart from young men joining the Watch, the 5th VBRH's shooting ranges at Taymouth, Fortingall, Aberfeldy and Grandtully were still echoing regularly to the sound of drill commands and gunfire. Gavin Campbell was now Colonel of the Battalion.

By the time Fyfe came to retire in 1899, all the black houses in Mill Street had been cleared away, a cemetery had been opened and an abattoir – known locally as 'the killing-house' – had been built, conveniently close to the station. Discreet rivalry between grandees had continued: Sir Robert Menzies had planted the line of trees along Poplar Avenue towards Weem, and the Marquess had responded by leasing Victoria Park to the town.

A photograph of Thomas Fyfe in top hat and tail-coat shows him near the end of his career. As the dignified seventy-three year old stationmaster prepared to leave his office for the last time, a letter was delivered to him from

Landlord (possibly taking snuff), barman and clients of the Black Watch Inn

Golf Clubhouse, erected 1896

Jones 4-4-0 tank locomotive, No 50(17) Aberfeldy, 1890s

Haggart's emporium in the 1890s

A showman's wagon at the Black Watch Monument, 1880s

Private carriage, probably the 3rd Marquess's, outside the newly opened Town Hall, 1989.

the Marquess. Gavin Campbell, who, as a boy, had almost certainly watched the first train arrive with Fyfe aboard, and who was now a Director of both the Highland and the Caledonian Railways, had arranged for Fyfe to be given an additional pension over and above the stationmaster's standard amount. Thomas Fyfe took his well-earned retirement and, like the rest of the townsfolk, awaited the coming of the twentieth century.

The Aberfeldy Bell-man makes an announcement

Home Rule, Women's Rights and War

Though two of its lairdly dynasties were shortly to vanish, Aberfeldy's twentieth century began as it was to go on, with young men heading off to war. First-footing had scarcely finished before volunteers of the 5th VBRH gathered in their full parade uniforms at the Armoury in Kenmore Street, following the Black Watch to the Boer War. Headed by their band of pipes and drums, they marched down to the station, and the *Perthshire Courier* reported that they were given 'a fine send-off' by a large crowd. They probably sailed to Africa in one of Sir Donald Currie's ships.

The Aberfeldy District Farmer's Club, chaired by W. Steuart Fothringham met and worried whether the Queen's health might be suffering as a result of the shocking carnage of 'Black Week' the previous December. At Christmas she'd sent boxes of chocolates to the soldiers in South Africa. William Macdonald sent his box home to his father, a mason in Dunkeld Street. Four months later Trooper Macdonald was killed.

There was no talk of the glory of war. Local people were not spared the realities: the *Courier* published a letter from a correspondent at the front. War, he wrote, had changed since the days of the Crimea: "Nowadays, the only thing seen is the dust thrown up by the bullets like a rainstorm on the surface of a lake. When a bullet strikes, you hear a grunt or a gurgle and the man collapses and doubles up. If hit in the arm or the leg, he spins around and falls. The worst thing is a bullet wound in the stomach, below the navel, which is mortal: the pain is excruciating and they howl like a shot hare; it sounds like a child screaming and is horrible."

In the comfort of Castle Menzies, eighty-three-year-old Sir Robert held a cinematograph evening with pictures of the war and portraits of the generals. He presented a sum of money, collected locally, to men of the Dull section of the 5th VBRH, off to join their comrades. He later opened Fisher's Steam Laundry – still going strong at the bottom of Home Street – but the great days of the Menzies dynasty, the family that controlled swathes of the valley for six centuries, had less than twenty years to run.

As the Boer war rumbled on, John Murray, Duke of Atholl, urged men from his estates to join the Scottish Horse, a cavalry regiment raised for the duration by his son. Troopers in their smart grey uniforms and blackcock-feathered slouch hats waited on the station platforms of Balnaguard and Ballinluig to begin their journeys to Johannesburg. Compared to men of many units, the Scottish Horse were at ease in the wide spaces of the veld. They fought bravely and were honoured by being converted into a permanent Imperial Yeomanry Regiment. When the Boer War ended in 1902, the soldiers were welcomed home and Aberfeldy organised its own town Pipe Band, made up mainly of men from the 5th VBRH.

Aberfeldy Station and staff in the 1900s

The *Courier* also gave space to the activities of the Scottish Home Rule Association. Home Rule was a key issue for Scots in the Edwardian era, along with the increasing strength of the trade unions and the emancipation of women. There was another issue: 'Landlordism', as it was called; it featured high on the Aberfeldy valley agenda. Some landlords were virtual despots, ruling their properties through the iron control of their factors, grieves and ghillies. On one occasion Sir Robert Menzies, whilst checking in the dark that one of his gamekeepers was doing his proper job, was mistaken for a poacher and so thoroughly beaten up that he had to spend a fortnight in bed; the ghillie was promoted. Sir Robert died in 1903, succeeded by a quieter, less robust son.

That same year, in a reference to Gavin Campbell, the 3rd Marquess, the following appeared in *Punch* :-

'In Braid Albyn'

From Kenmore to Ben More
The land is a' the Markiss's;
The mossy howes, the heathery knows,
An' ilka bonnie park is his;
The bearded goats, the toozie stots,
An' a' the braxie carcasses;
Ilk crofter's rent, ilk tinker's tent,
An' ilka collie's bark is his;
The muircock's craw, the piper's blaw,
The Gillie's hard day's work is his;
From Kenmore to Ben More
The warld is a' the Markiss's

The 'Markiss' probably smiled at this gentle dig at landlordism; he didn't know that in fact it was a lighthearted single-verse version of a longer, much harsher poem written about the 2nd Marquess's clearances sixty years earlier, as quoted in Chapter 19. Like the Menzieses at Weem, the Breadalbane Campbells' time was almost up.

In the meantime, the Marquess was involved in setting up an aerial ropeway from his quarry above Gatehouse. It brought stone in 3 hundredweight (152 Kg) buckets down to the railway station at the rate of ten tons an hour. Some blocks went to build houses in Market Street, but most were tipped into railway trucks and went for County Council road metal. Later, it was collected by the Council's own steam lorries. Gavin, the Marquess, was not a happy man: he

Fisher's Laundry, Home Street, Aberfeldy, founded 1900

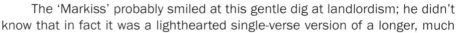

was fretting about his wife Alma's gambling addiction. Her ancestor Montrose had wrecked the Breadalbane Estates in 1645; it looked as if the Marchioness, at her gaming table in Taymouth's white quartz-walled estate dairy, was set do so again.

In Aberfeldy, people's lives were still very much defined by the church they attended, but now there were several shifts in loyalties. In 1900, the congregation of the Breadalbane Free Church – with its recent clock – merged with the smaller, older United Presbyterian Church, and renamed themselves the United Free. A significant group in the Free Church congregation refused to accept the very idea of such a linkage. The congregation was split, and the argument as to who should have services in Breadalbane Church – the `Free' or the 'United Free' – dragged on for six years. It was sufficiently serious for fights to break out in school playgrounds.

Possession of Breadalbane Church was eventually given to the United Free and so in 1907 the 'Wee Free' built their own church at the top of Chapel Street, not far from where the old Dissenter Chapel had once stood. Giving quiet Chapel Street yet another claim to religious fame, it was the first purpose-built 'Wee Free' church in the country. It is currently a charity shop, though its memory and its Gaelic singing are still valued by some in the town. Not to be outdone, the Episcopalians also built a church, St. Margaret's in Kenmore Street, almost always referred to as 'the English Church', now a private house.

Ballinluig station, change for Aberfeldy

Aerial ropeway from Gatehouse Quarry to Aberfeldy station

In order to accommodate the increasing number of people coming and going from the north side of Strathtay to Grandtully railway station, Grandtully Bridge was built, and more churches appeared. In addition to beautiful, peaceful St Mary's, Pitcairn, dating from the 1500s, two more Church of Scotland buildings were constructed: Grandtully Church built by the Steuart-Fothringhams in 1892, and Strathtay Church built in 1900. There was also an Episcopalian Church built in 1888 and a Roman

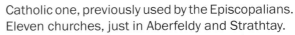

Grandtully station

St Mary's Church, Grandtully

Catholic one, previously used by the Episcopalians. Eleven churches, just in Aberfeldy and Strathtay.

By now, Aberfeldy had a thirteen-man fire brigade, a bowling green, tennis courts, a purpose-built Masonic lodge, a fine new Bank of Scotland in Bank Street; and a garage, Frazer's in Dunkeld Street, listed in Michelin's first British Guide. And the Aberfeldy Pipe Band had won the All-Britain Pipe Band Championship. Perhaps even more importantly, thanks to a Liberal landslide, everyone now had an old age pension, and, where necessary, unemployment benefit. And in 1909 Aberfeldy Cottage Hospital opened; young Dr MacKay, now in practice with his elderly father, was proving to be a fine and caring physician, as well as a passionate local historian.

In August 1910, the *Aberfeldy News* reported that Mrs Emmeline Pankhurst of the Womens' Social and Political Union visited Aberfeldy and spoke to a packed audience in the Town Hall. The stage was decked in green, white and purple, the colours of the Suffragettes. Mrs Pankhurst was actually only campaigning for votes for working women and equal rights in marriage. Many of Mrs Pankhurst's women listeners took a more radical stance than she herself; the idea of votes for all adults was gaining ground. A small number of men sat at the back; some of them heckled.

Editorials in local newspapers reveal that the Liberal landslide had put Home Rule firmly back on the agenda. The papers covered Sir Donald Currie's – and the Marquess's – generosity over the new Cottage Hospital, the Marquess's donation of the Birks and its waterfalls to the town, the new telephone exchange ("Frazer's Garage: Telephone Aberfeldy 25"), the new water supply and the building of McKerchar and MacNaughton's red stone emporium in Bank Street. The death of the quiet golfer, Sir Neil Menzies, last of the Menzies line, was also covered. But it was Home Rule that remained the burning issue. In 1914 the Scottish Home Rule Bill passed its Second Reading. Few people now recall that it was only prevented from reaching the Statute Book by war.

War: its declaration in August 1914 took Aberfeldy by surprise. The local weekly, the *People's Journal* had hardly spotted the impending crisis. In the previous months, just a handful of editorials had pondered the conflicts of interest between European powers. There had been one or two concerns over increased military expenditure across Europe. The Kaiser had been called a 'bloated militarist' and the word 'Armageddon' was once mentioned.

In July, the *Journal* recorded that a hive of bees at Weem School had thrown off a fine swarm. In passing, it mentioned that the assassination of Archduke Ferdinand in Sarajevo might hold "disturbing possibilities in regard to the Austrian Succession." But there was also an article about Captain John Wylie, a volunteer officer in the Black Watch Reserve. He had used a cinematograph in Aberfeldy Town Hall to show 'The British Army Film'. He had pointed out that

recruitment numbers were dropping and hoped that the film might encourage men to join the Army Reserve. The *Journal* did not mention that, back in 1908, the local men of the 5th VBRH had been disgusted at the offer of becoming part of a planned Territorial cyclist battalion; instead they had become 'H' Company of the 6th Battalion, the Black Watch. During normal working hours, John Wylie ran a music shop in Perth.

In late August, in an echo of the Boer War, 'H' Company, led by their pipers, marched from the Kenmore Street Armoury to Aberfeldy railway station. They were commanded by Captain John Wylie. A newspaper commented that "although somewhat youthful in their appearance, they looked ready and fit to do their duty for King and Country." Some of the boys had walked down from Glenlyon; on their way, they had paused in the sunshine at Ardtrasgairt to sing a farewell song to an old lady and her cats.

Aberfeldy Cottage Hospital, opened 1909

'H' Company's first duty was to defend the Forth Bridge. W&A Robertson, the shop in Aberfeldy Square, sent them 50 currant loaves. Special cheap rail fares enabled wives and families to visit them. By October, the Black Watch's one Recruiting Sergeant was hard at work; by February 1915, the army had to send two more Sergeants to join him. Young husbands from Aberfeldy's only tenements were a particular target. The tenements, in Breadalbane Terrace, were nicknamed 'The Happy Land' due to the large number of newly-weds. A twenty-bed hospital was set up at Provost Haggart's house, Eilean Riabhach, at the west end of Aberfeldy, run by nurses from the new Volunteer Aid Detachment, the VADs. Its first

Cameron's, newsagents in the Square, 1914. Note 'Home Rule' is mentioned on the placard bottom right

patients were Belgian soldiers. Serious fund-raising began, including, significantly, the 'Black Watch Prisoners of War Fund'.

'H' Company crossed to France in May 1915 and the grim drumroll of battles commenced: Neuve Chapelle, Ypres, Festubert. 1916: Arras, Vimy Ridge, Armentieres, Beaumont Hamel. 1917:

W&A vehicle outside shop in the Square. Ready to take currant loaves to 'H' Company by the Forth

6th Battalion Black Watch soldiers take a break on the Western Front

Arras again, Ypres again, Cambrai – by which time John Wylie the music seller had become a Colonel. As more senior officers came, were broken, and went, Wylie found himself several times in command of the entire 6th battalion. In 1917, he came home to lead yet another recruiting drive.

As the war went on, columns in local newspapers of local men killed and wounded – the 'Fought and Fell' pages – grew longer. The little photographs of the faces of the dead steadily increased in number, and grew smaller and smaller to fit the page. Details of specific battles became vague, but in May 1918, 'H' Company were back at Arras for the third time.

The Scottish Horse had also gone into action, albeit dismounted. It was not a cavalry war. They fought at Gallipoli, in Egypt, in Salonika, and in 1918 finished on the Western Front. Throughout the war, Scots regiments were regarded as aggressive shock troops with fine performance records in the front line, especially in attack. There was a price for this reputation: 26.4 per cent of them were killed compared to 11.8 per cent for rest of the British Army.

On July 28th, 1918, the 6th Battalion of the Black Watch, including 'H'

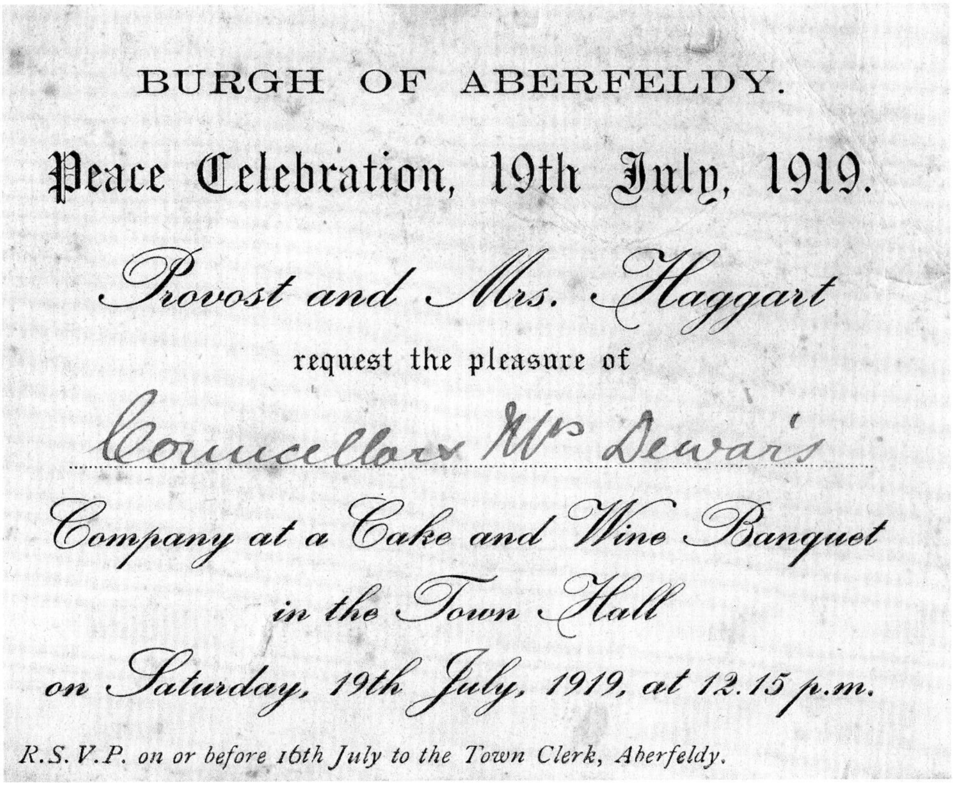

BURGH OF ABERFELDY.

Peace Celebration, 19th July, 1919.

Provost and Mrs. Haggart

request the pleasure of

Councillor & Mrs Dewar's

Company at a Cake and Wine Banquet

in the Town Hall

on Saturday, 19th July, 1919, at 12.15 p.m.

R.S.V.P. on or before 16th July to the Town Clerk, Aberfeldy.

Invitation to the Cake and Wine Banquet 1919

company, captured the village of Chambrecy. At the end of the day, 454 men of the battalion had been killed or wounded; only 140 were still standing. The French Government bestowed a Croix de Guerre on the entire battalion.

Though there were still volunteers at bayonet practice in Logierait and Aberfeldy, by 1918 the newspapers in the valley were discussing how politics after the war might look. They wondered what women who had shouldered serious responsibilities in nursing, farming, transport and munitions work might do. But a month after the Armistice, pages of photographs of dead and wounded soldiers were still appearing.

There was little rejoicing at the end of the 'Great War', as it had been called from the very beginning. So many mothers, wives and lovers were now alone. Up and down the valley over the next few years, in churchyards, in parks, at crossroads, on hillsides, in schools, in clubhouses, war memorials were erected, listing the names of the men and boys who were not coming home. On Saturday, 19th July, 1919, Aberfeldy held its Peace Celebration – 'a Cake and Wine Banquet' – in the Town Hall. And in June, 1921, the new War Memorial arch at the entrance to the Birks was dedicated. The guests, dressed in black, were predominantly women of all ages, with a sprinkling of older men.

Opening of Aberfedly War Memorial, 1921. Note absence of young men

THE BLACK WATCH STATUE AND GENERAL WADE'S BRIDGE, ABERFELDY

Captured German guns around Black Watch Monument, 1921

Between the Wars

Standing at his forge in Acharn, hammer in hand, Alec McKercher could see that Scotland in 1919 clearly was not going to be 'a land fit for heroes'. The Great War had given the old order a serious jolt. Men and women came back from their war experiences with a changed attitude. The old days of obedient deference to grandees and their representatives had been shot away in Flanders and Gallipoli. The Feeing Market in the Square vanished. All adult males and all women over 30 could now vote, and they responded by voting strongly for the new Labour Party. It rapidly became the largest political power in Scotland. Less attention was paid to Home Rule.

The days of the great estates in the valley were numbered. In 1919 the Government imposed 40 per cent death duties on estates valued at £2 million and over. The massive Menzies estate had already gone, effectively bankrupt, sold in November 1914, almost unnoticed in the clamour of war. Between 1918 and 1921, one fifth of Scotland changed hands. Some of the great aristocratic landowners' estates survived, often by paring away outlying parts, the Atholl Estate being an example. But by far the biggest local casualty was the Marquess of Breadalbane.

In 1921, while the town was building its first Council Houses, on the north side of Market Street, in Tayside Place and in Tayside Crescent, the Marquess sold up. In addition to enormous post-war tax bills and huge labour costs, he had another problem. Rumour had it that his wife Alma's gambling was out of control: she had allegedly lost £40,000 in one evening. According to a member of staff on duty that night, a shotgun had had to be gently removed from his Lordship's hands. Gavin Campbell offered his estate to the public in five enormous lots. No one could afford them.

There were other matters to occupy the valley, although local newspaper headlines were hardly earthshaking. Farmers were intrigued by the success of a motor tractor at Ballechin. It had ploughed three acres in a short day. There was a court case over washing lines at Killiechassie. At New Year, the 'Boots' at the Fortingall Hotel got fighting drunk, seriously injured three people and had to be tied to a chair until the police arrived.

In 1922, the Breadalbane Estate was broken into smaller pieces and sold to forty different buyers. The Loch Tay steamers went to the Caledonian Railway, although a year later, both the Caledonian and the Highland Railway, including the Aberfeldy branch, were swallowed by the LMS (London Midland Scottish Railway). When the estate contents were sold off, Aberfeldy got Taymouth Castle's fire engine, and the Marquess's coach went for virtually nothing. Almost all the buyers were local men. James Haggart, owner of Haggart's Woollen Mills and Provost of Aberfeldy from 1913 to 1949, in his own words 'bought the town' by purchasing the feu-duties of Aberfeldy, Duntaylor and Dunskiag.

Jock Allan at Alec McKerchar's forge

Taymouth Castle, its grounds and Kenmore village were purchased by the Taymouth Hotel Company, which opened its doors in 1923. The Marquess did not live to see it; his willowy widow Alma retired to a castle on the west coast and lived another ten years. Aberfeldy's great lairds had gone.

As the grand men faded and their estates disintegrated, two groups in the valley came to the fore: first the gentry, pocket lairds each with a farm and a stretch of moorland, Remony, Bolfracks, Chesthill, Edradynate and so on; next a solid middle class of shop-owners, farmers, doctors, teachers and lawyers, all of whom were employers in one form or another. These two groups effectively replaced the great lairds in terms of local power. Most people in the valley worked for them, apart from tradesmen such as joiners, plumbers – and blacksmiths like Alec McKercher.

The town remained more or less self-sufficient. There were dairies in Chapel Street and Burnside, and more milk came in from Dundavie, Cuil Farm and Weem. Thursday cattle auctions did well and the regular Special Sales brought animals from Glenlyon and Rannoch to be sold, then herded up Home Street to the station pens. McGrowther's in Dunkeld Street – currently 'Farmfresh' – with its array of rabbits and hares hanging outside, produced fine sausages and bacon.

There were three tailors, Scrimgeour up by the crossroads, McKerchar and MacNaughton by the bridge – with their vacuum-operated, serpentine Lampsen-tube system shooting cylinders of paperwork round the ceilings – and Haggarts down in Dunkeld Street. James Fisher, the man who had founded the coal-fired Steam laundry in 1900, ran a grocery, a seedsman's and a wine

merchant's business in Dunkeld Street. W&A Robertson's bakery that had produced the currant loaves for 'H' Company in 1914 was still going strong. 'W&As' – as it was commonly called – also supplied farm equipment, sold groceries and ironmongery, made lemonade, and had an elegant café, The Corner House, 'the finest suite of Restaurant Rooms in the Highlands'.

Trade picked up, even Alec McKercher's blacksmith's business at Acharn; but he was a man who could see how things might develop. He had seen motor cars pass his smithy, noticeably not requiring his services. Now, he decided to go into competition with Frazer's Garage down by Aberfeldy railway station. Frazer had bought an impressive fleet of ex-army Albion trucks. As they left in the morning – dodging cows leaving their byres behind the Palace Hotel, heading to graze on the golf course – the trucks took coal and building materials out as far

Alec McKerchar's first garage in Bank Street, with Ford model Ts

as Glenlyon, Loch Tay and Rannoch. Later in the day they brought back timber and farm produce, including tons of potatoes in the season, to the station yard. Frazer's also serviced limousines and shooting-brakes brought in on railway flat-trucks by sporting parties.

McKercher bought a showroom in Bank Street close to the red stone grandeur of McKerchar and MacNaughton's Department Store. At a time when almost all deliveries in the town were made by horse and cart, brand new Ford Model Ts gleamed outside Alec's garage. Perhaps even more importantly, he also sold the new must-have for farmers, Fordson tractors. As business built up, he reinvested; he bought the Breadalbane Arms Hotel. He ran taxis and set up another blacksmith's, close to the Black Watch Inn. He bought motor buses and catered for the Aberfeldy station to Loch Tay Steamer tourist trade – naturally calling at the Breadalbane Arms – and began to run regular bus services to places not served by the train. When David Frazer took his Albions out of service in protest at the new Road Tax, Alec went into haulage. Then he took another risk: he set up an Aberfeldy to Perth bus service in direct competition with the railway.

As the 'twenties went on, employment gradually became harder to find, especially after the 1926 General Strike. Even the local railwaymen struck briefly, a major problem for local firms and farms. The 1929 financial crash made things even worse. But the valley remained relatively untroubled by the difficulties in Scottish cities. Local newspapers reported matters such as the building of more Council houses in Chapel Street and the brief stay of the Duke and Duchess of York with Admiral Earl Beatty at Grantully Castle. Beatty was a keen golfer, often on the Aberfeldy course, sometimes despatching his caddie into the town for a dozen 'Silver Kings'.

But just before the 1929 money markets nose-dived and the financial world stood still, there were three significant local events. First, all women in the valley found they could now vote. Second, the Church of Scotland and the United Free Church settled their differences and merged; in Aberfeldy, though the two congregations at Breadalbane by the cross-roads and St Andrews up the Crieff Road remained obstinately in their separate churches, they knew that sooner or later the time would come when one church – or the other – would become redundant. A discreet struggle began. Third, the railway station burned down once more, and was swiftly rebuilt.

The stock-market crash developed into a major long-term depression. In 1932, when 65 per cent of Clyde shipyard men were out of work, and the three-funnelled Cunarder Queen Mary stood half-built and untouched for a second year, unemployment finally hit Aberfeldy. Ever since the Great War, men had been able to find some work at least, felling timber for the new Forestry Commission on Drummond Hill, or on the Bolfracks Estate or up in the Birks, but now those tasks were done. The massive stacks of timber beside the Commission's local headquarters at Dalerb pier near Kenmore disappeared. Just at the moment when work was most desperately needed, the sawmills fell silent and the logging horses, the traction engines and the bogie teams going to and from the station were all laid off. Those seeking assistance had to take the hated Means Test. Every penny of a household's income was scrutinised, and even if just one son brought money in, his cash had to support his parents and his brothers and sisters.

A charabanc about to depart for Kenmore Pier from Aberfeldy Railway Station

It was hard to find things to do; young men did odd jobs round the town or out in the farms; or just went for walks. The Masons, the Foresters, church collections and discreet gestures by members of Aberfeldy's middle class went some way to ease the burden. Since the war, the town's businesses had become used to yearly influxes of workers on holiday from Glasgow and Dundee, coming in by train to spend a happy week in the countryside. Many little shops and tradesmen depended on them, but as poverty and unemployment in the cities rose to new heights, fewer came. Aberfeldy's formerly well-attended annual Highland Games petered out in 1934.

By 1936, life was looking a little rosier, despite sudden small dramas: three-year old Alec Dewar, the future Precentor of the Aberfeldy's Free Church in Chapel Street, swallowed a penny, choked, was raced round the corner to Dr Mackay's house and, thanks to a professional wallop, had the thing knocked out of him by with just seconds to spare. Business was better again. Electricity lines reached the town. Once again, Alec McKerchar spotted the potential market and set up an electrician's business. By 1937 his team had wired up most of the offices, shops and larger houses in the town. Outwith the town however, it was still very common to draw water from the well, to use the family dung for fertiliser, to light the dark evenings with a double-burner paraffin lamp, and to take a candle to bed.

Along with the rest of the Aberfeldy business people, McKerchar was pleased that the number of day-trippers coming in on the train and taking the bus down to Loch Tay began to increase again. In 1937, the first long-distance motor coach arrived, from Manchester. Aberfeldy now had a proper sewage works, with the capacity for handling effluent not only from local sources but also from that of the summer influx of tourists. Village halls sprang up. Fortingall now had the splendid Molteno Hall; its previous hall migrated to the Camserney road end. And the newspapers reported that the Scottish National Party had come into existence, aiming for full independence rather than Home Rule.

Alec Mckercher's son Alistair had done well at Breadalbane Academy and was now training to take over the business. Aberfeldy Public School had been renamed Breadalbane Academy and designated a Senior Secondary School in 1922. It had been given a sports field and a gymnasium. Pupils from Killin, Glenlyon, Rannoch and other outlying areas were boarding weekly in Dunolly, (24 girls from 1930, later boys) and Craigtuil, (18 boys from 1936, later 60 girls). Boys and girls still come from Pitlochry to finish their education in Aberfeldy.

Another step towards modernity came with the opening of the Art Deco-style Birks Cinema in July 1939. But its opening was overshadowed by the looming international crisis, and almost everyone in the valley was resigned to the fact that there was going to be another war. This time, the writing was very clearly on the wall. The whole country had started to prepare.

In January 1939, the *Perthshire Advertiser* editorial was quite clear that: "If war does come, the Nazi militarists will pour death and destruction with such suddenness and over such a wide area that the war will be won before it has begun." People were advised not to hoard, but to store a little more food than normal. Later that month, the *Advertiser* added: "A new word has been invented by a Scottish newspaper – 'evacuees'. The trouble with a word of this kind is that it has probably come to stay." In February, the Aberfeldy Burgh Council met to discuss plans for dealing with theoretical 'evacuees' from Glasgow. The townspeople people were soon to welcome large numbers of this new class of person.

By the start of April 1939, once Germany had invaded Czechoslovakia, the country began to get ready. Again and again, the *Advertiser* editorials repeated that Churchill ought to be the man to lead. Recruitment for the Territorial Army and the Air Defence Corps began in earnest. The Scottish Horse began training with the new Bren gun and the Boys anti-tank rifle; they brought their Pipe Band to the Square and, along with the 6th Battalion of the Black Watch, started to recruit in Aberfeldy once again, as did the Royal Army Service Corps. The VAD nurses re-formed at Provost Haggart's house, and the Aberfeldy unit was inspected and pronounced ready to handle air raid victims and wounded soldiers.

In late April, just as national conscription was introduced, gas-masks for the town's population were delivered: large, medium and small. Police Sergeant Scott took charge of them. For everyone over the age of four, fitting took place at the Town Hall. Primary schools became fitting points in outlying areas. Logierait got theirs in May. Children got used to toting the black canisters on shoulder-straps. The Women's Voluntary Service began to enrol at the newly-sandbagged Town Hall. Other local women disappeared, away into nursing, or the Women's Royal Army Corps, the Auxiliary Territorial Service, the Women's Auxiliary Air Force, the Womens Royal Naval Service, and the Women's Land Army.

Air Raid Wardens gave a demonstration of the power of an incendiary bomb by exploding one at the bottom of Alma Avenue. In August, along with many other schools in country areas, Breadalbane Academy closed in order to prepare for the arrival of youngsters from Glasgow. Now, it was just a question of time, very little time as it happened.

On the 1st of September, Germany invaded Poland and two days later Chamberlain declared war. But evacuation had already begun. The September 2nd edition of the Perthshire Advertiser carried a photo of evacuees arriving at an un-named highland station. The Census records show – and the number of gas-masks delivered confirm – that number of people living in the town

Aberfeldy Home Guard, 1940

was 1,564. Over three days at the beginning of September 1939, a total of 1,150 boys and girls arrived at the station. For a town like Aberfeldy, this was a tidal wave of children. There were the inevitable culture clashes. Some of the children had nits, others had lived their entire lives on a staple diet of chips and 'jeely pieces', and most were horrified to see milk spurting from cows. But they were all made welcome. Some stayed on after the war, some subsequently settled here, and others still come back regularly. Alec McKerchar's buses were used for transporting them about.

The death-rain from German bombers did not materialise, though the town's emergency services practised for it. They staged a mock air raid on Kenmore Street: 'Casualties' were taken to the First Aid Post in Breadalbane Academy; Dr Swanson was in attendance. Aberfeldy found its role, not as a target but as a refuge, and a much appreciated one.

Apart from noisy Glaswegian children, a quietness descended. Even the cricket club closed. The Loch Tay steamers, already reduced to a summer-only service, were hauled out of the water, never to return. Food rationing was imposed; for a woman, the weekly allowance was four ounces (125g) of bacon, two ounces of butter – a quarter of a standard size pat – four ounces of margarine, four ounces of cooking fat, eight ounces of sugar, three ounces of sweets and two ounces of tea, the equivalent of 17 modern tea-bags. But most folk had friends or relatives on local farms, so rabbits and hares supplemented the diet, and chickens materialised in back gardens. Farmers suddenly found themselves to be the darlings of government; after the hard times of the 'thirties, subsidies came as a pleasant surprise.

Only in 1940 did the town really go into action. Over in France, it had become shockingly clear that the British Army – especially the Territorials – were wonderfully brave but badly trained and inadequately armed. As Black Watch soldiers surrendered at St Valery and others escaped at Dunkirk, Major Frank Macdonald, manager of the Breadalbane Arms took command of the local Home Guard. Home Guard soldiers had to be British males, aged between seventeen and sixty-five, and 'capable of free movement'. Macdonald and his men strung wires across the golf course to stop enemy planes landing. They patrolled Wade's Bridge, using the golf clubhouse as a guardpost. They dug trenches on the north side, and more up the Crieff Road to protect the little Birks bridge. Once duty was done, the mixed band of old men – and the more mature-looking youngsters – generally adjourned to the bar of the Breadalbane. The boys would be off into the thick of it soon enough, and many of the older men knew from first-hand experience what it would be like.

A stone blockhouse was built on the bank of the Tay, at the eastern pinchpoint where the river, the road and the railway came closest together, not far from the town end of the distillery. A pleasant bench now sits on its foundations. Another blockhouse, still in good condition, was built at the narrows of the road above Taymouth Castle. There was a brick air raid shelter at the top of Kenmore Street, on the south side. A siren was mounted on the fire station and a new fire engine with a more powerful pump was brought in. Aberfeldy was as ready as it could be.

Local people organised a Great Free Gift Sale to raise money for the Red Cross Agriculture Fund. Among hundreds of items auctioned that day were an overcoat, a churn, a three-tier cake stand, a pair of budgerigars, a pair of knicker hose, and half a ton of coal to be collected at the station. Better-off farmers and lairds gave sheep, lambs, stags, even bulls. Farmer Michael McDiarmaid entered a ewe lamb for his son John, and brought the boy home a corgi puppy. Humbler clachans did their bit: at Ardtrasgairt, Dugald Carmichael, Donald Frazer and Miss J. Burnet between them gave three shillings and a bag of potatoes.

Taymouth Castle became the No 1 Base Hospital and HQ for General Sikorski's Polish Army. Castle Menzies, requisitioned, became the Polish Motor Transport Depot, and Alec McKercher's vehicles found themselves in use for military purposes. The Poles in their blue outfits, often smelling of shaving scent, were a big hit with the local women. During the later filming for the TV series *Scotland's War*, one Aberfeldy lady, Isobel Morris, remarked: "Well, let's face it, our Scotsmen are not all that courtly, nice as they are. With the Poles there was an excessive clicking of heels, kissing of hands and just general adoration of womenfolk – which we're not accustomed to here." Many Poles stayed on after the war, not simply because the Russians had now occupied their homeland. The valley retains a happily unusual number of Polish surnames.

Brochure for the 1940 Red Cross Great Free Gift Sale

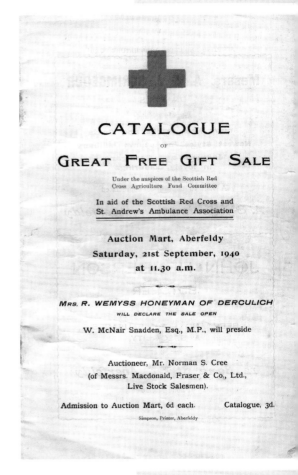

CATALOGUE
OF
GREAT FREE GIFT SALE

Under the auspices of the Scottish Red Cross Agriculture Fund Committee

In aid of the Scottish Red Cross and St. Andrew's Ambulance Association

Auction Mart, Aberfeldy
Saturday, 21st September, 1940
at 11.30 a.m.

MRS. R. WEMYSS HONEYMAN OF DERCULICH
WILL DECLARE THE SALE OPEN

W. McNair Snadden, Esq., M.P., will preside

Auctioneer, Mr. Norman S. Cree
(of Messrs. Macdonald, Fraser & Co., Ltd., Live Stock Salesmen).

Admission to Auction Mart, 6d each.   Catalogue, 3d.

Simpson, Printer, Aberfeldy

*Polish Army
at Taymouth
Castle. Corporal
Leon Lugowski
standing far left*

Moness House, requisitioned from the man who had bought it twenty years before at the break-up of the Breadalbane Estate, was converted into a home for the Glasgow evacuee children. The Crown Hotel became a hostel for Polish women working at Taymouth Castle. Provost Haggart's Eilean Riabach House, which had been a hospital for Belgians in the First War, now turned into a Polish Army Convalescent home. Most men and women in the valley settled to the nightly ritual of listening to the six o'clock news on the wireless. The Home Guard practiced by firing across Loch na Craig at the hillside opposite, but tragedy struck when the captain and first mate of the *Queen of the Lake* were killed during grenade practice.

Dutch, Canadian, Australian and New Zealand soldiers – none able to get to their real homes whilst on leave – were welcomed into local families. There is a wartime film of an Australian soldier, a Canadian sailor and a New Zealand pilot arriving in Aberfeldy by train and being taken off for their tea to different houses. At the start of the film, the Square looks painfully deserted – 250 local men and more than a few women had gone off to war – but the 'boys from the Dominions' were there in time for the Aberfeldy Gala. They watched the sheepdog trials and tried eightsome reels with sprightly oldies – and one or two attractive youngies – in the Square. Later they did a spot of fishing and, with cattle ever-present on the course, played a round of golf. They also paired off with three of the dancing young ladies and went for romantic walks. For servicemen watching the film later, whilst baking in Africa, sweltering in Burma, or slogging their way up through Italy, Aberfeldy must have seemed very close to paradise. The film crew used local people, several of whom are still alive.

Sometimes on Saturday nights, Aberfeldy Square ceased to be paradise, especially when the Birks Cinema turned out. As local townspeople and wounded Polish soldiers, having stood rigidly to attention for the National Anthem, trailed out to the waiting McKercher buses in the Square, too late for a quick drink, occasional fights would break out. But visitors were generally extremely well-behaved. They took tea in 'Mortali's', now 'The Fountain', or carried out chips from the shop behind the café. The Mortalis were a popular family; surprisingly they remained free, unlike many other Italians – those in Dunkeld for example – who were interned, away on the Isle of Man.

News of what had happened in Glasgow during the nights of the 13th and 14th of March 1941 sent a shudder round the town, especially at Breadalbane Academy and up at Moness House. The truly shocking devastation of the Clydebank Blitz justified the uprooting of all those Glasgow children then in Aberfeldy. Rumours of more than 500 people killed were bad enough, but, when the real figures were found to be well over 1000 dead with as many again injured, the Government suppressed them. However, by October 1943, as the men of the 6th Battalion of the Black Watch and the troopers-turned-gunners of the Scottish Horse fought their way up Italy, as Lancaster bomber crews flew nightly raids over Germany, as the Wehrmacht were driven back across Russia, and as the Japanese slowly retreated across the Pacific, it was becoming clear that such a ferocious attack on Glasgow was unlikely to occur again. Football matches on the Breadalbane Academy playing field between the 'vacs' and the 'locals' ceased, the city children went home and the school returned to normal.

The Crown Temperance Hotel, home for Polish women on military service

BANK STREET, ABERFELDY.

By that time, Scotland was effectively being ruled by one man, Tom Johnston, Secretary of State for Scotland. Churchill had surprised many by appointing such an unlikely candidate to this post. A socialist journalist before the First World War, Johnston had written a powerful attack on Scottish aristocracy, ironically entitled Our Scots Noble Families. But Johnston was a tough, effective, inclusive leader. On one occasion, Churchill was heard to remark: "Ah, here comes the King of Scotland." And Tom Johnston had a dream for the highlands, a dream that was to have a direct connection with Alec McKercher and his electrical business, and a lasting effect on the Aberfeldy valley.

A McKerchar bus in the Square, Aberfeldy

Bridgend, 1945. Note army uniforms and military truck

Never had it so Good

VE Day (Victory in Europe) and then VJ Day (Victory over Japan) came and went with celebrations and parades. Children from that time now recall how impressed they were with small details, the bright colours of the flags and bunting, and evening trains leaving the station fully-lit. Aberfeldy celebrated the return of peace characteristically: happy that farming subsidies were set to continue, its Young Farmers set up an Agricultural Show. But the real change for most people in the valley came in 1948. The post-war Labour Government's National Health Service, National Insurance Scheme and Old Age Pension brought a new sense of security. Down at the railway station, the signs were changed to 'British Railways'. The ageing Caledonian tank engines sported new lion-and-wheel emblems on their sides, swiftly smothered in grime.

The Cottage Hospital became the Obstetric unit for North Perthshire, and a young doctor, 'Wattie' Yellowlees, back from grim days of fighting in Italy and Germany, began his rounds. Wattie joined the legendary Dr Jack Swanson, a tireless campaigner for the improvement of healthcare facilities in the valley. The Aberfeldy practice covered an enormous area: an emergency at the top of Glenlyon could occupy a doctor for almost an entire day. Wattie learned to watch out for signals in outlying post offices and shops. A broom standing upright in a tin at Strathtay meant that he should stop for a message from the surgery and probably miss his lunch once again.

Alec McKercher had become a pillar of the community. He had served on the Town Council for many years. On Saturday the 18th of August 1951, a parcel arrived at the office for the Crieff bus that had just left. Alec's son Alistair threw the parcel into a car and raced up the road after the bus. At the little bridge above Gatehouse, he is believed to have crashed head-on into an Austin Princess coming downhill. His death threw a pall over the town; he had been seen by many as one of the town's future leaders. It was not long before Alec, too, died and the business was sold; but Alec and his like had brought Aberfeldy into the modern age.

Things were moving forward: besides the success of the post-war socialist agenda, Home Rule for Scotland resurfaced. In 1949, while smart new red post vans began to motor up and down the valley, often taking the 'messages' to outlying farms, signatures were being gathered for the Scottish Covenant. Its organizers chose the word 'Covenant', because of all its old associations with Scots anti-establishment protest. By 1950, the year that the Stone of Destiny was kidnapped from Westminster Abbey – there is a rumour that the Stone spent time under the floor of Dull Church – over a million and a quarter Scots had signed this petition, but the impetus soon dissolved again in arguments over full independence or various alternative forms of devolution.

Meanwhile, the people in Aberfeldy read about the government's new

housing policy and watched as German prisoners-of-war, still here, erected quick-build houses, so-called 'Prefabs' below Market Street. Work began on new Council Houses in Moness Crescent and Moness Avenue. There was a drama when part of Breadalbane Academy burned down; the fire had begun, embarrassingly, in the Domestic Science room with its new gas-fired cooking facilities.

Some in the town frowned when tennis was permitted on Sunday outwith church hours. Golf remained forbidden. Most were pleased to see the old gas streetlights replaced by electric ones. Many bemoaned the final demise of W&A Robertson's and its replacement by the Co-op. The Co-op took over premises on the south side of the Square and down Dunkeld Street: it had a draper's, a butcher's, a shoe shop, a dairy, an ironmonger's, a grocer's, and a car hire business. Its green lorries delivered coal from the station. Everyone pondered plans drawn up for an increase of the town's population from 1500 to 3000, with an industrial area, a roundabout at the crossroads and even an airfield.

The town's children still left school on or even before their fifteenth birthday. Alec Dewar was one of only three who stayed on in his year. As a member of the Free Church congregation, he was unaffected by the acrimonious coming-together of the two Church of Scotland/United Free congregations on either side of the Aberfeldy crossroads; but he was surprised that some of his pals joined the Episcoplian – the 'English' – Church, until he found out that the 'Piskies' respected the Sabbath only until mid-day; and they had ping-pong and billiards tables in a hall behind the church.

Young Betty Allan liked to get home from school, scramble into old clothes and go off down to the market to watch the cattle in the pens. Sometimes she

The familiar van of the S.C.W.S. Retail Service saves the housewife in this area time and trouble by bringing the necessities of life to her door. It saves money, too, for Dividend is paid on purchases.

For the year 1950, the sum of £9,614 in DIVIDEND was returned to Aberfeldy area housewives. Are YOU saving on your shopping the S.C.W.S. way?

S.C.W.S. RETAIL BRANCH

THE SQUARE, ABERFELDY.   TELEPHONE — ABERFELDY 19

★ Aberfeldy Co-op. Restaurant caters for Breakfasts, Lunches, Teas.   Special Terms to School Children.

✱ The Co-operative Garage, ABERFELDY, offers Cars and Lorries for hire — specialises in Motor Repairs.

24

was allowed to hold the heads of horses at the smithy below the 'Black Watch' whilst her blacksmith father – who had worked for, and had got on well with Alec McKercher – shoed them; she liked to talk to the big gentle beasts.

Taymouth Castle stood deserted after the Polish troops left. It was in no condition to be re-opened as a hotel, and besides the times were not right. In 1950, it became a school for the National Civil Defence Corps. The Government were mindful of Russia's atomic power; a complete village was built in the castle grounds, then deliberately destroyed so that rescue squads could get realistic nuclear air-raid practice. It was a far cry from the grandeur of Queen Victoria's visit.

A new Queen came to the throne in 1953. Local people recall the day because it was ferociously cold for June, and many of the festivities and sports events were chilly affairs. As rationing finally stopped – sweets were the last to

Dam building in the 1950s. No hard hats, protective boots or safety harnesses

go – work began on the hydroelectric dams, slowly bringing Tom Johnston's dream to life. Retired from politics at the end of the war, he became Chairman of the Scottish Hydro-Electricity Board. As Johnston himself said, he wanted to have "a jolly good try at a public corporation on a non-profit basis to harness highland water power for electricity."

Trucks began to rumble through the town, over Wade's bridge on their way to the 'The Schemes'. As the dams rose at Lochan na Lairige, Lubreoch, Loch an Daimh and Stronuich, vast camps were built by construction companies. Endless convoys of trucks and buses trundled up and down the long twisting road through Glenlyon. On one stormy Sunday night Alec Dewar, now working for the GPO's telephone department, was called out to mend a phone line in the glen. On his way home in the early hours, his van's path was blocked by a massive blown-down oak. Only too aware of the chaos that would be caused to trucks on their way to the 'Schemes' the following day, he clambered over the tree-trunk, tramped down to the road and clamped his ladder to the side of ghillie Jock Fisher's house. He climbed up and clipped his phone to the line. He had just made contact with the Aberfeldy operators in their flat above the Post Office, when Jock's bedroom window was thrown open and a shotgun was thrust against Alec's head: 'Jock! Don't shoot! It's me, Alec!' He finished his call to the Burgh Surveyor in the comfort of Jock's kitchen with a cup of tea.

The workers on the 'Schemes' needed huge quantities of food and drink. On Saturday nights, the town would be invaded by busloads of thirsty men, down from the dams with plenty of money. More than a few former Polish soldiers and German ex-prisoners-of-war stayed on to become members of the tough, highly-skilled 'tunnel tiger' teams. Besides providing good employment for local people, there were many Irish workers on these massive feats of civil engineering.

By 1961, the dams were complete and electricity was flowing down the valley. Houses, farms and businesses were supplied with cables to their door free of charge, in return for a guaranteed consumption figure, and were then wired in, often by McKercher electricians, although Mckercher's had been taken over by a Mr Jones by then. One householder was allegedly delighted

A timber team pose at a local sawmill

with the new system, but only switched on his new bulbs nightly in order to light his candles.

Apart from the 'Schemes', the early 'fifties were a quiet time in terms of developments in the valley. Traffic lights were experimented with on Wade's bridge, a new Police station in Kenmore Street was built, and the Forestry Commission continued to be an important employer. The test of a good forester remained whether he could split a standing match with a two-handed axe. Horses were still by far the commonest form of traction on local farms. In the town, cattle still trailed back from their grazing up in the fields by the Old Crieff Road, leaving signatures across the Square, in which the Pipe Band would play on Saturday nights. 1957 was marked by a spectacular but fatality-free train crash on the Aberfeldy line, and in the same year Castle Menzies, by then a virtual ruin, was effectively given to the Clan Menzies Society by a local farmer.

By 1959, the valley was enjoying stability and prosperity. Rationing was a thing of the past, though it still coloured views on food and waste. A sense of British togetherness lingered from the war, over-riding the brief post-war move towards nationalism. Most people remembered the hard times of the 'thirties and were grateful. Wages were good and there was full employment. Two-parent families were the absolute norm. Domestic service had almost gone, and 'Dailies' were in great demand by the better-off. Families in real trouble received Public Assistance. When necessary, boots were provided by Breadalbane Academy to children without them. Crime and poverty were virtually unknown. Most people tended to agree with Conservative Prime Minister Harold Macmillan when he claimed that Britain had 'never had it so good'.

As the 'fifties slipped into the 'sixties, despite the ever-present threat of the 'four-minute warning' of Russian ballistic missile attack and nuclear obliteration, life in the valley was generally calm. Aberfeldy Auction Market was still going strong and the valley's reputation for fine cattle was outstanding. To this day, there is an Aberfeldy Spring Sale in Stirling, now the nearest auction site.

Golf was finally permitted on Sundays. The Cottage Hospital got a new Labour Room. Dr Wattie Yellowlees set up his surgery at Inzievar at the Aberfeldy crossroads and, when GPs were finally allowed to have paid staff,

Birks Cinema programme December 1949

Sonia his wife was finally relieved of the burden of being receptionist, nurse, unofficial psychologist and secretary. The population slipped from its 1901 figure of 1506 to 1407 in 1961.

The sense of wellbeing continued until the mid-sixties. As the 1960s Statistical Account for Logierait pointed out: "There is at present no unemployment in the parish, the main occupation being farming." The key crops were exactly as before: oats, turnips and potatoes. The number of horses dwindled: one or two farms kept them on; Alastair Duncan Millar at Remony kept his for a while yet. Further west, Mervyn Brown at Ardtalnaig kept a pair, but when one died and the other, broken-hearted, died shortly after, he didn't replace them. The ubiquitous little grey 'Fergy' tractor puttered into every farmyard, where their rusting remains linger to this day. Agrochemicals were being used much more frequently, and dairy farms had almost gone. The two hundred year old trend of linking small farms together to make bigger ones continued. Potato lifting in October was still very important; women and visiting gangs did the work; children had finally been exempted and allowed to stay at school. More and more visitors were coming on holidays. Both tourists and commercial travellers were using bed-and-breakfast accommodation.

Telephones were now common. Television had arrived but reception was still patchy. The valley was more-or-less self-sufficient in terms of entertainment. There was a Gaelic class, a pipe band, a choir, a gun club and a dramatic society. There were a myriad of other clubs: cricket, football, golf, bowling, curling, badminton, athletics, horticultural, agricultural. There was the Red Cross, the SWRI, the Church of Scotland Women's Guild, the Freemasons, the Foresters, the Boy Scouts, the Girl Guides, the Cadet Force, the Youth Club and the Boys Brigade. There were concerts, whist drives, dances, sheep dog trials, ploughing matches, fishing competitions, the Gaelic Mod, the Birks Cinema and occasional highbrow visits to Pitlochry Theatre's great tent. And there was the

British Legion; one local soldier fighting with the Kings Own Scottish Borders in the murderous jungles of Malaya was astonished and touched to receive a Christmas present from the Legion two years running.

The town remained more or less unaffected by the 'fifties and 'sixties crazes. There were no juke-boxes, no milk-bars, no teddy-boys, no coffee-bars, not much rock n' roll and limited Beatlemania. A night out at the Birks Cinema satisfied most. But people were still leaving the valley. The Statistical Accounts once again raised the century's-old cry: "For the great majority of the parish's young men and women of ambition there is no alternative but to migrate to the already densely-populated industrial belt in the Lowlands or elsewhere to earn their living."

Provost and Mrs JD Haggart returning from a military parade, 1945. The Provost is wearing the Aberfeldy Burgh Chain of Office

A sheep-shearing team at a 'clipping' in the hills, 1959

Aberfeldy Pipe Band in the station yard, 1953, with visiting Pitlochry Pipe Major Wilson

Aberfeldy Young Farmers' Club Outing 1962

Toboganning on the Crieff Road, 1963

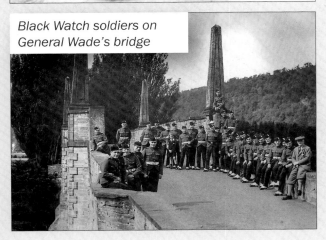

Black Watch soldiers on General Wade's bridge

Aberfeldy Auction Market Catalogue, February, 1962

ABERFELDY AUCTION MARKET
CATALOGUE
— OF —
GREAT ANNUAL SPRING SALE OF
1600
STORE CATTLE
— AT THE —
Aberfeldy Auction Market
— ON —
Thursday, 15th February, 1962

SALE AT 10 A.M. PROMPT

NOTICE TO BUYERS
TERMS OF SALE—CASH

All Purchases must be Settled for and Cleared on Day of Sale.

Purchase-Notes and Delivery-Orders will be got from Clerk of Sale when the Lots are settled for; and, on handing Delivery-Order to Shepherds in charge, they will give delivery, and assist in trucking.

The correct numbers of each Lot will be given at time of Sale.

When Lots require to be cut, the Auctioneers reserve the right to send their Yard Shepherd to do so.

Payment will only be taken in money, or Cheques vouched by Bankers' Letters.

Disputed Sturdy Sheep shall be decided by the Yard Shepherd.

Every assistance in Trucking, for the accommodation of Buyers, will be arranged as far as possible by the Auctioneers, who will not be responsible for loss or damage incurred thereby; and to prevent mistakes in Trucking, the Address must be left in writing with the Cashier.

NOTICE TO CONSIGNERS

The Shepherds and Herds in charge must remain beside their respective Lots, take them to and from the Sale-Ring, and count and deliver to Buyers on receiving Delivery-Order; also truck, if desired. Should the Shepherd not be in attendance at the time his Lot falls to be Sold, it may be passed over and taken at end of Sale.

All Stock is at the Consigner's risk until taken delivery of by the Buyer.

MACDONALD, FRASER & CO., LIMITED
AUCTIONEERS AND LIVE STOCK SALESMEN

Advertisement for Tigh-an-Loan Hotel, Fearnan

Young men continued to join the Black Watch. Whilst Scotland was at peace, these men fought their way through Korea, Indonesia, Indo-China, Malaya, Kenya, Cyprus and Aden. Just like their fathers, their grandfathers and their ancestors, they returned to the valley with tales of places and experiences unknown to most. The town was never without soldiers on leave from one battlefield or another. But they no longer came and went by train: on the 3rd of May 1965, Aberfeldy witnessed the departure of its last train, a victim of Dr Beeching's ferocious pruning of the rail network. The branch was precisely two months short of its centenary. The station site, off Moness Terrace, is now a public carpark and recycling area. For a further forty-three years, the 'Station Hotel' continued to mystify visitors who looked in vain for a corresponding railway station. It is now the 'Schiehallion'.

By rights the valley should have been healthier than the old days. As one Statistical Account quaintly put it: "Improved hygienic policy has abolished the former promiscuous byre, sty and stable." There were now three doctors in the valley, strongly supported by a network of District Nurses. But as Wattie Yellowlees unceasingly pointed out, the diet of the valley folk had changed very much for the worse, the key devils being sugar and white flour. Some say every valley household should posses a copy of his book *Doctor in the Wilderness*. True to their principles of healthy eating and locally-grown organic food, Wattie and Sonia set up Aberfeldy's

Drivers and Conductors of McKerchar's buses, late 1940s

The Aberfeldy Show, Victoria Park, late 1950s

first allotment on the other side of the river at Boltachan. Tinker families in their tents continued to amaze the doctors with their hardihood. Wattie once received a tinker patient and gasped: 'Your head's half-open, Morag!' He got the reply: 'He hit me wi' the axe, doctor.'

People in the valley took notice when Winnie Ewing became the first Scottish Nationalist MP in 1967. They remained unaffected by the student protests of the following year, but really sat up and listened when, that same year of distant tear-gas and riots, in Perth, the Conservative Opposition Leader Edward Heath committed his party to a Devolved Assembly for Scotland. It was not as simple as Heath imagined, and his was not to be the party for it.

Mrs Lugowska, daughters and staff in kitchen of Coshieville Hotel prepare for a wedding, early 1950s

Last Train about to leave, 3rd May, 1965

The Square in the early 1960s

Towards 2000

As the 'Swinging Sixties' drew to a close, new ideas and new values appeared, often in conflict with established views. People were generally better off and cared much less than their parents about what their elders or the churches thought of them. Youngsters relished satire. Newspapers spoke of a battle between family values and flower-power, but disrespect for what was seen as old-fashioned did not mean that the upcoming generation ceased to care about their valley.

A cadre of younger people now found that they could help their community in ways that were outwith the conventional institutions. They bypassed the churches and the various branches of worthy national organisations, yet still made major contributions to local people's welfare. The groups that formed – the Raft Race fund-raising team, for example – also ignored the discreet class structures that existed in other organisations.

In 1970 – the year in which the Black Watch were granted the Freedom of Aberfeldy – BP struck gigantic oil reserves in the North Sea off Aberdeen. It quickly became apparent to Scots that the recently elected Conservative Government under Edward Heath was not going to allow Scotland to become another Norway. Westminster pocketed the new oil revenues and used them as financial analgesic to ease the migraines of militant unionism and outdated British industry.

During the winter of 1972/73, while the unions arm-wrestled with the Heath Government and business-people in London struggled to hold meetings and write reports by candlelight, here in the valley thinking men and women grew seriously concerned about the increasing divide between politicians and ordinary people, and by what they saw as government ineptitude. Their worry deepened over the next two years, as inflation spiralled, the price of oil shot up after the Arab-Israeli war, and 73 percent of the value of the leading 30 companies trading on the London Stock Market vanished. There was a real feeling that, as one local farmer put it: 'the balloon might go up', and Highland valleys such as Aberfeldy might find themselves having to take management of local resources into their own hands. It was time to explore methods of making the community self-sufficient. An ad hoc group of local farmers, builders, doctors, lairds, shopkeepers and architects met and planned practical ways for the valley to renew itself.

'Wattie' Yellowlees, the doctor who had arrived in Aberfeldy after the Second World War, was now a pillar of the community, known for his strong views on the doubtful physical health of the valley. He had argued for years against conventional curative-based medical wisdom and vigorously maintained that much ill-health could be prevented by better diet. Now he and the other members of the group took the initiative. In September 1974, they issued the 'Aberfeldy Group Manifesto'.

The Manifesto stated that, in the group's opinion, we in Britain had: "ceased producing enough wealth to pay our own way in the world; we are surviving only by borrowing colossal sums from abroad. In view of the failure of any of the political parties to face the reality of the situation, or to put forward policies which will ensure our survival and then our prosperity, and because of our concern at the drift of events, we are agreed ...", and it listed the following causes for concern: non-existent national food security, lack of long-term care of the soil, water pollution, failure to link inferior food quality with bad health, extravagant use of fossil fuel energy, and dependence "on the whim of money-lenders".

ABERFELDY GROUP
MANIFESTO

In this Autumn of 1974 Britain is facing disaster. Inflation is raging at about 20% per annum; we have ceased producing enough wealth to pay our own way in the world; we are surviving only by borrowing colossal sums from abroad. In view of the failure of any of the political parties to face the reality of the situation, or to put forward policies which will ensure first our survival and then our prosperity, and because of our concern at the drift of events, we are agreed on the following three statements:

1. In the face of increasing world population and dwindling food stocks no country can have security without producing to the utmost food from its own land for its own people.

2. Any country which is dependent for its standard of living on the whim of money-lenders can have no true independence.

3. When nations over-develop their industries and neglect the husbandry of the soil, the quality of life of that nation sooner or later deteriorates.

We therefore conceive it as our duty to discuss, and if possible to reach the following objectives:-

1. To urge by every means possible government policies which will enable our agriculture and horticulture to make Britain self-supporting in essential foods and in the requirements for their production.

2. To grow in the land of the upper Tay Valley as much food as possible in as much variety as possible for consumption by those living in the valley, and for sale of surpluses to any who want to buy.

3. To achieve these objectives without impairing soil fertility for the future, without polluting our surface waters, and without the extravagant use of fossil fuel energy.

4. To spread the knowledge of the relationship between soil fertility, food and health.

September 1974

The Manifesto proposed a countrywide policy for food security and a local policy for producing a wide range of properly-grown food for local people. It hit the national headlines. The newspapers chose to laugh; the valley was portrayed as a community of doom-obsessed hippies. The politicians, all of whom had been criticised, stood aside. But the attitude of the group brought other people with alternative views to the area. A team from Hull College of Higher Education brought in a squad of students and they produced detailed plans for local food schemes, allotments, renewable energy from small hydroelectric systems and wind turbines. Perhaps parts of these new plans – multiple small holdings, part-time farmers, group labour sharing – were too far-reaching for some of the original members of the group and this may have diluted the Manifesto's impact.

In any case, a year later, the group lost any chance of exercising its will politically when the Aberfeldy Burgh Council was abolished. The days of the 'Meet and Greet' gatherings in the Town Hall, when each electoral hopeful

Aberfeldy Manifesto, 1974

made his or her case to the local people, were over. In the eyes of most, the Community Council that replaced the Burgh Council was by comparison a talking shop. At the same time, much of the final decision-making further up the ladder – planning for example – moved from Perth to Dundee. The new two-tier local government became party-politicised, much to the disgust of men such as Alastair Duncan Millar of Remony. Duncan Millar had been a local Councillor since the end of the war. With his charm, acumen and broad-based approach he had consistently secured what was best for the area. Against opposition he had, for example, ensured that the valley got its fair share of Council Housing. At the time of its final meeting in May 1975, he had been Chairman of the Perth and Kinross Council.

But Aberfeldy was not done yet. There were other ways the community might improve itself. There was a fine Town Hall, sure, but what was needed was a Community Centre, a place where people could get fit, mend damaged muscles, swim, play table tennis and billiards, learn how to shoot, or just meet for a coffee. In 1976, a year of wonderful sunshine in which Labour's Dennis Healey had to ask for money for Britain from the IMF, two local hotels – Aileann Chraggan and Coshieville – challenged each other to a raft race down the Tay from Kenmore to Aberfeldy. Its aim was to raise money for a Community Centre. The Aberfeldy Raft Race – copied by many others since – became an institution run with humour and professionalism, until it was brought to a stop fifteen years later as larger and larger groups of visitors led to alcohol-fuelled

The Aberfeldy Raft Race 1989

*Breadalbane
Academy, 2007*

incidents. However, sufficient money had been raised by the races and by similar fund-raising activities to persuade the new Perth and Kinross District Council to back the project. Through its own efforts, the valley got its Community Centre and Sports Complex. It was completed in 1993, right beside Breadalbane Academy.

The school itself was going from strength to strength. There were now nearly 500 children, with over 100 pupils boarding in the town. Dunolly was now for boys and Craigthuil for girls, and Gilbert Price was hostel-master of 30 boys in another house up at Dunallan. Class sizes were being reduced, and corporal punishment was finally banned.

In 1979, Margaret Thatcher and the Conservatives came to power. She was determined to promote 'self-help', to smash the unions, to allow free market capitalism, and to encourage privatisation, including Tom Johnston's not-for-profit Scottish Hydro-Electric Board. Her attitude to Scotland was a continuation of the Heath policy: Whitehall control. Government cutbacks hit employers like the Forestry Commission. Most of the thirty men still working on Drummond Hill were laid off.

As before, local people carried on regardless. In 1981, the *Atholl and Breadalbane Community Comment*, a local open newspaper was first published. As its editor, Brendan Murphy put it: "Founded on sweat capital and voluntarism, it was supported through advertising from generous and tolerant local businesses." *Comment* saw itself as both a voice and a stimulant for local businesses, including farming, and from the outset it had the stated aim of setting up a local community radio station.

*Advertisement
for Palace Hotel*

Aberfeldy
with the Tay
in full flood

Two local farming co-operatives were set up. The first, Tayfresh Producers, encouraged local farmers to grow broccoli, cauliflowers, calabrese, Brussels sprouts and leeks, which they then sold on to major supermarkets. It came to an end after a few years' success, due to lack of suitable local manpower and difficulties competing with larger growers and co-operatives. But the second, Highland Glen Producers is still a very successful operation involving several local farms and marketing 70 percent of all the lamb exported from the valley.

In 1987, the Conservatives suffered a heavy defeat in Scotland, and made matters worse in April 1988 by introducing the Poll Tax, just in Scotland. Mrs Thatcher threw fuel on the fire a month later by addressing church leaders in Edinburgh and equating Conservative values with those of Christianity. As a direct reaction, a Convention of almost all the bodies representing Scotland, except the SNP, came together in 1990 to produce detailed plans for a Devolved Assembly. Significantly the Convention's aims were fully supported by the Labour Party.

In 1992 another bridge was placed across the Tay at Aberfeldy. It was and is a technological marvel: the first bridge in the world to be constructed using fibreglass. This was also the year in which *Radio Heartland* took to the airwaves. *Comment*, together with its business forum Locus, had been campaigning for a local radio for a decade: *Heartland* is still going strong and, in some parts of the valley, is often the only radio station available other than endless long-wave cricket commentary.

Tinker families only finally disappeared in the 'nineties. The word 'tinker' itself did not carry the pejorative baggage it had in other parts of Scotland. Local tinkers called themselves as such; they felt the word differentiated them from New Age Travellers and Romany Gypsies and properly reminded other people of their extraordinary, centuries-old tinsmithing expertise. Though fond of drink, tinkers generally had a good reputation in the valley; farmers were often glad to have their labour. Anyone in the valley who has heard Jess Smith sing – or has read her book *Tears for a Tinker* – will have sensed the timeless and unique

quality of tinker culture. It became rarer and rarer to find their caravans and mobile homes parked on secluded by-roads in the summertime.

But a new slightly wealthier class of visitor had begun to appear in the local hotels and bed-and-breakfasts, and many in the area began to see the potential advantages – long argued for in *Comment* – to persuade these people to stay longer and to come back regularly. Time-share schemes at Moness and Kenmore began to book up all year round, significantly increasing local trade.

Running the gauntlet of planning authorities, owners of redundant farmhouses and steadings started to convert them into holiday accommodation. By the late 'nineties, albeit in a worrying development for young local couples, house prices had started to rise dramatically and new houses were beginning to appear. Tourists were converting to residents, and this in no way affected the steady number of visitors who brought their caravans to the valley each summer.

Artists and writers – including greats such as Turner and Burns – had been coming to the valley since the 1800s, but in the 1970s and 1980s, a new generation of painters and writers made the valley their home. Several local people settled to creative work, too: Wattie Yellowlees, now retired from his role a Senior Partner in the Aberfeldy Practice had already proved himself to be a convincing author. Now he took up pottery. His beautiful mugs and bowls, sold in the very-successful Aberfeldy Art Gallery, adorn many a valley home as well as Perth Museum. Like Thomas Fyfe and Alec McKerchar before him, Wattie saw the way things could go in the valley and he and his like have undoubtedly influenced life here for the better.

So where are we now?

Now and Ahead

One day during the Second World War, the boom of an exploding grenade echoed down the valley. Two men lay dead. But which two? The tragedy occurred within living memory but, depending on who tells the story, it could have been any two of at least four people, and it could have occurred in at least two places. The nearer history comes to the present, the slipperier it becomes. Two more examples, one national and the other local: in 2000, Tom Devine, a respected historian, wrote of Scotland's economy: "In the private sector, the jewel in the crown is finance." He added that Scotland was: "now as famous for electronics manufacture as it had been for shipbuilding in earlier generations." And here in the valley, there are three different versions of Alistair McKerchar's tragic death; and no death certificate.

What was absolutely certain, however, was that by 1996 the system that had replaced the old Town Councils was unloved. The twenty-year-old, two-tier Perth District/Dundee Region was scrapped, and Perthshire and Kinross became a Unitary Authority. The new structure came hardly any nearer to replacing the directness of local government previously exercised by the old Aberfeldy Burgh. The Aberfeldy valley now came into the area of the Highland Ward, with three local Councillors out of the total of forty-one.

A year later – the year in which the Black Watch were the last military unit to leave Hong Kong – New Labour came to power under Tony Blair. A referendum on devolution for Scotland showed that by far the majority of Scots wanted their own Parliament and their own tax raising powers. On the 12th May 1999, guided by Donald Dewar, after two hundred and ninety-two years, Edinburgh welcomed a Scottish Parliament once more.

In November 2001, Dun Coillich, 1,100 acres of local hill ground, came up for sale. The hill looks down on Glengoulandie, in the lee of Schiehallion. A group of local people once again took matters into their own hands. As Robin Hull, one of the group's leaders wrote: "The aim was to return Dun Coillich to a state that might have existed had man not altered the ecology; but this must be addressed as a scientific experiment." Under the weighty title of the Highland Perthshire Communities Land Trust, the group obtained substantial grant aid and badgered local people until, after several scares – and with the help of a major benefactor – in 2002 they had sufficient funds to buy the land. Robin Hull referred to Dun Coillich as: "a rather unremarkable hill," but he was underplaying its new value as a place not only for scientific work and observation, but also for local recreation and education, year-round.

In 2003, the 1st Battalion of the Black Watch went into action in Iraq and lost six of its men; but this was the end of its activities as an independent regiment. Amid ferocious protests, in 2006 it was amalgamated into the Royal Regiment of Scotland. It was, however, permitted to call itself 'The Black

December 2009: 3rd Battalion, the Royal Highlanders march past the Black Watch Inn, back from operations in Afghanistan with the loss of five men. The Regiment had been raised 269 years before, less than half a mile away

Watch, 3rd Battalion' and its soldiers proudly continued to wear the legendary Red Hackle on their headgear. More men were soon to lose their lives in Afghanistan. The regiment had come a long and distinguished way from that day in 1740 when the Independent Companies paraded beside General Wade's bridge.

Here meanwhile, the growing colony of artists, writers and poets has flourished. The Aberfeldy Gallery found itself joined by three others. Fortingall, followed by Fearnan and Grandtully organized annual art exhibitions in their village halls. Several residents set up studios. Writing groups and bookclubs began to meet. The range of restaurants increased. The two founding establishments of the Raft Race, the Ailean Chraggan and the Coshieville, continued to welcome guests. In 2005, the old watermill in the centre of the town, which had been closed and empty for three years, was converted into a bookshop, a café and a gallery, although its machinery was carefully left in place. Former commercial properties in the town began to be converted into living accommodation.

So, where are we now? More and more tourists are coming to – and coming back to – the area, providing a real boost to the local economy. The attention and efficiency of the local Tourist Information Office in the former Congregational Church in the Square impresses thousands of visitors annually.

A canoeing competition at Grandtully, 1971. Nearly forty years later, this is a national venue

But some local people, especially farmers, are worried that the valley is becoming too dependent, in the words of Brendan Murphy, Editor of *Comment*, on 'the monoculture of tourism'. Tourism may be transitory in the longer-term, but farming will remain a vital component of local life.

In any case, the centuries-old consolidation of smaller farms into larger ones goes on. For example, in 1939 the 180 acre Mains of Murthly farm was operating much as it had done for a hundred years. It employed 3 men and a handful of casual tinkers. They grew oats, turnips and potatoes. They had hay, grazing and pasture for 22 cattle. Forty years later, by the late 1970s, the farm had expanded to 600 acres. Adjacent small farms had been taken over, farms that had supported families until the 1940s and had since lain idle, their farmhouses and cottages often deserted. By 2004, Mains of Murthly was employing 12 staff, plus part-timers and foreign students. They were concentrating on bush fruit and oilseed rape, they had pasture for 60 cattle and 1000 ewes, and they also produced hay. Almost all of the farm's lamb was sold out of the valley through Highland Glen Producers. There were eight holiday cottages and a furniture showroom, all converted from former farm buildings. There was also a separate pig boar stud.

In 1881, 113 people lived on 11 of the farms between Aberfeldy and Grandtully. In 1981 that number had dropped to 13, a brutal change typical of the whole valley from Glenlyon and Kenmore to Logierait. But by 2004 the number in the same area had tripled to 39. At the time of writing, the total number of people in Aberfeldy town is a little under 2000. In 1961 it stood at 1,407. Compared to the rest of Scotland, the statistics show that the valley has an older and slightly wealthier than average population, with a marginally higher than normal number of widows, divorcees and remarried couples, and a significant increase in families with young children.

Betty Allan – now Betty McNab and a grandmother – puts her finger on a feature not easily noticed by visitors: "There are still good employers in the town: Fisher's Laundry, Barhaul, Willie Grieve, Blairish Restorations; several other small companies, mainly to do with building and transport."

James Fisher would be delighted to see the development of his laundry. It now has four branches across Scotland and employs about forty people locally on a full-time basis with a further forty part-timers in the summer months. Barhaul, essentially a haulage, plant hire and building materials company, began in Aberfeldy in 1997 and also employs about forty people. Among other things, they carry out crushing and transport work for the MiSWACO barytes mine. Barytes, a very heavy mineral essential to the oil industry, has been mined in the hills east of Loch Kinardochy since the 1980s. The mine is the only operational underground mine in Scotland; it employs 15 staff of whom 10 are full-time miners. This figure would rise if a second mine could be opened to a world-class ore-seam in the hills north of Strathtay.

WB (Willie) Grieve – now Aberfeldy Groundworks – are also major employers. Besides major work on contracts such as hydroelectric schemes, the company has worked with archaeologists and historians on projects linked to Scotland's past, including the Scottish Crannog Centre, the Birks of Aberfeldy, and further afield at places such as Hopetoun House. Along with others such as Barhaul, it has taken an active part in local sponsorship, particularly for young people.

Inside the barytes mine

With the laundry, the mine, the distillery and the various companies involved in transport and construction, Aberfeldy is considerably more 'industrial' than many comparable highland towns. Wordwright Communications, publishers of *Comment* since 1997, are based in the town and provide an excellent and invaluable administrative support service to many small businesses.

The valley has long been known for its walks and its hills, but now new businesses have developed around the river and the cycle path network. Several small companies have set up in the valley to cater for outdoor activities, such as hill-walking, mountain-biking, kayaking and rafting. Grandtully is now on the national map as a centre for canoeing competitions and training.

Some say the real power is no longer held by local employers but by distant bureaucrats. Does the valley need a stronger, more direct local government with fiscal powers? Many people think that having only three councillors for the vast area of the Highland Ward means they're unable to carry much weight among the thirty-eight other Perth and Kinross Council members. As Betty McNab put it: "It was easy when there was a Town Council. If something worried you, you only had to pop into the fish shop and talk to Councillor Peter MacGregor; or you might meet the Provost in the street." Whether such local government should take the form of a body for the valley alone or, as some maintain, it should be a beefed-up version for the entire Perthshire Highland Ward area remains a moot point. What is certain is that, in an echo of the originality of the earlier Manifesto, in November 2002, Aberfeldy declared itself a Fairtrade Town, the first in Scotland; and in doing so it clearly sees itself as the hub of the geographical Upper Tay.

Life for schoolchildren has changed, too. By 2007, there were no more boarders at Breadalbane Academy. Although pupils are bussed in from Pitlochry and further afield, parents from Glenlyon for example have to take their children down the glen to Fortingall to meet the school bus. In 2008, amid considerable local trepidation, Breadalbane Academy and the Community Centre with its swimming pool were demolished. The school moved into Portakabins. Bereft of their pool, local swimmers met undaunted in a local café for a chat after replacement activities such as yoga, tai–chi and pilates.

A new combined community centre and school is under construction, using public/private finance. There will be places for another 150 children and the education and sports facilities will be greatly improved. The campus will be for the community as a whole. Local people will be able to swim again and take advantage of new amenities such as a dance studio and a climbing wall. But distant shareholders will be involved, and however grand the building may be, the men and women who fought so hard to raise funds for its predecessor will no longer be able to marvel at what they achieved as they swim lengths under the new roof. There is the bigger question of how the local economy will survive if governments continue to privatise profit and nationalise loss.

And life in the valley is not all roses. As Betty McNab mused: "What's different about now? Well, there's a lot more vandalism, drugs and violence, never there when Aberfeldy had a Police Sergeant and two Constables, who knew the youngsters' faces and knew who their parents were. People have a lot more money now; they can get what they want, more or less, but when they watch television, they see they could get a lot more. There's maybe less community spirit." Others maintain that, though it has certainly changed, the community spirit is still there, as strong as ever.

Despite current crises, now is probably the best time ever to have lived in the valley, certainly for the majority of its inhabitants rather than just a privileged few. As in the rest of Scotland, better education has given children opportunities unavailable to their grandparents; there is a benefit system if needed and a small pension for later. Locally, there are excellent shops, an enormous range of goods and foodstuffs, active churches, good recreation spaces – in particular an award-winning playground in Victoria Park – and an excellent medical practice.

The Cottage Hospital has celebrated its centenary. Despite being under fairly constant siege from bureaucrats over the years, it is still seen as an important contributor to the wellbeing of the community. The art-deco Birks Cinema may have a new lease of life, and Taymouth Castle may live again. As has already happened in other European countries, public transport in the area will – has to – improve.

The days of clan warfare, of destruction and starvation, of the Fiery Cross, of Poor Relief, of the Logierait Poorhouse, of snooping church elders, of overbearing lairds, are gone. But Aberfeldy's highland past is still celebrated in the annual August Highland Games and the simultaneous Menzies Clan Gathering, both so successful that their site has been moved from Victoria Park – where the Aberfeldy Show reinvented itself in 1945 – to a field on the north side of the Tay, close to where the Black Watch originally mustered.

Around the time when Pale John became first Earl of Breadalbane, the Lady of Lawers made a number of grim prophecies. Her house still sits silent and ruined by the lochside. When she was alive, the Breadalbane Campbells

were less than half way through their steady rise to enormous power, but the Lady correctly foretold their complete disappearance from the valley. She was also right to foresee that sheep would replace men on the hills; although even the sheep are now going. One of her predictions, however, has not as yet come true: that the temperature on Ben Lawers would sink so low as to destroy everything within a seven mile radius.

In 2010, the SNP are in government in Scotland, and they have eighteen out of forty-one seats in the Perth and Kinross Council. Whether or not we become a separate nation once again, we will still worry about climate change, global overpopulation, conservation, renewable resources and food security. Though we can do nothing directly about global overpopulation, here we have land, timber, water and resourceful people. If the weather becomes warmer, perhaps we may be able once again to exploit the large areas of land on higher ground formerly in cultivation. If wetter, our water will flow more strongly and our woodland will still grow. If we shut our eyes, there is space for wind-turbines. In some parts of Europe, nearly every roof now sports a solar panel or two; perhaps this valley could do with a little more sunshine for that, but the technology is improving.

Several estates along the valley built hydroelectric systems around the turn of the last century for their own electricity supply, and at least one converted to selling power to the national grid. The new private hydroelectric schemes, of which there are seven currently in operation and at least another five planned, are all designed to supply power to the grid. One of them – a 'run-of-the-river'

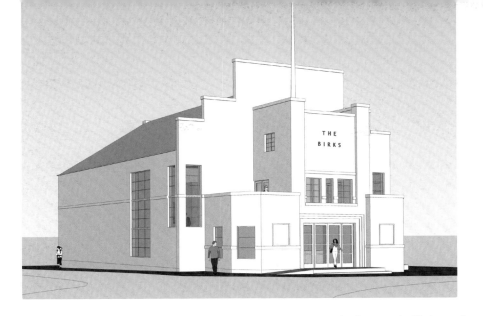

scheme and virtually invisible – has a power output equivalent to half that of the 1951 power station below the massive Lubreoch dam. Lubreoch is one of three 1950's power stations that use water from behind the huge dams in Glenlyon; together, Lubreoch, Lochay and Cashlie have an installed capacity of 62 MW. In total, the new schemes will have more than a fifth of that capacity, a very significant contribution with allegedly sufficient power for at least 12,000 homes, and with much less visual impact than the 1950s dams, magnificent though most people consider those mighty structures to be.

Here again, as technology develops and equipment becomes cheaper and more easily available, it is safe to say that more small schemes will come into use, even for individual households. After all, the Lady of Lawers also predicted that one day there would be a mill on every burn. But one local hydroelectric scheme took nine years to jump all the bureaucratic hurdles placed – often without warning – in its path.

Sheer public demand may well sweep some of the more extreme regulations aside, though local opinions differ: isn't there a risk that that no amount of carefully-assembled data will prevent unintended consequences? Isn't the present management of these regulations more geared to protecting agency jobs than anything else? Are some schemes being put forward which seriously endanger other local interests such as tourism? Isn't the implementation of these schemes a missed opportunity to reintroduce Tom Johnston's not-for-

New Breadalbane Academy and Community Campus under construction, February 2010

Birks Upper Falls, frozen for the first time in 29 years, January 2010

profit – or at least consensus – approach? As so often before, the valley is full of disagreement over a burning issue, though this time it is unlikely that anyone will die for their views.

The advent of the computer has done little locally to stem the need for administrators. As an example, in 1970 Breadalbane Academy had one part-time secretary. By 2007 it had six computer-literate full-timers. Perhaps the instant-access-to-information internet, even more than writing, is really bringing home yet another of the Lady of Lawers' predictions, that the quill of a goose will destroy man's memory. But the internet has enabled more and more people to work from home, so home for many salary-earners no longer needs to be in the Central Belt. As one local farmer said: 'Edinburgh and Glasgow are coming closer.'

Television and the internet have provided us with more than enough entertainment to keep us amused and interested during the long dark winter evenings. Just as the days of Gaelic story-telling by the fireside have long gone, so the days of some local organizations may be numbered, but there will always be a need for local societies and committees to take an interest in and fight for whatever issue is important at the time. And the valley has a good record in this respect.

People new to the area are pleased to find that local shops can supply a vast range of products, and next-day delivery vans bring anything that cannot be bought here. Probably the fresh air, the freedom, the quietness – or perhaps just the phenomenon of people smiling and talking to each other in the town – will offset whatever the newcomers may miss about the cities. More and more of the houses once occupied by highland families, and which later fell empty and into disrepair, have since been refurbished as holiday cottages and second homes. Perhaps some of them will once again echo year-round to the shouts of children.

***

In the Introduction to this book, I made a personal comment. Since then I have tried to keep myself out of the story. As a resident who loves this area deeply, I will make one more remark: the sense of community, which I personally find so astonishingly strong in the Aberfeldy valley, has changed and may well change again. But it will not fade. This place does something to people who come here. Time and again, over the years – on, say, one of Robert Burns' 'lightsome days' – when the sun shines, the Tay sparkles, and all the hills and fields and woods looks their most ravishing, I watch people grin at each other and use phrases like: "You'd need to go a long way to find anything better than this," or just: "This is why we're here!"

Good Luck! A postcard from the '50s

ACKNOWLEDGEMENTS

- The Royal Commission on the Ancient and Historical Monuments of Scotland for permission to reproduce two photographs from their collection
- The Black Watch Regimental Museum for permission to reproduce five images from their collection. Special thanks to Tommy Smyth
- Perth and Kinross Heritage Trust for permission to reproduce a photograph of the replica logboat. Special thanks to Steve Timoney
- The Scottish National Portrait Gallery for permission to reproduce six portraits in their collection
- The National Railway Museum/Science and Society Picture Library for permission to reproduce the LMS railway poster
- The AK Bell Library for permission to reproduce many photographs from their collection. Special thanks to Sara-Ann Kelly, Marjorie Donald and Yvonne Bell
- The Perth Museum for permission to reproduce three photographs and the portrait of Gavin Campbell of Glenfalloch. Special thanks to Maria Devaney and Paul Adair
- Perth and Kinross Council Archive for permission to reproduce the photograph of Aberfeldy Fire Brigade
- Linda Cracknell for permission to reproduce her photograph of a ring-marked stone
- Gladys Meek for permission to draw on her extensive photographic collection
- John McDiarmid for permission to reproduce images from his extensive collection of memorabilia
- *Comment* for permission to reproduce three photographs. Special thanks to Brendan Murphy
- The Mitchell Library for permission to reproduce the portrait of the 2nd Marquess of Breadalbane
- Jamie Stormonth-Darling for drawing the aerial sketchmap of the area for the endpapers
- Kari de Koenigswarter for her sketch of the Dunfallandy Stone
- Nickloai Globe for all his care in the layout of the book
- Jayne Ramage for her work on the three diagrams
- The Aberfeldy Common Good Fund for permission to reproduce images from Dr Mackay's *Aberfeldy Past and Present*
- Dewars Ltd for permission to reproduce a photograph of the Aberfeldy Distillery. Special thanks to Jacqui Seargeant
- Robin Baker Architects for permission to reproduce the artist's impression of the Birks Cinema
- The Railway Correspondence and Travel Society for the photograph of the locomotive *Aberfeldy*
- Fellow-Members of the Breadalbane Heritage Society

with many thanks

Whilst I take full responsibility for any errors or omissions, this book is really the result of the efforts of the local community: so many people in the area have given me hospitality and kindness, shared their time, their tea and their memories with me, trusted me with treasured possessions, books, portraits, photographs and maps – and consistently made me laugh. I'd like to thank:-

Jane Anderson
Mervyn Brown
Alec Dewar
Charlotte Flower
Janet Fry
Alistair Gillespie
Sandy Goodyear
Neil Hooper
John Jack
Allan Mackie
Pam McDiarmaid
Fiona Grant
Colin Liddell
Betty McNab
Gilbert Price
Michael Riddell
Bert Shearer
Zanna Steuart Fothringham
Barbara Stewart
Sandy Wilson
Watty Yellowlees
Elaine Whewell
Janet Wotherspoon

Some local folk have, among other forms of encouragement, been brave enough to wade through earlier drafts and to comment diplomatically but firmly. I thank Hamish and Malize McBride, Henry Steuart Fothringham, Jimmy Stewart, and my wonderful loyal writing-buddies, Polly Pullar, Linda Cracknell and Jamie Grant.

As well as reading an entire draft, Jayne Ramage has been constantly supportive, and her husband Kevin, my editor and publisher, has been astonishing: without his kind, eagle-eyed attention and broader judgement, this book would simply not be what it is.

Lastly, I'd like to thank two people in particular: my brother-in-arms, Frank Woods, who has marched with me, chapter by chapter, every step of the way; and Kari de Koenigswarter who knew whenever I needed help – often before I did – and was absolutely and always there.

BIBLIOGRAPHY

Aberfeldy and District Tourist Association: *Aberfeldy and District, the Official Guide*, Wm Culross & Son, 1972

Ashmore, PJ: *Neolithic and Bronze Age Scotland*, BT Batsford/Historic Scotland, 1996

Barlow, L & Smith, RJ: *Uniforms of the British Yeomanry Force, No8*, Spellmount Ltd, 1985

Barnett, TR: *The Road to Rannoch*, Robert Grant & Son, 1924

Barthorp, M: *Jacobite Rebellions 1689-1745*, Osprey Publishing, 1982

Black, N: *From a Hollow on the Hill*, 1999

Black Watch Regimental Trustees: *The Black Watch Photographic Archive*, Tempus Publishing, 2000

Bowie, W, Innes, C: *The Black Book of Taymouth*, privately circulated by the Marquis of Breadalbane, 1855

Breadlabane Archaeological Society: *Strathtay History Trail*, 1970

Breadalbane Heritage Society: *Around Aberfeldy, a Historical Trail*, 1994

Breadalbane Heritage Society: *Around Aberfeldy, "Fit Vestibule for Heaven"*, 1998

Breadalbane Heritage Society: *Cupmarked Stones in Strathtay*, from *In Scotland Magazine*, 2005

Brodie, I: *Steamers of the Tay*, Stenlake Publishing, undated

Buchan, J: *Capital of the Mind*, John Murray, 2003

Burl, A: *The Stone Circles of the British Isles*, Yale University Press, 1976

Butter, R: *Kilmartin*, Kilmartin House Trust, 1999

Byrom, B: *Old Killin, Kenmore and Loch Tay*, Stenlake Publishing, 2004

Calder, A: *James Maclaren, 1853-1890, Arts and Crafts Architect*, Royal Institute of British Architects, 1990

Calder, A: *James Maclaren, Arts and Crafts Pioneer*, Shaun Tyas, 2003

Cameron, JC ed: *Views of Aberfeldy*, JC Cameron, undated

Campbell, D: *The Lairds of Glenlyon*, privately published, 1886, 2nd edition Clunie Press, 1984

Campbell, D: *The Book of Garth and Fortingall*, privately circulated for Sir Donald Currie, 1888

Campbell, D: *Reminiscences and Reflections of an Octogenarian Gael*, The Northern Counties Newspaper and Printing Company Ltd, 1910

Coleman, R, Perry, D: *Moated Sites in Tayside and Fife*, Tayside and Fife Archaeological Journal, Vol 3, 1997

Cooke, A: *Stanley, From Arkwright Village to Commuter Suburb 1784-2003*, Perth & Kinross Libraries, 2003

Cornforth, J, Hughes-Hartman, G: *Inverary Castle*, The Pilgrim Press, 1990

Cruikshank, G: *The Battle of Dunnichen*, The Pinkfoot Press, 1999

Cumming, E: *Hand, Heart and Soul, the Arts and Crafts Movement in Scotland*, Birlinn, 2006

Cummins, WA: *The Age of the Picts*, Sutton Publishing Ltd, 1998

Cunningham, AD: *A History of Rannoch*, AD Cunningham, 1984

Cunningham, AD: *Tales of Rannoch*, Perth & Kinross District Libraries, 1989

David, S: *Churchill's Sacrifice of the Highland Division, France 1940*, Brasseys, 1994

Devine TM: *The Scottish Nation, 1700-2000*, Penguin Books, 1999

Dewar, AD: *Castle Menzies*, The Pilgrim Press, 1980

Dixon, N: *The Crannogs of Loch Tay*, The Scottish Trust for Underwater Archaeology, 2000

Driscoll, S: *Alba, The Gaelic Kingdom of Scotland, ad 800-1124*, Birlinn/Historic Scotland, 2002

Duff, D: *Queen Victoria's Highland Journals*, Webb & Bower, 1983

Duncan Millar, A: *Countryman's Cog*, Wm Culross, 1990

Fawcett, R: *St Andrews Castle*, Historic Scotland, 1992

Fenwick, K, Sinclair, NT: *The Perth and Dunkeld Railway*, The Highland Railway Society, 2006

Fraser, D: *Highland Reflections*, Wm Culross, 2004

Fraser, D, Notley, B: *Killiecrankie*, National Trust for Scotland, 1997

Fraser, W: *The Red Book of Grantully*, privately circulated

Ferguson, M: *Rambles in Breadalbane*, Thomas Murray & Sons, 1891

Fergusson, B: *The Black Watch, a Short History*, Woods & Co, 1955, Revised edition, reprinted 1974

Firsoff VA: *In the Hills of Breadalbane*, Robert Hale Ltd, 1954

Fisher, J: *Memories of an Aberfeldy Childhood*, Impact Communications, 1989

Foster, SM: *Picts, Gaels and Scots*, BT Batsford/Historic Scotland, 2004

Gillies, WA: *In Famed Breadalbane*, 1938, 2nd edition Clunie Press, 1980

Gordon, S: *Highways and Byways in the Central Highlands*, Macmillan & Co, 1948

Goring, R: *Scotland, The Autobiography*, Penguin Viking, 2007

Grant, F: *Old Aberfeldy, with Weem, Fortingall and Glenlyon*, Stenlake Publishing, 2009

Grove, D: *Dunstaffnage Castle*, Historic Scotland 2004

Henderson, S: *Memories of Old Aberfeldy*, Church of Scotland, undated

Hindmarsh, E: *Fortingall Sewer, Data Structure Report*, AOC Archaeology Group, 2007

Hingley, R: *Settlement and Sacrifice, the Later Prehistoric People of Scotland*, Birlinn/Historic Scotland, 1998

Hooper, N: *Fortingall Kirk and Village*, Perth & Kinross Heritage Trust, 2003

Hooper, N: *Journals of the James Maclaren Society*, The James Maclaren Society, all volumes to date

Houston, RA, Knox, WWJ: *The New Penguin History of Scotland*, Allan Lane, The Penguin Press, 2001

Hull, R: *Ravens over the Hill*, Perth & Kinross Libraries, 2004

Irvine Robertson, J: *Atholl in the Rebellion of 1745*, Wordwright Communications, 1994

Irvine Robertson, J: *The First Highlander*, Tuckwell Press, 1998

Irvine Robertson, J: *Scotland's Heartland*, Heartland Publishers, 2001

Jamieson, F: *Drummond Castle and Gardens*, The Grimsthorpe and Drummond Castle Trust, 1993

Jauncey, J: *Blair Castle*, The Pilgrim Press Ltd, 1999. Also 1982 edition

Jeffrey,E, Jeffrey,B, Petrie,C: *Childhood Memories of Camserney*, Pioneer Associates, undated

Kelly, SA & Merchant, J: *Treasures of the AK Bell Library*, Perth & Kinross Council, 2008

Kennedy, J: *Folklore and Reminiscences of Strathtay and Grandtully*, The Munro Press, 1927

Kerr, J: *Wade in Atholl*, The Atholl Experience, 1985, reprinted from *The Transactions of The Gaelic Society of Inverness*, Volume LIII

Kerr, J: *Queen Victoria's Scottish Diaries*, Eric Dobby Publishing, 1992

Kerr, J: *Life in the Atholl Glens*, Perth & Kinross District Libraries, 1993

Konstam, A: *The Forts of Celtic Britain*, Osprey Publishing, 2006

Lamont-Brown, R, Adamson, P: *Victorian and Edwardian Perthshire*, Alvie Publications, 1985

Liddell, C: *Pitlochry, Heritage of Highland District*, Perth & Kinross District Libraries, 1993

Liddell, C: *Pitlochry, a History*, Watermill Books, 2008

Macgregor, AA: *Wild Drumalban*, W&R Chambers Ltd, 1927

McGrigor, M: *Anna, Countess of the Covenant*, Birlinn Ltd, 2008

Mackay, ND: *Aberfeldy Past and Present*, The Town Council of Aberfeldy, 1954, facsimile edition 2000

Mckean, J: *Charles Rennie Macintosh, Architect, Artist, Icon*, Lomond, 2008

McKerracher, A: *Perthshire in History and Legend*, John Donald Publisher, 1988

Mackintosh, J: *Holidays in the Perthshire Highlands*, Turnbull & Spears, undated

McLaughlan, T, Skene, WF: *The Book of the Dean of Lismore*, Edmonston and Douglas, 1862

Maclean, F: *A Concise History of Scotland*, Thames & Hudson, 1970

McLellan, A, Campbell, JL: *The Furrow Behind Me*, Routledge & Kegan Paul, 1962

Macmillan, H: *The Highland Tay*, H Virtue & Co, 1901

Macrae, J: *Eilean Donan Castle*, J Arthur Dixon, 1978

Martine, R: *Supernatural Scotland*, Robert Hale, 2003

Maxwell, G: *A Gathering of Eagles, Scenes from Roman Scotland*, Birlinn/ Historic Scotland, 1998

Michelin Tyre Co Ltd: *Michelin Guides*, 1911, 1993, 2008

Mileham, P: *The Yeomanry Regiments*, Canongate Academic, 1985

Mileham, P: *The Scottish Regiments, 1633-1936*, Spellmount Ltd, 1988, new edition 1996

Miles, H: *Fair Perthshire*, John Lane The Bodley Head Ltd, 1930

Miller, J: *The Dam Builders, Power from the Glens*, Birlinn Ltd, 2002

New Lanark Conservation Trust: *The Story of New Lanark*, 2003

Peterson, HL: *The Book of the Gun*, Paul Hamlyn Ltd, 1963

Philippou, P, Hands, R: *Battleground Perthshire*, Tippermuir, 2009

Prebble, J: *Culloden*, Penguin Books, 1967

Prebble, J: *Glencoe*, Penguin Books, 1968

Prebble, J: *The Highland Clearances*, Penguin Books 1969

Prebble, J: *The Lion in the North*, Penguin Books, 1971

Prebble, J: *Riot*, Wordwright Communications, 1996

Rees, J: *Never an Old Tin Hut*, The Aberfeldy Golf Club, 1994

Reid, S: *Like Hungry Wolves, Culloden Moor, 16th April, 1746*, Windrow & Green, 1994

Reid, S: *Highland Clansman 1698-1746*, Osprey Publishing, 1997

Ritchie, A: *Scotland BC*, HMSO/Historic Scotland, 1988

Ritchie, A: *Meigle Museum*, Historic Scotland, 2006

Roberston, S, Young, P: *Daughter of Atholl*, Abertay Historical Society, 1996

Robotham, R: *On Highland Lines*, Ian Allan, 2000

Scott Morton, R: *Traditional Farm Architecture in Scotland*, The Ramsay Head Press, 1976

Scottish Hydro-Electric plc: *Power from the Glens*, 1994

Sinclair, DM: *By Tummel and Loch Rannoch*, John McKinlay, 1989

Sinclair, NT: *Highland Railway: People and Places*, Breedon Books Publishing Ltd, 2005

Smith, J: *Jessie's Journey*, Mercat Press, 2002

Smith, J: *Tales from the Tent*, Mercat Press, 2003

Smith, J: *Tears for a Tinker*, Mercat Press, 2005

Smith, WAC: *Tayside's Last Days of Steam*, Stenlake Publishing, undated

Smurthwaite, D: *The Complete Guide to the Battlefields of Great Britain*, Michael Joseph Ltd, 1995

Stansfield, G: *Perthshire and Kinross-shire's Lost Railways*, Stenlake Publishing, undated

Stewart, Alexander: *A Highland Parish*, Alex Maclaren & Sons, 1928

Stewart, Alexandra: *Daughters of the Glen*, Leura Press, 1986

Stewart, D: *Sketches of the Character, Institutions and Customs of the Highlanders of Scotland*, 'New Edition', A&W Mackenzie, 1885

Taylor, DB: *Circular Homesteads in North West Perthshire*, Abertay Historical Society, 1990

Thoms, LM, Breeze DJ Hall DW: *First Contact – Rome and Northern Britain*, Tayside and Fife Archaeological Committee, Monograph 7, 2009

Thomas, C, Strachan, D: *Around Aberfeldy, a Brief History*, Breadalbane Heritage Society/Perth & Kinross Heritage Trust, 2008

Thomas, J: *The Scottish Railway Book*, David & Charles, 1977

Vallance, HA: *The Highland Railway*, Newton Abbot, David St John Thomas, 1938, 1985 edition extended by Lambert, AJ

Watson, D: *A Simple Introduction to the Stone Circles and Standing Stones of Perthshire*, Simple Guides Scotland, 2006

Wheater, H: *Aberfeldy to Glenlyon*, Appin Publications, 1981

Wheater, H: *Kenmore and Loch Tay*, Appin Publications, 1982

Wheater, H: *Killin to Glencoe*, Appin Publications, 1982

Wilkinson-Latham, R: *Scottish Military Uniforms*, David & Charles, 1975

Williams, R: *Sons of the Wolf*, House of Lochar, 1998

Wood, S: *The Scottish Soldier*, Archive Publications, 1987

Wooliscroft, DJ, Hoffman, B: *The Romans in Perthshire*, Perth & Kinross Heritage trust, 2005

Wooliscroft, DJ, Hoffman, B: *Rome's First Frontier*, Tempus Publishing Ltd, 2006

Woosnam-Savage, RC (ed): *1745, Charles Edward Stuart and the Jacobites*, Glasgow Museums, 1995

Yellowlees, WW: *Food and Health in the Scottish Highlands*, Clunie Press, 1985

Yellowlees, WW: *A Doctor in the Wilderness*, Janus Publishing, 1993

About the Author

Ruary Mackenzie Dodds' maternal family tree is littered with Stewarts of Dull and Robertsons of Logierait. He was educated in England at Gresham's School. He worked for ten years for Michelin, finishing as Company Secretary of one of their subsidiaries. He then joined Canning, an international business language training outfit based in London and worked with them for eighteen years, finishing as Operations Director. He is Chairman of the Dragonfly Project, a Registered Charity based in East Anglia, which raises public awareness of the beauty, fascination and plight of dragonflies He lives and writes poetry and prose in Glenlyon – and suffers from an obsession with trains.

Index

(**Bold** denotes a photograph or map)

Aberdeen 16, 66, 105
Aberfeldy
    Aberfeldy (Dewar's) Distillery **115,** 117
    Aberfeldy Show **153**
    Anglo-Normans in region of 27–9
    Art Gallery 160, 162
    Auction Market 147, **151**
    Bank of Scotland 126
    Bank Street 29, 76, 85, 90, 111, **111**
    Bell-man **122**
    Birks Cinema 136, 141, **148,** 165, **167**
    Bridgend (1945) **142**
    Burgh Council of 115, 137, 156, 161
    Burgh of, Peace Celebration invitation (1919) **129**
    Burnside/Black Street 75, **78**
    Cadet Force 148
    Cameron's Newsagent **127**
    Chapel Street/Factory Street 75, 82, **82, 84**
    charabanc for Kenmore Pier **135**
    cholera outbreak 86
    Community Centre 157, 158, 165
    Congregational Church 83, 107, 112, **112,** 163
    Corner House Restaurant **133**
    Cottage Hospital 126, 127, **127,** 165
    council houses in 144
    Crown Hotel **141**
    Curling Club 98
    dancing in square **144**
    Debating Society 90, 101
    disruption in Church affairs 92–5
    Dunkeld Street 105, **109**
    early road locomotive in Bank Street (1872) **106**
    Fairtrade Town 164
    Feeing Market Days 108
    Fire Brigade **127**
    flooding and bad harvests 61
    Football Club 113
    Foresters Society 148
    Frazer's garage 126
    Free Church 94
    Gaslight Company 97, 102
    Golf Club and course 79, 116–17, **120**
    Groundworks (WB Grieve) 163
    Group Manifesto 155–6, **156,** 164
    Highland Games 136, 165
    Home Guard **138**
    Home Street 108, 113
    Kenmore Street 76, 88, 90, 105
    Last train from (1965) 152, **154**
    Laundry in Home Street **124**
    MacGregor incursions on 44
    map (1753) **78**
    Market Square 77
    Masonic Lodge 126
    McKerchar bus in Square **142**
    Mill Street 85
    Moness Terrace 116, 152
    Over Milton/Bank Street 75
    Palace Hotel 133, **158**
    Pankhurst, Emmeline visit 126
    people's lives, improvements and prosperity in 72–3
    Perthshire Rifle Volunteers 99–100
    Pipe Band 126, **150**
    Police Station 147
    Poplar Avenue 119
    Post Office 79, 80, 117
    potato crop failures 97
    Prefabs in Market Street 143, 144
    Prince Charles Edward at Wade's bridge 66
    private carriage outside Town Hall **121**
    private owner wagon at station **114**
    Public School 106, **110,** 114
    Raft Race **157,** 162
    Rifle Volunteers 108
    Romans in proximity of 15–16
    Royalty, visits of 91–2
    St Andrew's Church 113, 114, **115**
    Secondary School 106
    showman's wagon at Black Watch Monument **121**
    sketch looking west (1868) **103**
    Spring Sale 147
    Square (1856 drawing) **82,** (early 1960s) **154**
    station 101, 103, **124**
    Station Hotel/Schiehallion 152
    steam locomotive at **121**
    stone circles in region of 9
    Taybridge Drive 114
    Taybridge Road 106
    timber team at local sawmill **147**
    toboganning/Crieff Road **151**
    Tourist Office 107
    Town Hall 121
    Victoria Park 165, **166**
    view from Blairish **116**
    view from north **112**
    villages in region of 42–3, 90
    Wade's bridge at 65, 72, 75, 81, 84
    War Memorial 129, **130**
    washing day in **110**
    Watermill 85, 162
    Yacht *Alma* (aground in Bank Street) 105
    Young Farmers **151**
    Young Ladies Institutes 106
    Youth Club 148
Abthanage of Dull 32, 42
Abyrfealdybeg 29, 75
Abyrpheallaidh 28
Acharn 70

Achloa 70
Act of Union 61
Adam, William 63
Aerial ropeway to Aberfeldy Station **125**
Agricola 15, 17
Ailean Chraggan 88, 157, 162
Air Defence Corps 137
Air Raid Wardens 137
Alamo siege 84
Alba 24
Alexander II 27
Alexander III 27, 31
Alister, R. 87, 89
Allan, Jock (at McKerchars forge) **132**
Alma 99
American Civil War 103
American War of Independence 80, 82
Amulree 54
Anglo-Normans 27, 28, 29, 32, 33, 34
Anglo-Saxons 20, 23, 24
Angus (King of Atholl) 23
Antonine Wall 17
Aquitaine 28
Ardtalnaig 15
Argyll, county of 9, 22, 23, 24, 27
Argyll, Earl of 48, 57, 60
Argyll, Marquis of 50
Argyll (land of the Gaels) 19
Argyll Militia 66, 67
Arisaig 65
Army Reserve 127
Ashanti wars 106
Athfotla' (New Ireland) 22
Atholl, district of 18, 21, 22, 27
Atholl, Duchess of 103
Atholl, Dukes of 10, 62, 63, 71, 76, 81, 82, 101
Atholl, Earls of 28, 29, 31, 32, 33, 36, 48, 49
Atholl, Marquess of 57, 59
Atholl, William of 66
Atholl and Breadalbane Community Comment 158, 160,
       163, 164
Atholl and Breadalbane Ploughing Society 85
Atholl and Breadalbane Times 116
Atholl Brigade 61, 66, 67
Atholl family 57, 59, 69, 79
Atholl Mormaers 23
Atholl Wrights' Brotherly Society 85
Auction Mart 113, 114
Australia 87
Austrian Succession 126
Auxerre 19
Auxiliary Territorial Service 137
Ayrshire 54, 56

Badenoch, Alexander Stewart, Earl of Buchan, Wolf of 34,
       35, 36
Balbridie 8
Ballechin 48
Ballinluig 101, 123, 125
Ballinluig Station **125**
Balliol, John 31
Balliol family 27
Balloch Castle 41, 47, 48, 52, 53, 54, 57
Balnacraig 12
Balnaguard 72, 91, 102, 123
Banff 34
Bannockburn, Battle of 32
Barhaul 163
Baron's Hall 91

barytes mine **164**
Bath 57, 59
Beatty, Admiral Earl 135
Beeching, Doctor Richard 152
Beltane 86, 105
Ben Lawers 166
Benachie 16
Birks of Aberfeldy 70, 77, **79,** 126, 163, **168**
Bishop of Iona 23
Bishop of Murray 35
Black Death 43
Black Watch 62-71, 81, 84, 99, **99,** 113, 118, 119, 123, 127,
       128, 137, 139, 141, 152, 155, 161, 162
    soldier, original uniform (1742) **64**
    soldiers at General Wade's bridge **151**
    soldiers on the Western Front **128**
    Third Battalion, Royal Highlanders **162**
Black Watch Inn **108, 120,** 134, 145
Black Watch Monument 114, 121, **130**
Blackhill 85
Blair Atholl 47
Blair Castle 52, 57, 65, 66
Blair, Tony 161
Blairish Restorations 163
Boece 15
Boer War 114, 118, 123, 127
Bolfracks 42, 61, 66, 104
    quarry at 64, 91
Bonnie Prince Charlie 65
Boy Scouts 148
Boys Brigade 148
Brander Pass 19
Breadalbane, district of 47, 53
Breadalbane, Earls of - see Campbells
Breadalbane, Marquesses of - see Campbells
Breadalbane Academy 105, 106, 136, 144, 147, **158,** 165,
       168, **167**
Breadalbane Arms 1, 24, **90,** 91, 134
Breadalbane Cricket Club 104
Breadalbane Estate 63, **77,** 131
Breadalbane Fencibles 81
Breadalbane Football Club **117**
Breadalbane Free Church, Aberfeldy 94, **95,** 117
Breadalbane Highland Gathering 117
Breadalbane woollen mill 86
Bridge of Lyon 95
British Empire 119
British Legion 149
British Railways 143
Britons 18, 23, 24
Brochan 39
Bronze Age 7
Brooklyn 71
Bruce, King Robert 28, **30,** 31, 32, 33, 34
Bruce family 27
Burns, Robert 160

Caithness, county of 34, 56
Caithness, Earl of 54
Caithness, Mary Countess of 54
Caledonians 14, 16, 17
Calgacus 17
Cameron, Donald 73
Cameron, Rev of Logierait 92
Cameron family 27
Campbell, Alma, 3rd Marchioness of Breadalbane 116,
       125, 131
Campbell, Archibald, Earl of Argyll 46
Campbell, Archie Roy 65, 68, 69, 71

Campbell, Colonel John 47
Campbell, Duncan, 2nd Laird of Glenorchy 42
Campbell, Duncan, 2nd Laird of Glenlyon 44
Campbell, Gavin, 3rd Marquess of Breadalbane **104**, 114,
  115, 119, 122, 124, 126
Campbell, John, 4th Earl of Breadalbane 77, 79, 80
Campbell, John, 2nd Earl of Breadalbane 62, 69
Campbell, John, 2nd Marquess of Breadalbane 15, **87**, 88,
  89, 91, 92, 93, 94, 95, 97, 98, 104
Campbell, John, 7th Laird of Glenlyon 61, 62
Campbell, John, 3rd Earl of Breadalbane 71, 75, 76, 77, 82
Campbell, Mad Colin, 3rd Laird of Glenlyon 41
Campbell, Pale John, 1st Earl of Breadalbane 53-62, **55**,
  165, 166
Campbell, Sir Colin, 6th Laird of Glenorchy, Grey Colin 41,
  44, **44**,
Campbell, Sir Colin, 8th Laird of Glenorchy **47**, 48
Campbell, Sir Duncan, 7th Laird of Glenorchy, Black
  Duncan 53, **54**
Campbell, Sir John, 10th Laird of Glenorchy 53
Campbell, Sir Robert, 9th Laird of Glenorchy 51, 52
Campbell clan 43, 45, 48, 49, 54, 57
Campbells of Argyll 44
Campbells of Balloch 75
Campbells of Breadalbane 66, 75
Campbells of Glenorchy 34, 43, 44, 53
Camserney 8, **86**
Canada 71, 88
Carlisle Castle 68
Carpow 5
Carse Farm 9
Castle Dow 11
Castle Menzies 42, **43,** 52, 59, 61, 139, 147
Catholicism 58
Cawnpore 99
Celtic chieftains 27
Celtic Earls of Atholl 27
Celtic language 14, 19
Celtic royal families 20
Celts 18
Cerialis 15
Certified Teachers 110
Chamberlain, Neville 138
Charles I 46, 47, 48, 49, 51
Charles II 51, 52, 53
Christianity 18, 159
Church of England 46
Church of Iona 23
Church of Rome 23
Church of Scotland 45, 78, 83, 93, 144
Churchill, Winston 142
Churchyard Yew, Fortingall 8
Clark, Miss 106
Clarke, Rev Donald 97
Clifton 66
Clochfoldich 28, 31, 90, 106
  Laird of 41
Cloichfoldich 103
Cloichran 87
Cluny burn 28
Cluny Ferry 102
Cluny Rock 11
Clydebank Blitz 141
Co-op (SCWS) 144, **145**
Comment 158, 160, 163, 164
Commercial Bank 113
Commissioners for the Forfeited Estates 69, 70, 75, 76
Comrie 15, 17
Comrie Bridge and ford site **48**

Comrie Castle 48
Comyn, Sir John (Earl of Badenoch - Red Comyn) 28, 31
Comyn family 27, 33
Conservatives 159
Constantine I 24, 27
Constantine II 25
Cope, General Sir John 65, 66
Corryarack 65
Coshieville 9, 48, 65, 88, 162
Coshieville Hotel **153,** 157
Covenanters 53
Craig na Cailleach 3
Craigianie 25
Craigthuil 158
Crannogs 10, 12, **12**
Crieff 19, 63, 67
Crimean War 99
Crockett, Davy 84
Croftmoraig 8, **9,** 70
Cromwell, Oliver 51, 52, 56
Cuil-an-Daraich Poorhouse 101
Culdares 61
Culloden 68, 69
Cumberland, Duke of 67, 68
Cup-and-ring, near Camserney **8**
Currie, Sir Donald **107**, 114, 116, 119, 123, 126
Cymbeline, King of Britons 15

Dacians 17
Dalginross 15
Dalnacardoch 63, 65, 88
dam building 1950s 146
Daniel, Colonel 51
Daniel Stewart's Free School 90, 106
David I 20
David II 34
de Bercleys 34
de Erthe, Baillie Hugo 31, 33
Declaration of Arbroath 32
Deeside 8
Derculich 103
Devolved Assembly 159
Dewar, Alec 144, 146
Dewar, Donald 161
Disruption in the Kirk 93, 94, 97, 100
Domesday Book 33
Donald, King of the Argyll Scots 23
Douglas, John of Kenmore 66
Douglas clan 41
Drummond Hill 11, **14**
Duff, Rev David 83, 85, 86, 92, 93, 95, 97
Dull Village 9, 14, 31, 35, 36, 50, 54, 65, 66, 73, 79, 81, 84,
  87,103
  Dull Church **20**, 143
  fairs and markets, decline of 90
  Free Church support 94
  Irish missionalres and monasteries 19, 20
  MacGregors raid on 44
  parish choice of minister 45
  Rev Menzies of 81
  sack of monastery at 23–4
  standing stones at Carse Farm **9**
Dumfries 31
The Dun 14
Dun Coillich 161
Dun Geal 12, **12,** 13
Dun MacTuathall 14
Dunacree 12
Dunallan 158

Dunbar 28, 31, 32, 51
Dundai 12
Dundavie 12
Dundee 14, 41, 51, 62, 101, 103, 136
Dunedin 14
Dunfallandy Stone 21, **21**
Dunkeld 1, 14, 23, 24, 25, 57, 77, 88, 90
Dunkirk 139
Dunolly 158
Duns 10
Dunskeig 12
Duntaggart 12
Duntuim 12, 87, 88, 98
Durham 47
duthchas,' concept of 57

East India Company 71
Easter Aberfeldy 2, 38, 42, 50, 52, 75
Easter Cluny 59
Edinburgh 1, 18, 21, 27, 29, 52, 61, 63, 69, 94, 113, 159,
    161, 168
Edinburgh Brigade 66
Edradynate 28, 29, 59, 100, 103
Education Act 1872 105, 106
Edward I 28, 29, 31, 32
Egypt 113
Elgin Cathedral 35
Emperor Augustus 15
Emperor Septimius Severus 17
English Church 125
English Civil War 49
English Puritan religionists 49
Eonan 19
Episcopalian Church 78, 125, 144
Essex 29
Established Church 97, 100, 105
Ewing, Winnie 153
Extermination of the Scottish Peasantry' (Alister, R, 1853)
    89

Falkirk 63, 66, 105
Fearnan 50, 66, 75, **76**, 162
Fegan, Peter **107**
Feldy burn 19, 29
Fendoch 15, 17, 28
Ferdinand, Archduke 126
Ferguson, Fergus 65
Ferguson ,Fergy' tractor 148
Fiery Cross 50, 66, 67, 165
Fife 18, 21, 41
Fife Light Horse 115, 116
Fifth Volunteer Battalion Royal Highlanders **100**, 115, 119,
    123
Fingal 39
Finlarig Castle, Loch Tay 48, 51
First World War 60, 64, 71, 126-131
Fisher, James 163
Fisher's Laundry 123, 124, 163
Fitzalan family 27
Flanders 60, 64, 71
Flemyng family 34, 42, 73, 75, 76, 77
    lace factory 85
Flodden, Battle of 39, 41
Fonab 59
Ford of Lyon 49, 72
Forestry Commission 135, 147, 158
Forfar 18
Forteviot 18, 23, 24
Fortingall 4, 7-9, 11, 34-5, 50, 69, 71, 80, 103, 162, 165

fairs and markets, decline of 90
fort at 28
local market at 37, 79
Metellanus' castle at 15–16
monastry at **19**, 20, 23, 24
murder of MacGregors at 44
old church at **95**
Pictish sculpture in **21**
Sabbath behaviour at 45–6
Fortingall Hotel 43
Fortingall Long Cairn **5**
Fortrenn 18
Forty-third Regiment of Foot 64
France 27
Free Church 93, **95**, 97, 100, 105, 117, 144
Free Church schooner Breadalbane 97
Freemasons 148
French Revolution 80, 82
Friends of the People of Scotland 81
Frontinus 15
Fyfe, James 105
Fyfe, Thomas 101, **102**, 104, 106, 107, 108, 113, 114, 116,
    118, 119, 160

Gaelic language 34
Gaelic Mod 148
Gaelic-speaking Scots 22, 23, 24
Gallows Hill 18
Garth 12
Garth Castle, Keltney Burn 35, **36**, 41, 52
Garth House, Fortingall **119**
Gask Ridge 15
General Assembly of Kirk of Scotland 45, 46, 47, 83, 93,
    94
General Strike 134
George I 61
George II 64
German ex-prisoners-of-war 146
Girl Guides 148
Glasgow 54, 69, 81, 113, 136, 168
Glassie 70
Glen Cochill 39
Glen Dochart 43
Glen Quaich 63, 67, 87
Glen Sassunn 28
Glenalmond 15
Glencoe massacre 61
Glendochart 32
Glengoulandie 44, 48, 65, 80, 161
Glenlyon 2, 19, 25, 60, 67, 146
    Alan Stewart's return from Culloden 68
    Anglo-Norman fort remains 28
    Charter granting lands 32
    clan battles in 42
    clans cleared from crofts 87
    Dissenter preachers in 83
    farm closures 163
    guarding western approach to Aberfeldy 15
    Hydro-Electric dams in 167
    MacDiarmids of 34
    McNab of 39
    Royalists versus pro-Kirk forces 49–51
    sale and transfer of lands 57
Glenorchy 19, 32
Glenquaich 61, 66
Goddodin 18
Graham, James, Marquis of Montrose 49, **50**, 51, 58,
    59–60
Grandtully 4, 8, 18, 48, 94, 99, 163, 164

canoeing at **162**
St Mary's Church **46, 126**
Standing Stone on Haugh of **8**
Grandtully Bridge 125
Grandtully Church 125
Grandtully Distillery 102
Grandtully Station **126**
Grania 39
Grants 27
Grantully 29, 72
Red Book of Grantully 9, 41, 56
Grantully Castle **40**, 41, 42, 53
Grieve, WB 163

Hadrian's Wall 17
Haggart, James 131
Haggart, P & J 113, 116, **121**
Haggart, Provost and Mrs JD **149**
Halidon Hill, Battle of 41
Hall of the Court of Regality 69
Hastings 27
Havana 71
Healey, Dennis 157
Heath, Edward 153, 155
Hebrides 32, 97
Hekla (Icelandic volcano) 10
Highland Brigade 113
Highland Glen Producers 159, 163
Highland Host 54
Highland Perthshire Communities Land Trust 161
Highland Railway 101, 103
Highland Ward 164
Hill Forts 10
Home Guard 139, 140
Home Rule for Scotland 118, 126, 131, 143
Hong Kong 161
Hopetoun House 163
House of Lords 94
Hughes, Captain 69
Hull, Robin 161
Hull College of Higher Education 156
Hydro-Electric Schemes 146–7

Ice Age 3
Imperial Yeomanry Regiment 123
Inchtuthil 15, 17
Independent Companies 162
Indian Mutiny 99
Inverness 34, 101, 105
Iona 19, 22, 23, 24, 25
Ireland 3, 18, 23, 24, 81, 102
   Home Rule for 114
   potato blight in 97
   workers from 146
Iron Age 11
Ironsides 51, 53
Isle of Man 141
Isle of Wight 104

Jacobites 58-67
James I 36, 58
James II 41
James III 42
James IV 35, 37, 39
James VI and I 44, 46
James VII and II 58
Jesus Christ 18
Johannesburg 123
John de Strathbogie (Earl of Atholl) 28-36

Johnston, Tom 142, 146, 158, 168

Kells 24
Keltney 72
Keltney Burn 35, 36
Kenmore 1, 12, 48, 76, 54, 76, **79,** 83, 86, 88, 91, 103
   church pillaged at 50
   Evangelical speakers, dispute over 93
   farm closures 163
   Glenorchy land, boundary of 41
   hanging of Gregor Roy at 44
   installation of Pale John's minister at 53
   local market at 37, 63, 90
   losing trade to Aberfeldy 77
   MacNaughtons at 34
   passenger steamers at 113
   pier at 92
   Royalist *versus* pro-Kirk forces 45–8
   school established at 51
   timeshare schemes 160
   volunteers against French invasion threat 99
   water mill at 70
Kenneth MacAlpin 24, 25
Killiechassie 66, 68, 69, 99, 103
Killiecrankie 58, 59, 69
Killin 67, 76, 88, 113
Kilmartin 9
Kiltyrie 87
Kings of Pictland 23
Kings of Scots 24, 31
King's Own Scottish Borderers (KOSB) 149
Kinross 18
Kirk of Scotland *see* Church of Scotland
Kynachan 65

Labour Party 131, 159
Lady of Lawers 165-168
Lady of the Lake 113, **118**
Lagg 102
landlordism 124
Latin 14, 19, 20
le Grand, Captain Patrick 31
Leicestershire 70
Leith 66
Lewis 34
Liberal Party 107
lint mills 69
Loch an Daimh 146
Loch Awe 19, 43
Loch Derculich 13
Loch Kinardochy 70, 163
Loch-na-Craig 63, 77
Loch-na-Lairige 146
Loch Tay 2, 3, 13, 15, 19, 23, 28, 43, 50, 53, 54, 67, 75, 83,
   88, 92
Loch Tay Steamboat Company 113
Lochay 167
Logierait 2, 7, **10,** 11
   battling minister from 59
   civic importance of, decline in 103
   clearances in 71, 72
   farm closures 163
   Ferry 24, **111**
   Hall of the Court of Regality, disuse of 69
   James Edward Stuart, standard raised near 61
   local market at 37, 90
   parish boundaries 79
   parish choice of minister 45
   Pictish artefacts at 21

poorhouse at 101, 165
    Roman Fort remains 28
    Talorgan's Court 23
Logierait Agricultural Show 117
Logierait Church **84**
Logierait Logierait Hotel **111**
Logierait Sheriff Court 36
London 28, 29, 47, 52, 53, 57, 64, 69
London Midland Scottish Railway 131
London Stock Market 155
Lord Nairn 67, 68
Lorn 22
Lothian 23
Lower Milton 29
Lowlands 152
Lubreoch 146, 167
Lugowska, Mrs **153**
Lyon Bridge 7

Mac-an-t'Sassunaich 28
Mc'Ara, Duncan 71, 73
McDiarmid, Duncan 105
McDiarmid, James 71
MacDiarmid clan 34, 42, 43
MacDonald, Rev Robert 86
MacDonald clan 49, 50, 51
MacDonalds of Glencoe 58, 59, 60
MacDonalds of Lochaber 45
MacDonnells, Irish clan 49, 50, 51
MacDougall clan 32
MacGregor, Gregor Roy 44
MacGregor, James, Dean of Lismore 44
McGregor, John 84
MacGregor, Peter 164
MacGregor clan 34, 39, 43, 44, 45, 57
Macintosh, Charles Rennie 116
MacIvor clan 42, 43
Mackay, General Hugh 58, 59
McKerchar, Alec 134, 136, 138, 139, 142, 143, 145, 160
    Garage in Bank Street **134**
McKerchar, Alistair 143
MacKerchar, James 117
McKerchar bus drivers 152
McKercher electricians 147
Maclain, Alasdair, Macdonald clan chief of Glencoe 60
Maclaren, James 116
Macmillan, Harold 147
McNab, Betty 163, 164, 165
MacNab, Lieutenant-Colonel Francis 81
MacNaughton clan 34, 70
McNaughton's 126
Macpherson clan 66
Magersfontein 118
Mains of Murthly 163
Mar, Earl of 62
Marcus Aurelius 17
Mariota 35
Mary, Countess of Caithness/ Breadalbane 57
Mary, Queen of Scots 44
Masonic Lodge 90
means test 135
Meggernie 29
Meggernie Castle 41, **43**
Menzies, Captain James 61, 62
Menzies, Captain of Culdares 63
Menzies, Robert and James 58
Menzies, Sir Alexander, 1st Baron 27-33
Menzies, Sir Alexander, 9th Baron 44
Menzies, Sir Alexander, 11th Baron 49, 50

Menzies, Sir Archibald 58, 60
Menzies, Sir Duncan,12th Baron 51, 52
Menzies, Sir James, 10th Baron 41
Menzies, Sir John, 4th Baronet 81
Menzies, Sir Neil, 6th Baronet 87, 92,
Menzies, Sir Neil, 8th Baronet 126
Menzies, Sir Robert, 2nd Baron 29
Menzies, Sir Robert, 7th Baron 35
Menzies, Sir Robert, 3rd Baronet 65
Menzies, Sir Robert, 7th Baronet 100, **108,** 111, 114, 119, 123, 124
Menzies, William 51
Menzies Castle 62, 66
Menzies clan 34, 42, 44, 49, 53, 58, 75, 86
Menzies Clan Gathering 165
Menzies, Clan Society 147
Menzies Highlanders 92
Menzies of Comrie 66
Menzies of Culdares 66
Mesnieres 27
Metellanus 15
Meyners (Menzies) Sir Robert de (Chamberlain of Scotland) 27
Militia Act 81
Millar, Alastair Duncan 157
Milton 28
Milton, Over and Nether 50
Milton, Upper and Lower 42
MiSWACO barytes 163
Monck, General George 51, 52, **52,** 53
Moness 2, 29, 34, 42, 50, 73, 160
Moness bridge 85
Moness burn 19, 63, 75
    wheel-driven meal mill 85
Moness Estate 75, 77
Moness House **74,** 104, 140
Mons Graupius, Battle of 16, 17
Montreal 71
Montrose, Duke of 104
Morenish 87
Mormaers 18, 24
Mortalis 41
Moulinearn 61
Murphy, Brendan 158, 163

Nairn 34
Napoleon III 99
National Civil Defence Corps 145
National Covenant 47, 48, 51
National Health Service 143
Nechtan (Over-King of the Picts) 23
Nether Milton 2, 75
New Age Travellers 159
New Labour 161
New Lanark 71
New York 71
New Zealand 87
Newcastle 47
Norfolk 70
Normandy 27
Norsemen 24, 25, 27
North British Fusiliers 66

Oban 22
Obstetric Unit for North Perthshire 143
October trysts 69
Old Age Pension 143
Oliphant, Sir William 31, 32, 33
Paine, Tom 82

Paisley 70
Paldy Burn 19, 63, 75
Palladius 19
parish boundaries, 1862 map of **80**
Penny Post 90
Perth 15, 17, 18, 23, 24, 29, 32, 37, 50, 51, 53, 54, 62, 71, 103
Perth and Kinross Council 161, 164, 166
Perth and Kinross Heritage Trust 5
Perth County, Ontario 88
Perth Museum 160
Perth to Dunkeld Railway 101
Perthshire Advertiser 137
Perthshire *Courier* 123
Perthshire Rifle Volunteers 99, 115
Pictish Atholl Mormaers 27
Pictish crosses 21, 23
Pictish language 14
Pictland 20, 21, 23, 24
Picts 16, 18, 22, 23, 24
Pinkie Cleugh, Battle of 41
Pitcairn 100
Pitilie 85, 86, 98
Pitlochry 1, 148
Pitnacree **6**, 7, 8, 9, 99
Plague Stone 95
Poland 138
Polish Army at Taymouth **140**
Polish Motor Transport Depot 139
Polish soldiers 146
Poll Tax 159
Pontius Pilate, Governor of Judea 16
Poor Box 38, 50, 79
Poor Law scheme 105
Poor Relief 165
The Pope 32
Pormahomack 20
Preston 62
Prestonpans 66
The Pretender 61, 62
Prince Albert 91
pro-Kirk Covenanters 45, 51
Puritan English Parliament 51

Queen of the Lake, construction of **118**

Radio Heartland 159
Ragman Roll 28, 32
Rannoch 32, 35, 42, 44, 65, 66, 80
Rawer 70
Red Comyn 32
Red Cross 148
Red Cross Agricultural Fund **139**
Reformation Parliament 45, 46
Regiment of Foot 60
Regiment of Perthshire Foot 47
Restoration of Charles II 57
Rich, Lady Mary 53, 54
River Danube 19
River Forth 15
River Lyon 1, 9, 23, 28, 48, 57, 61
River Tay 2, 3, 5, 8, 9, 15, 17, 19, 23, 24, 25, 27, 28, 29, 57, 61, 63, 72, **159**
River Tummel 23, 28, 59, 65
River Tweed 17
River Tyne 17
Robert II 34
Robertson, Laird of Fearnan 62
Robertson, W. & A. **128**, 133, 144

Robertsons of Rannoch 66
Roman Catholic Church 78, 125
Roman Empire 16, 17, 18, 27
Romans 14, 15, 16, 18, 19, 28, 33
Romany Gypsies 159
Rome 15, 17, 18, 19, 23
Rosetta Stone 22
Ross 71
Ross, Countess Euphemia of 34
Royal Army Service Corps 137
Royal Highlanders 162
Royal Regiment of Scotland 161
Royal Scottish Museum 21, 24
Royalist Robertson clachans 50
Royalist Stewart farms 50
Royalists 45, 53

Saint Adamnan 19, 23, 25
St Andrews 23, 24, 104
St Andrews Church, Edinburgh 93
Saint Brandon 19
Saint Carmac 19
Saint Cedd 19, 23
Saint Chadd 19
Saint Columba 19, 24
Saint Cuthbert 19
Saint Dabhi 19
Saint Luag 19
St Mary's Church, Grandtully **46**
Saint Muireach 19
Saint Ninian 19
Saint Palladius 19
Saxons 19
Scandinavia 3
Schiehallion 14, 69, 161
Scone 23, 24, 32, 62
Scotland 3, 5, 11, 14, 24, 25, 27, 29, 32
Scots 22, 24
Scots Gaelic 14
Scots Prayer Book (Anglican-style) 47
Scottish Covenant 143
Scottish Crannog Centre **5**, 163
Scottish Enlightenment 77, 82
Scottish Government 58, 60, 61
Scottish Home Rule 124, 126
Scottish Horse 123, 128, 137, 141
Scottish Hydro-Electric Board 146, 158
    dam building (1950s) **146**
Scottish National Party 136
Scottish Parliament 47, 48, 49, 51, 52, 161
Scottish Reform Bill 86
Scottish Society for the Propagation of Christian Knowledge(SSPCK) 73, 77
Scottish Women's Rural Institute (SWRI) 148
Sebastopol 99
Second Adiutrix Legion 15
Second World War 137-142, 161
Seventy-fifth Regiment of Foot 71
sheep-shearing **150**
Sheriff Court 90
Sherrifmuir 62
Shetlands 18, 21
Sikorski's Polish Army 139
Sinclair Earl of Caithness 56
'Sketches of the Highlanders' (David Stewart of Garth) 72
Skye 34
Smith, Adam 79
Smith, Jess 159
Southey, Robert 84

Stanley 71
Statistical Accounts 83
Steuart, John of Grantully 54, 59, 62
Steuart, Sir Thomas, 12th Laird of Grantully 51, 54, **56,** 57
Steuart, Sir William, 9th Laird of Grantully 45
Steuart, Sir William of Grantully, 7th Baronet, 101
Steuart-Fotheringham family 125
Steuarts of Grantully 42, 65
Stewart, Alan of Woodend 66, 68
Stewart, Alexander, Earl of Buchan, Wolf of 34, **35,** 36
Stewart, Charles of Inchgarth 65
Stewart, Elizabeth 1
Stewart, General David of Garth 35, **72**
Stewart, Neil Gointe (The Fated) 35, 43
Stewart, Patrick of Ballechin 59
Stewart, Patrick of Drumcharry 65
Stewart, Rev Donald 95
Stewart, Robert, Laird of Garth 71
Stewart, William of Garth 65, 80, 81
Stewart clan 42, 43
Stewart Kings 41
Stewart of Crossmount, Donald 1
Stewart of Garth, Statue of General at Keltneyburn **72**
Stewarts clan 33, 53
Stewarts of Ballechin 61, 65, 84
Stewarts of Crossmount 39
Stewarts of Garth 42, 44, 65, 84
Stewarts of Grantully 36, 49
Stirling 41, 51, 53
Stirling Castle 32
Stix 70
Stone Age 7
Stone of Destiny (Stone of Scone) 29, 143
Strathclyde 18, 23
Strathmore 21
Strathtay 13, 24, 28, 48, 50, 65, 70, 95, 99, 103, 163
Strathtay and Breadalbane Railway 101, 102
Strathtay Farmers Friendly Society 85
Stronuich 146
Stuart, Charles Edward 65, 66
Stuart, James Edward 61, 62
Stuart kings of Scotland 34
Sudan 113
Sutherland 34
Swanson, Jack 143
Sybilla's Island, Loch Tay 42, 48, **48,** 52

Talorgan 23
Tay Bridge 63
Tayfresh Producers 159
Taymouth 29, 81, 101, 125
Taymouth Castle 90, 91, **92, 93, 94,** 97, 101, 103, 139, 145, 165
Teaching Certificate 106
Telford, Thomas 84
Tempar 65
Territorial Army 137
Tertullian 18
Thatcher, Margaret 158, 159
Tigh-an-Loan Hotel **152**
Tighnalechan **67,** 68
Tippermuir 50
Tirinie 109, 116
Toiseachs 18, 24, 33
Tominteold 70
Tomnacroich 18
Tomtewan 14, **88**
Tourist Information Office 162
The Trinity 20

Tullichuil Farm 8
Tullochcroish 65
Tummel Bridge 1
Turner, J.M.W. 160
Twentieth Valeria Victrix Legion 15

United Church 144
United Free Church 125
Upper Milton 2, 29
Upper Tay 164

Vale of Atholl 47
Venicones 15, 18
Victoria Park 119
Victoria (Queen) 91, 92, **96,** 103, 114, 123, 145
Victory in Europe 143, 144
Victory over Japan 143
Vikings 23, 24, 25, 27
Volunteer Aid Detachment 127, 137

Wade, General George (later Field-Marshall) 1, 2, 29, **63,** 64, 65
    roads built by 76
Washington, George 71
Wee Free Church 125
    see also Free Church; United Free Church
Weem 50, 79, 103
    agricultural expansion 63
    archaeological remains at 9
    destruction of Weem Castle 35
    fairs and markets, decline of 90
    Free Church support 94
    Friends of the People of Scotland 81
    grant of land to Earl of Atholl for support of Edward I of England 28
    MacGregor raids on 44
    Menzies clan in control of lands 42
    monastery remains at 20
    parish choice of minister 45
    ploughing match at **85**
    Rev MacDiarmid of 81
    sacking of monastery at 24
    school established at 54
    turnpike road through 88
Weem Castle 41, 92
Weem Church 27, **85**
Weem Inn **62**
Weem Rock 11
Welsh 14
West Highlands 102
Westminster 99, 119, 158
Whitby 23
William of Orange 58, 59, 60
William the Conqueror 27
Women's Auxiliary Air Force 137
Women's Guild (Church of Scotland) 148
Women's Land Army 137
Women's Royal Army Corps 137
Women's Royal Naval Service 137
Women's Voluntary Service 137
Worcester 51
Wordwright Communications 164
Wylie, John 87, 97, 104, 126, 128
    letter concerning meal for the poor from **98**

Yellowlees, Walter 143, 153, 155, **160**
York, Duke and Duchess 135

Books about Aberfeldy and the surrounding area, available from The Watermill Bookshop in Aberfeldy...

To order (under £50 add £2.50 carriage, over £50 post free), write to:
The Watermill, Mill Street, Aberfeldy, PH15 2BG,
Telephone 01887 822896 • www.aberfeldywatermill.com

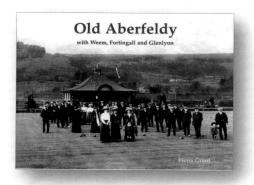

Old Aberfeldy
by Fiona Grant. 59 photographs and notes covering Aberfeldy, Weem, Fortingall and Glenlyon. £7.99

Old Killin, Kenmore and Loch Tay
by Bernard Byrom. Pictoral guide. £7.99

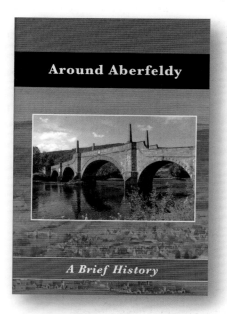

Around Aberfeldy
by Clare Thomas and David Strachan
Fourth edition of booklet particularly covering archaeological sites, first published in 1970. £3

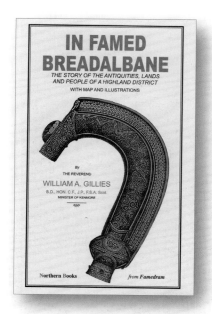

In Famed Breadalbane
by William Gillies. A history of the area from Roman times to the 1960s and especially the rise and fall of the Campbells. £20 hardback.

A Doctor in the Wilderness
by Walter Yellowlees
Thirty-three years as a GP, organic gardener, writer and lecturer, viewed through the author's experience living and working in the Aberfeldy area. £12.99

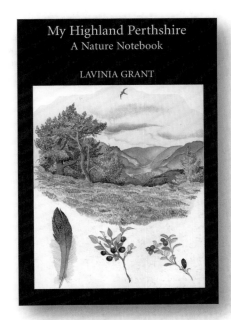

My Highland Perthshire
by Lavinia Grant
The author spent thirty years observating nature and the seasons around Loch Tay and Drummond Hill. Beautifully illustrated with the author's watercolours and sketches. Published by The Watermill, 220 pages, with more than 100 colour plates, hardback. £20

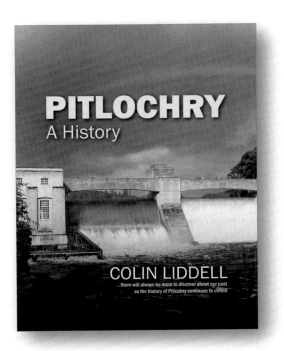

Pitlochry - A History
by Colin Liddell
A comprehensive history of Pitlochry and district, from the Ice Ages to the present and covering the whole area from Strathtummel to Logierait and Straun to Enochdhu. Published by The Watermill, 256 pages, with over 275 images and photos, hardback. £20